EDITIONS SR

Volume 17

The Five Aggregates

Understanding Theravāda Psychology and Soteriology

Mathieu Boisvert

Published for the Canadian Corporation for Studies in Religion / Corporation Canadienne des Sciences Religieuses by Wilfrid Laurier University Press

1995

Canadian Cataloguing in Publication Data

Boisvert, Mathieu, 1963-
The five aggregates : understanding Theravāda psychology and soteriology

(Editions SR ; 17)
Includes bibliographical references and index.
ISBN 0-88920-257-5

1. Theravāda Buddhism – Doctrines. 2. Theravāda Buddhism – Psychology. 3. Salvation (Buddhism).
I. Canadian Corporation for Studies in Religion.
II. Title. III. Series.

BQ7235.B65 1995 294.3′91 C95-932239-6

Cover design by Leslie Macredie

Printed in Canada

The Five Aggregates: Understanding Theravāda Psychology and Soteriology has been produced from a manuscript supplied in camera-ready form by the author.

Order from:
WILFRID LAURIER UNIVERSITY PRESS
Waterloo, Ontario, Canada N2L 3C5

Table of Contents

List of Tables

Acknowledgements

Although most books are attributed to one single author, various individuals and many factors contribute to the development of any manuscript. As the theory of dependent origination suggests, there is no initial cause (or authorship), but merely a succession of inter-dependent events that are responsible for what comes into being. As an author, I am simply one of these necessary conditions, and I truly wish to express my gratitude to all those who have contributed directly or indirectly to my work.

More especially, I wish to thank my parents and my whole family who offered me the emotional and financial support needed to undergo all these years of study. Venerable Jāgara and S.N. Goenka also played a crucial role in providing the inspiration needed to pursue my objective. Richard Hayes' humble yet apposite comments proved to be pivotal in the elaboration of my argumentation, and in encouraging me to persevere. I am further indebted to A.K. Warder and Ravindra Panth, both of whom showed an extreme amount of patience in teaching me Pāli. My style and rhetoric have also been reviewed by a legion of editors, starting with Diana Allen, Raynald Prévèreau, Stephen Jones, Philip Moscovitch and Lisa Kosuta. The writing of this book would not have been possible without the help of many other individuals (and circumstances), for which I am extremely grateful.

This book has been published with the help of a grant from the Canadian Federation for the Humanities, using funds provided by the Social Sciences and Humanities Research Council of Canada. A grant in aid of publication was also provided by the *Comité des publications* of Université du Québec à Montréal.

Foreword

In Buddhist philosophy, the theory of the five aggregates (*pañcakkhan-dhā*) of realities, or real occurrences known as "principles" (*dhamma*), is the analysis of what elsewhere is often called the "problem" of matter and mind. In Buddhism, to separate these would be to produce a dilemma like the familiar one of "body" and "soul" (are they the same or different?). But the resolution is different. Whereas the "soul," according to Buddhism, is a non-entity and the problem therefore meaningless, consciousness is as real as matter. The tradition emphasizes that consciousness is inseparably linked to matter: there can be no consciousness without a body; although there could be a body without consciousness, it would not be sentient.

Matter and consciousness are two of the "aggregates"; the other three link them, or rather show them inseparably bound together in a living being. These are, to use Boisvert's translations, "sensation" (*vedanā*, variously translated as "experience," "feeling," etc.), "recog-nition" (*saññā* or "perception") and "karmic activities" (*saṅkhāra*, "forces," "volition," etc.). Sensation — being either pleasant, unpleasant or neutral — can occur only in a body which is conscious. Similarly, recognition occurs solely when consciousness is aware of sensations. The karmic activities, sometimes restricted to volition (*cetanā*), were gradually elaborated to include about fifty principles, from "contact" (*phassa*, the combination of a sense organ, its object and consciousness), energy and greed to understanding, benevolence, compassion and attention.

In what are supposed by many to be the earliest Buddhist texts, the five aggregates are taken for granted, as if pre-Buddhist thought generally accepted them. Boisvert argues that they are a theory intrinsic to Buddhism and extracts from the texts the passages needed to explain them and show that these five, in this order, are required to describe and understand the process of "transmigration" (or "rebirth"). The greater part of the book (chaps. 2 to 6) clarifies the nature of the individual aggregates. "Recognition" has usually been found the most obscure, to the point of elision in translation. But Boisvert shows that this aggregate is central to the transmigration process since it links desire (*taṇhā*, "craving") to sensation. Release (*nibbāna*) requires that recognition be replaced by understanding (*paññā*). The reactions of the aggregates with the external world are clarified by their interaction with each other. The ultimate argument relates the aggregates to conditioned origination (*paṭiccasamuppāda*), the essentially Buddhist description of transmigration. Through this analysis the proper sequence of the aggregates is established.

Boisvert has been able to use *BUDSIR*—the Bangkok *Mahidol University Databank* of 1989—to search exhaustively for contexts in Pāḷi literature. It is to be hoped that he will search further and clarify more Buddhist terminology.

A.K. Warder
Toronto

Abbreviations

References to primary sources are given by the abbreviation of the source used, followed by a lower-case Roman numeral indicating the volume number and an Arabic number indicating the page. For example, a quotation from the third volume of the *Dīghanikāya*, p. 238 would be listed as **D. iii, 238**.

A.	*Aṅguttaranikāya*
AA.	*Aṅguttaranikāya* commentary (*Manorathapūraṇī*)
AbhS.	*Abhidhammattasaṅgaha*
AbhA.	Commentary on the *Abhidhamma* excluding the *Dhammasaṅgaṇi* and the *Vibhaṅga* (*Pañcappakaraṇatthakathā*)
AbhK.	*Abhidharmakośa*
It.	*Itivuttaka*
Ud.	*Udāna*
Kvu.	*Kathāvatthu*
Th.	*Thera-Therīgāthā*
D.	*Dīghanikāya*
DA.	*Dīghanikāya* commentary (*Sumaṅgalavilāsinī*)
Dh.	*Dhammapada*
DhA.	*Dhammapada* commentary
Dhs.	*Dhammasaṅgaṇi*
DhsA.	*Dhammasaṅgaṇi* commentary (*Atthasālinī*)
Nid.	*Niddesa (Mahā)*
Net.	*Nettipakaraṇa*
Ps.	*Paṭisambhidāmagga*
PsA.	*Paṭisambhidāmagga* commentary
Pug.	*Puggalapaññatti*
M.	*Majjhimanikāya*
MA.	*Majjhimanikāya* commentary (*Papañcasūdanī*)
Mil.	*Milindapañhapāli*
Ymk.	*Yamaka*
Vin.	*Vinayapiṭaka*
Vbh.	*Vibhaṅga*
VbhA.	*Vibhaṅga* commentary (*Sammohavinodanī*)
Vsm.	*Visuddhimagga*

S.	*Saṁyuttanikāya*
SA.	*Saṁyuttanikāya* commentary (*Sāratthappakāsinī*)
Sn.	*Suttanipāta*
SnA.	*Suttanipāta* commentary

Introduction

The following study presents a detailed analysis of each of the five aggregates (*pañcakkhandhā*); its primary intention is to establish how the Theravāda tradition views their interaction. It therefore attempts to clarify the fundamentals of Buddhist psychology by analyzing one of the earliest classifications of the conditioned phenomena (*saṅkhata-dhamma*)—the five aggregates—investigating the role that these aggregates play in the cognitive process and explaining how they chain us to the wheel of misery. Once the individual meaning of each of the five aggregates is conceptualized, we try to understand the relation that exists between each of them. This explains the reason for the nomenclature of the five aggregates in the specific order found in canonical literature. Evidence against both Mrs. Rhys Davids' view that "the primary reason for the *khandha*-division was practical ... and not scientific"[1] and Th. Stcherbatsky's opinion that the order in which the aggregates appear is merely "a gradual progress from coarseness to subtleness"[2] is also presented. By demonstrating that the customary taxonomy hints at a psycho-physical process present in every individual, I have clarified the significance of the traditional order of the five aggregates, and this significance is far greater than Stcherbatsky suggested. By using computer technology,[3] I feel that the results of this

---

1 C.A.F. Rhys Davids, trans., *Buddhist Psychology: A Buddhist Manual of Psychological Ethics. A Translation of the Dhammasaṅgaṇi from the Abhidharmapiṭaka* (Delhi: Oriental Books Reprint Corporation, 1975), p. 55.

2 Th. Stcherbatsky, *The Central Conception of Buddhism and the Meaning of the Word "Dharma"* (Delhi: Motilal Banarsidass, 1970), p. 19.

3 By using a databank containing the whole Pāli canon [BUDSIR databank, designed by Mahidol University, Bangkok, 1989], I was able to make a thorough contextual analysis of the concept of *pañcakkhandhā* and of each of its members. This task was made possible by the Vipassanā Research Institute, Igatpuri, India, who allowed me to use their databank. Without this tool, I could have never accomplished what I had set out to do. Using "masks" [a "mask" is used in computerized searches to find variations on a word or string of characters; for example, searching for "**khandh**" will find "*khandhā*," "*khandhānaṃ*," "*pañcakkhandhā*," "*rūpakkhandhassa*," etc.], I searched for every occurrence of the word *khandha*, standing on its own, in whatever declensions it appeared, or as a member of a compound—thus incorporating the more specific term of *pañcakkhandhā*. The same procedure was followed with each of the five aggregates. Whenever a reference was found, it was stored on disk with

research are exhaustive in the sense that they take into consideration the entire Pāli canon. These results not only explain the psycho-physical workings of the individual, but also shed light on the mental process which, according to the Pāli *sutta* (texts known as the discourses of the Buddha), constitutes the grounds of transmigration.

The aim of this study is not to discover what the Buddha actually said about the five aggregates, nor what his intended meaning was, for it is impossible to state with conviction that any particular texts were spoken by the Buddha himself. Although many scholars have attempted to offer a chronological classification of various canonical texts, a consensus has not been reached. For example, H. Saddhatissa claims that the *Suttanipāta*, a work mainly containing verses, "is one of the oldest collections of Buddhist discourses in the Pali canon,"[4] while A.K. Warder is of the view that prose texts of the *Dīghanikāya* "are more authentic in their preservation of the utterances and dialogues of the Buddha."[5] Moreover, it is very likely that advances in linguistics will raise questions about the originality of Pāli texts. A definitive statement as to the originality of Pāli canonical texts does not lie around the corner! My concern here is not so much with what the Buddha said, but rather with the position that the Theravāda tradition supports. This school, which has regulated the lives and beliefs of millions of people for over two millennia, has elaborated an intricate scholastic and commentarial tradition. Undoubtedly, there is a huge chronological and geographical gap between the time the Buddha uttered his discourses (the fifth and sixth centuries B.C.E., in North India), and when they were written down for the first time (most probably the first century B.C.E., in Sri Lanka). It is highly probable that either certain elements present in the "original" canon were "forgotten," or that passages not

the actual paragraph in which the word occurred. Although many of these references were repetitions, the amount of data collected was enormous: more than seven megabytes. I then proceeded to catalogue these passages according to their implications. Most of the references only defined the five aggregates (*pañcakkhandhā*) as matter (*rūpa*), sensation (*vedanā*), recognition (*saññā*), karmic activity (*saṅkhāra*) and consciousness (*viññāṇa*). Many others simply stated that the five aggregates—or any of them—are transient, or devoid of "self." Passages were then compiled and, through a detailed analysis, I was able to frame a structure that circumscribed the meaning and the function of each of these aggregates.

4 H. Saddhatissa, trans., *The Suttanipāta* (London: Curzon Press, 1985); note on back cover.

5 A.K. Warder, *Introduction to Pali* (Delhi: Motilal Banarsidass, 1980), p. viii.

uttered by the Buddha himself were "remembered." Another seven centuries separate the actual writing down of the canon and the elaboration of most commentaries. Again, this gap offers more grounds for those arguing that the exegetical literature is not necessarily consistent with "original" Buddhism. Since "original" Buddhism is a tradition that we have not yet discovered, we cannot prove whether the exegetical literature is or is not consistent with the primeval tradition.

We can postulate, however, that since the commentarial tradition was incorporated within the Theravāda tradition itself, the latter must have insured that the former was consistent with every aspect of its own theory. The Pāli *sutta*, the *abhidhamma* (the scholastic literature), and Buddhaghosa's commentaries have all been accepted as integral parts of the Theravāda tradition. Consequently, I have assumed that the Theravāda tradition itself must have assured the integrity of a text before accepting it. This study of the five aggregates will be based on the whole of the Pāli canonical literature, and will refer to the commentaries whenever certain canonical passages seem unclear. This book will therefore analyze the five aggregates within the Theravāda tradition as a whole.

According to Buddhist texts, the entire universe, including the individual, is made up of different phenomena (*dhamma*). Although all these phenomena are reduced to transitory entities by the theories of impermanence (*anicca*) and selflessness (*anatta*), Buddhism classifies them into different categories in order to explain the conventionally accepted concept of person. The three concepts of bases (*āyatana*), elements (*dhātu*), and aggregates (*khandha*) constitute different schemes for classifying the various phenomena. Although the aggregates are nothing but a "convenient fiction,"[6] the Buddha nevertheless made frequent use of the aggregate scheme when asked to explain the

6 In his *Buddhist Dictionary*, Nyānātiloka emphatically remarked that these five aggregates "merely form an abstract classification by the Buddha, but that they as such ... have no existence. [It is] Due to a lack of understanding ... that the five Khandhas are often conceived as too compact, too substantial, so to speak, as more or less permanent entities, whereas in reality, as already stated, they as such, never exist; and even their representatives have only an evanescent existence" (Nyānātiloka, *Buddhist Dictionary* [Colombo: Frewin, 1956] p. 77). These five aggregates are therefore classified under the heading of conventional truth (*sammutisacca* or *vohārasacca*) as opposed to "truth in the highest sense" (*paramatthasacca*) to which the theory of dependent origination (*paṭiccasamuppāda*) belongs. The *Milindapañha* clarifies the distinction between these two levels of truth (Mil. 160).

elements at work in the individual. According to this scheme, what we conventionally call a "person" can be understood in terms of five aggregates, the sum of which must not be mistaken for a permanent entity since beings are nothing but an amalgam of ever-changing phenomena. According to the Theravāda *sutta* literature, the human personality is composed solely of the five aggregates,[7] and to perceive any of these as the self leads to a particular kind of wrong view known as "the view that the body is existing [permanently]" (*sakkāyadiṭṭhi*).[8] If the entire personality is confined within these five aggregates, the Buddhist theory of perception—and of "misperception" as well—should become clear through an understanding of their interrelation.

The five aggregates are variously translated as matter or form (*rūpa*); sensation, emotion or feeling (*vedanā*); recognition or perception (*saññā*); karmic activity, formation, or force (*saṅkhāra*); and consciousness (*viññāṇa*). Nevertheless, I believe that to rely solely on these standard translations is ultimately misleading, primarily because the concepts that some of these terms represent are heavily loaded with connotations inapplicable to the textual context in which the actual Buddhist aggregates were initially defined. For example, the term *vedanā* can be restricted neither to physical sensations nor to mental emotions or feelings, since the Pāli tradition itself informs us that *vedanā* can arise both on the body and in the mind.[9] Moreover, the *Saṁyuttanikāya* states that one should "dwell observing the impermanence of pleasant sensations *on* the body,"[10] thus implying that the term *vedanā* refers not only to an emotional "feeling," as Mrs. Rhys Davids has put forward, but also to a physical sensation occurring on the body. However, other passages such as "all mental objects culminate (flow) into *vedanā*"[11] stress the fact that *vedanā* is not a mere physical element, since it is influenced by mental contents. Yet

7 M. i, 229

8 M. i, 130, also M. i, 140-41 and A. ii, 128.

9 As we will see in Chapter 3, the *Saṁyuttanikāya* presents a fivefold classification of the concept of *vedanā*, where the first two divisions (*sukhindriyā* and *dukkhindriyā*) refer to pleasant and unpleasant physical *vedanā*, the third and fourth (*somanassindriyā* and *domanassindriyā*) are pleasant and unpleasant mental *vedanā*, and finally, the fifth (*upekkindriyā*) consists of neither pleasant nor unpleasant physical and mental *vedanā* (S. v, 210).

10 *So kāye ca sukhāya ca vedanāya aniccānupassī viharati* (S. iv, 211).

11 *Vedanāsamosaraṇā sabbe dhammā* (A. iv, 339).

most scholars adopt a certain translation for *vedanā* without first clarifying this nuance, thus leading the reader to think that *vedanā* is solely either physical or mental.

This confusion may be partially due to the fact that Sanskrit and Pāli sources, in most instances, fail to provide descriptive definitions of the five aggregates, let alone any treatment of their interrelationship. It is essential, therefore, to establish the deeper meaning of each of these elements, and then to explain their complex interaction. Since the Pāli literature illustrates these concepts with words of the same etymology, determining their meaning is more difficult than if they were paraphrased. For example, the *Majjhimanikāya* explains the meaning of *vedanā* thus: "it is called 'sensation' because it 'senses.'"[12] This problem is solved by discerning a definition of each aggregate through a systematic contextual analysis of every reference found in the Theravāda canon. By amalgamating all the passages where each of the aggregates is mentioned, I clarify their meanings and their implications to Buddhist doctrine.

Another problem arising from the study of the aggregate theory is whether the order of their nomenclature is purely random or has a certain significance. The fact that the five aggregates are always presented in the same order throughout Pāli literature does not necessarily imply that anything significant can be deduced from this very order. The Pāli canon was not written down until three or four centuries after the death of the Buddha and certain mnemonic devices had to be elaborated to facilitate its memorization. The sequence, then, may have become standard primarily as a pedagogical means to ease memorization. As noted above, Rhys Davids and Stcherbatsky wondered why this particular order was chosen rather than another, and they each put forward a different explanation. Rhys Davids suggested that the order of the aggregates was purely practical and not scientific; but she did not elaborate on what she meant by "practical." Stcherbatsky, on the other hand, hypothesized that the order reflects a gradual process from coarseness to subtlety. While it is true that the order, starting with "matter" and ending with "consciousness," seems to reflect this gradual process, we will see that the "material" aggregate possesses elements which stand on the same level of subtlety as the "consciousness"

12 *Vedeti vedetīti kho āvuso, tasmā vedanā ti vuccati* (M. i, 293).

aggregate.[13] My intention, however, is not to refute Stcherbatsky's argument, but to show that the reason for the particular order of the aggregates is grounded in something much more important than this "gradual process." In fact, I show that there was an underlying reason for choosing this particular order: the nomenclature of these five aggregates had to be in total accord with the theory of dependent origination (*paṭiccasamuppāda*; literally "arising on the ground of a preceding cause"). Although the theory of dependent origination is traditionally approached as the highest truth, and the five aggregates as conventional truth, I present evidence that these levels of truth are not merely juxtaposable, but represent different expressions of the same process.

The *paṭiccasamuppāda* could very well be considered the common denominator of all the Buddhist traditions throughout the world, whether Theravāda, Mahāyāna or Vajrayāna. The canonical texts of the Theravāda tradition portray Bhikkhu Sāriputta as saying that "whoever understands the *paṭiccasamuppāda* understands the teaching of the Buddha, and whoever understands the teaching of the Buddha understands the *paṭiccasamuppāda*."[14] In the Vajrayāna tradition, a similar view is expressed by the present Dalai Lama who states that the fundamental precept of Buddhism is this law of dependent origination.[15] Regardless of the tradition, we can clearly see the importance attributed to this theory. The *paṭiccasamuppāda* seems to constitute a fundamental tenet of Buddhism, indispensable for realizing and understanding the implications of Buddhist philosophy.

The theory of dependent origination is usually divided into twelve links (*nidāna*), each of which conditions the following one. The order presented below, where one link conditions the next (for example: "on account of ignorance, karmic activities arise": *avijjāpaccayā saṅkhārā*), is traditionally referred to as the "normal" order

13 Such elements are included in the list of secondary material elements (*upādārūpa*) on p. 39.

14 After this statement, an implicit correlation between the *paṭiccasamuppāda* and the five aggregates is established: *Yo paṭiccasamuppādaṁ passati so dhammaṁ passati, yo dhammaṁ passati so paṭiccasamuppādaṁ passatīti. Paṭiccasamuppannā kho pan' ime yadidaṁ pañcupādānakkhandhā.* "In fact, the five clinging-aggregates are dependently-arisen" (M. i, 190-91).

15 Gyatso, Tenzin, *Freedom in Exile: The Autobiography of the Dalai Lama* (New York: Harper Collins, 1990), p. 10.

(*anuloma*).[16] The *paṭiccasamuppāda* is also often presented in reverse order (*paṭiloma*), which simply indicates that if one link is eradicated, the next is also eradicated.[17]

Table 1
The Twelve Links of the Chain of Dependent Origination

1.	Ignorance	(*avijjā*)
2.	Karmic activities	(*saṅkhāra*)
3.	Consciousness	(*viññāṇa*)
4.	Mind and matter	(*nāmarūpa*)
5.	Six sense-doors	(*saḷāyatanā*)
6.	Contact	(*phassa*)
7.	Sensation	(*vedanā*)
8.	Craving	(*taṇhā*)
9.	Clinging	(*upādāna*)
10.	Becoming	(*bhava*)
11.	Birth	(*jāti*)
12.	Old age, death, ...	(*jaramaraṇa*, ...)

The chain of dependent origination is often approached as a causal theory. We usually speak of causality when we say "there being this, there appears that." Yet we have to stress that a substantial cause from which the effect was generated cannot be deduced from the *paṭiccasamuppāda*. As Stcherbatsky remarked:

> In this sense the logical law of Causation is the reverse of the real law of Causation. A cause is not a reason. The cause is not a sufficient reason for predicating (or predicting) the effect. But the effect is a sufficient reason for affirming apodictically the preceding existence of its cause.[18]

16 Literally [combing] "in the direction of the hair."

17 The usual wording of this reverse order would run thus: "From the thorough eradication of ignorance, karmic activities are eradicated." *Avijjāya tveva asesavirāganirodhā saṅkhāranirodho*.

18 Th. Stcherbatsky, *Buddhist Logic* (New York: Dover Publications, 1962), 1:311.

Each of the links of the chain of dependent origination is, therefore, necessary for the emergence of the next element; yet none can definitely be perceived as a cause sufficient to engender the following link.

Since this complex chain of causation is always said to give rise to suffering,[19] the deactivation of any of the twelve links is bound to break the causal process and to eliminate suffering. According to the Pāli canon, both the chain of dependent origination and the five aggregates are responsible for suffering (*dukkha*). The Buddha stated repeatedly that the root of all suffering lies in the five clinging-aggregates,[20] which represent the psycho-physical constituents of the individual. This is further evidenced by the *Mahāvagga* of the *Aṅguttara-nikāya*,[21] where an intimate relation between the five aggregates and the theory of dependent origination is established.[22] In this specific discourse, a description of the four noble truths is offered in terms of the *paṭiccasamuppāda*. Therein, the first noble truth follows the standard canonical rendering and ends with the following phrase: "in short, the five clinging-aggregates are suffering."[23] Yet the description of the two following truths does not comply with the paradigmatic rendition. Instead, they are depicted in terms of the theory of dependent origination. The noble truth concerned with the arising of suffering is simply explained by the *paṭiccasamuppāda* in normal order, while the noble truth of cessation of suffering is defined by the *paṭicca-samuppāda* in reverse order. It is clear, then, that the *paṭicca-samuppāda*, traditionally seen as an explanation for the arising and the eradication of suffering, is intimately related to the theory of the five aggregates.

The *paṭiccasamuppāda* is a theory that establishes the connectedness of all the phenomena. Since it deals with all the phenomena of existence, it becomes evident that the different schemes

19 "This [the *paṭiccasamuppāda*] is the origin of the entire mass of suffering." *Evam etassa kevalassa dukkhakkhandhassa samudayo hoti.*

20 The "clinging-aggregates" (*upādānakkhandhā*) are basically the same as the "five aggregates" except that the former are responsible for binding the individual to the cycle of birth, death and rebirth (*saṁsāra*). I shed more light on the nuances between the two concepts on p. 20 and following).

21 A. i, 176-77.

22 Étienne Lamotte has already noted this relation (Étienne Lamotte, "Conditioned Co-Production and Supreme Enlightenment," in O.H. de A. Wijesekera, ed., *Buddhist Studies in Honour of Walpola Rahula* [London: Gordon Fraser, 1980], p. 119).

23 ... *saṅkhittena pañc'upādānakkhandhā dukkhā* (A. i, 177).

used to classify them can be traced within the *paṭiccasamuppāda* itself. The five aggregates are merely a classification of the various phenomena of existence, and this taxonomy ought to be applicable to the *paṭiccasamuppāda* as well. I therefore offer evidence supporting the correlation between the five aggregates and the links of the chain of dependent origination; the establishment of such a relationship will clarify the meaningfulness of the traditional nomenclature of the five aggregates.

The Theravāda tradition holds that certain links of the chain of causation are limited either to the past, present or future. In other words, as exemplified in Table 2, different links constitute different temporal divisions.[24] Although this chronological division is not expressed explicitly in the Pāli canonical literature itself, it is supported by Anuruddha,[25] and is taken for granted by the tradition.[26] What is unclear, however, is the reason for clear delineation and theoretical distinction among these three divisions. Since the past is nothing but the aging of the present, and the present the actualization of the future, each temporal division has to be seen as the paraphrasing of, or a different perspective on, the two other divisions. Furthermore, Étienne Lamotte, commenting on a diagram similar to the one below, stressed that "Le tableau dressé ici se refère à un groupe de trois existences découpé [*sic*] artificiellement dans la suite infinie des existences s'intégrant dans un *Saṁsāra* qui n'a pas eu de commencement."[27] Since these divisions are merely arbitrary, the links of the *paṭiccasamuppāda* that were classified under a certain time period could have been easily classified under another. What comes under "past" could have been under "future" or "present," and vice versa. Therefore, it becomes evident that elements belonging to a specific time period represent a process similar to the one reflected by the elements

24 *Tattha tayo addhā ... Katham? Avijjā saṁkhārā atīto addhā jāti-jarā-maraṇam anāgato addhā majjhe aṭṭha paccuppanno addhā ti tayo addhā*. Anuruddha, "Abhidhamma-tthasaṅgaha" (*J.P.T.S.*, 1884, 1-46), p. 36. "There are three periods. Ignorance and karmic activities belong to the past; birth, old-age and death belong to the future and the middle eight [links] belong to the present."

25 As Mrs. Rhys Davids pointed out in her revised edition of Shwe Zan Aung's translation of the *Abhidhammatthasaṅgaha* (Shwe Zan Aung, trans., *Compendium of Philosophy: Abhidhammatthasaṅgaha* [London: P.T.S., 1967], p. 189, n. 4).

26 See Nyānātiloka, *Buddhist Dictionary*, p. 120.

27 Étienne Lamotte, *Histoire du bouddhisme indien: des origines à l'ère Śaka* (Louvain: Institut Orientaliste, 1967), p. 43.

belonging to another. Ignorance and karmic activities operate on the same principles as birth and old age and death, and as the eight middle links. The physical and psychological elements at work in the individual remain the same whether in the past, present or future. Stated differently, the theory of dependent origination could run thus: within one lifespan (links 11-12; birth and old age and death), one keeps generating karmic activities (link 2) because of ignorance (link 1), and this generation of karmic activities due to ignorance is more easily understandable by examining the process described by the eight middle links.

Table 2
The Three Temporal Divisions of the *Paṭiccasamuppāda*

Past	1. *Avijjā* (Ignorance) 2. *Saṅkhāra* (Karmic activities)
Present	3. *Viññāṇa* (Consciousness) 4. *Nāmarūpa* (Mind & Matter) 5. *Saḷāyatanā* (Six sense-doors) 6. *Phassa* (Contact) 7. *Vedanā* (Sensation) 8. *Taṇhā* (Craving) 9. *Upādāna* (Clinging) 10. *Bhava* (Becoming)
Future	11. *Jāti* (Birth; Rebirth) 12. *Jarāmaraṇa* (Old age and death)

Equally striking is that the division of the chain of causation into three time periods implies the presence of the five aggregates in each of these periods, for individuals (themselves composed of the five aggregates) must experience this process within each of the periods.[28]

28 This perspective was already put forward by Vasubandhu in his *Abhidharmakośa*: *Ya eṣa skandhasantāno janmatrayāvastha upadiṣṭaḥ | sa pratityasamutpādo dvādaśāṅgas trikāṇḍakaḥ | pūrvāparāntayor dve dve madhye 'ṣṭau paripūriṇaḥ* || (AbhK. iii, 20). Louis de La Vallée Poussin has translated this passage as follows: "Cette série de

Although the interrelation between the temporal divisions and the working of the aggregates within each of the divisions could be demonstrated, my research has focussed on the middle division (i.e., links three to ten), for it is the most detailed temporal division and the one wherein the process is most readily observable. Through this study, I am able to clearly establish the correlation between Buddhist soteriology and psychology, depicted respectively by the *paṭicca-samuppāda* and the five aggregates. By correlating some of the links of the chain of dependent origination with the five aggregates, it becomes clear that these links share the same order as the traditional nomenclature of the five aggregates, and that the latter fulfill the same function as the links of the *paṭiccasamuppāda*.

No attempt has ever been made before to explicitly connect both doctrines, and to state which links of the theory of dependent origination refer to which particular aggregate. In fact, scholarly research on the five aggregates in general is almost nonexistent.[29] Although many works have been published on Buddhist psychology, very few deal with the Theravāda tradition. While the mental process, in terms of the five aggregates, is a key aspect of Buddhism, it has never been thoroughly analyzed, nor been given more than the slightest academic attention. Most works on Buddhism enumerate the five aggregates and only offer a short description for each of them. David Kalupahana only devotes four continuous pages to the discussion of the five aggregates in his treatise entitled *The Principles of Buddhist Psychology*. Étienne Lamotte (*Histoire du bouddhisme indien*), A.K. Warder (*Indian Buddhism*), Steven Collins (*Selfless Persons*) and E.R.

---

skandhas que nous avons vu se développer dans trois existences, c'est le Pratītyasamutpāda qui a douze membres en trois parties, deux pour la première, deux pour la troisième, huit pour celle du milieu" (Louis de La Vallée Poussin, *L'Abhidharmakośa de Vasubandhu* [Bruxelles: Institut Belge des Hautes Études Chinoises, 1980], 2:60-61).

29 Beside H.V. Guenther's *Philosophy and Psychology in the Abhidharma* (Delhi: Motilal Barnarsidass, 1974); *Ecstatic Spontaneity* (Berkeley: Asian Humanities Press, 1993); and *Wholeness Lost and Wholeness Regained* (Albany: State University of New York Press, 1994); E.R. Sarathchandra's *Buddhist Theory of Perception* (Colombo: Ceylon University Press, 1958); Anagarika Govinda's *The Psychological Attitude of Early Buddhist Philosophy* (London: Rider and Company, 1961); R.N. Reat, *Origins of Indian Psychology* (Berkeley: Asian Humanities Press, 1990); and the first part of David Kalupahana's *The Principles of Buddhist Psychology* (Albany: State University of New York Press, 1987), the literature dealing with this precise subject is virtually non-existent.

Sarathchandra (*Buddhist Theory of Perception*) only mention them in passing. For example, Lamotte only explains succinctly the transitory and selfless character of these five aggregates without even trying to explain the role they fulfill.[30] The most extensive studies on the five aggregates so far are those of Bhikkhu Bodhi,[31] Jui-Liang Chang[32] and Rupert M. Gethin.[33] However none of these articles contains a rigorous examination of the nature and interrelation of each of the aggregates. Most of Gethin's and Bodhi's articles are devoted to the relation between the aggregates and the four noble truths and the difference between *khandha* and *upādānakkhandha*, whereas Jui-Liang Chang is primarily concerned with correlating the concepts of *khandha*, bases (*āyatana*) and elements (*dhātu*). This absence constitutes a gaping hole in the field of Buddhist studies, for although the five aggregates are seen as responsible for the arising of suffering, no academic research has established how the function of each of these aggregates chains beings to the cycle of birth, death and rebirth. I am convinced that without a thorough understanding of the five aggregates, we cannot grasp the liberation process at work within the individual, who is, after all, nothing but an amalgam of the five aggregates.

The first step, before proceeding to establish the function of each of the five aggregates, is to clarify what is meant by the Pāli concept of *khandha* and to describe the connotations of this concept at the time of the Buddha. The first chapter therefore focusses on explaining the concept of *khandha* itself and on contextualizing this conception within the wider Indian and Buddhist frameworks. It also clarifies the distinction between the "five clinging-aggregates" (*pañcupādāna-kkhandhā*) and the "bare" five aggregates (*pañcakkhandhā*). The five following chapters discuss each of the aggregates and hint at the place they could occupy among the eight middle links of the *paṭicca-samuppāda*. I follow the traditional order of nomenclature, starting with matter (*rūpa*) and ending with consciousness (*viññāṇa*), for my intention is also to show that this particular order reflects the eight middle links

30 Lamotte, *Histoire du bouddhisme indien*, p. 30.

31 Bhikkhu Bodhi, "Khandha and Upādānakkhandha," *Pali Buddhist Review* 1(1) (1976): 91-102.

32 "An Analytic Study on Three Concepts of 'Skandha,' 'Āyatana' and 'Dhātu'" [Chinese: Che hs[e]ueh lun p[v]ing] (*Philosophical Review* 8 [January 1975]: 107-21).

33 "The Five *Khandhas*: Their Theatment [*sic*] in the *Nikāyas* and Early *Abhidhamma*," *Journal of Indian Philosophy* 52 (1986): 35-53.

of the *paṭiccasamuppāda*. In order to arrive at a clear and precise definition of each of the aggregates in these five chapters, I will first analyze the etymology of the terms and study the canonical references that shed light on their function. The seventh chapter is threefold. It first establishes a correlation between the five aggregates and the *paṭiccasamuppāda*. This correlation is then used as an argument to contest the theory that the traditional nomenclature of the five aggregates is purely random. The implication of these findings is finally briefly analyzed in light of the process involved in traditional Theravāda meditation (*vipassanā*).

Chapter 1

The Concept of *Khandha*

Buddhism differs from other religions in that no room is allotted for an ultimate reality corresponding to the concept of "self." Most Buddhist traditions view the entire universe (and the individual as well) as composed of different, irreducible phenomena (*dhamma*). Although these phenomena serve as a common denominator for different Buddhist doctrines, their number and classification vary from one school to another. Nevertheless, most schools have elaborated numerous approaches for the purpose of analyzing reality. One of these consists of the division of these elements into two categories: conditioned (*saṅkhata*) and unconditioned (*asaṅkhata*). The larger conditioned category refers to all conditioned (that is, having a beginning and an end) phenomena of existence. The *Aṅguttaranikāya* describes the conditioned phenomena as possessing three characteristics: arising, passing away, and impermanence;[1] while the unconditioned phenomena are referred to as causeless[2]—this being defined as *nibbāna*.[3] The Theravādins and the Sarvāstivādins differ as to the constituents of the unconditioned-group; the former allows only *nibbāna* in this category,[4] while the latter considers space (*ākāśa*) and two kinds of *nibbāna* (*pratisaṁkhyānirodha* and *apratisaṁkhyānirodha*[5]) as unoriginated principles. The phenomena in the major group, generally known as the conditioned-group, are responsible for elation and depression[6] because they inherently lead to an inaccurate perception of reality. This group

---

1 A. i, 152.

2 *Katame dhammā asaṅkhatā? Yo eva so dhammo appaccayo—so eva so dhammo asaṅkhato* (Dhs. 193).

3 *Katame dhammā asaṅkhatā? Nibbānaṁ—ime dhammā asaṅkhatā* (Dhs. 244).

4 Lamotte, *Histoire du bouddhisme indien*, p. 675.

5 This first type of *nibbāna* refers to the eradication through wisdom of already existing defilements, while the second type refers to the obstruction through meditation (*dhyāna*) of any future defilements.

6 M. iii, 299.

is further classified into five aggregates:[7] *rūpa* (matter), *vedanā* (sensation), *saññā* (recognition), *saṅkhāra* (karmic activities) and *viññāṇa* (consciousness)—which alone stand as the constituents of the individual.

Etymology of the Term *Khandha*

The term *khandha* (or its Sanskrit equivalent, *skandha*) was already used in pre-Buddhist and pre-Upaniṣadic literature. One of the oldest Indian treatises on semantics and etymology, the *Nirukta*, holds that the general meaning of *skandha* in the Veda is restricted to "the branches of a tree" since they "are attached to the tree."[8] It is interesting to note that the word "trunk," which stands for the union of all the branches of the tree, is one of the connotations of the Pāli term *khandha* as well.[9] The author of the *Nirukta* also alludes to a secondary meaning, viz. "shoulder," which is derived from the same root (*skandh* = "to be attached"), and is used in this peculiar sense because the shoulder "is attached to the body."[10] We find a similar usage in the Pāli canon: the *Saṁyuttanikāya* and the *Visuddhimagga* use the word *khandha* to designate shoulder.[11] Some later pre-Buddhist texts, such as the *Chāndogya Upaniṣad*, use the word *skandha* in the sense of "branches" referring to the three branches of duty: *trayo dharmaskandhāḥ yajñaḥ*

---

7 *Saṅkhataṁ rūpaṁ sankhataṁrūpan ti yathābhūtaṁ na pajānāti. Saṅkhataṁ vedanaṁ. Saṅkhataṁsaññaṁ. Saṅkhate saṅkhāre. Saṅkhataṁ viññāṇaṁ saṅkhataṁviññāṇanti yathābhūtaṁ na pajānāti* (S. iii, 114).

8 *Skandho vṛkṣasya samāskanno bhavati. Ayamapītaraskandha etasmādeva. Āskannaṁ kāyo* (Lakśman Sarup, ed. and trans., *The Nighaṇṭu and the Nirukta: The Oldest Indian Treatise on Etymology, Philology and Semantics: by Yakṣa* [Delhi: Motilal Banarsidass, 1977], vi 18).

9 S. i, 207; D. ii, 171-172; Sn. 282, etc.

10 *Skandho vṛkṣasya samāskanno bhavati. Athamapītaraskandha itasmād eva. Āskannaṁ kāye. Ahiḥ śayataupaparcanaḥ pṛthivyāḥ* (Sarup, ed. and trans., *The Nighaṇṭu and the Nirukta*, vi, 18).

11 *Atha kho māro pāpimā kassaka-vaṇṇam abhinimminitvā mahantam naṅgalaṁ khandhe karitvā.* ... "So Mārā the evil one, taking the shape of a farmer, bearing a mighty plough on his shoulder" (S. i, 115). *Tasmā pathamaṁ sīsaṁ makkhetvā khandhādīni makkhetabbāni.* "Therefore, having first anointed the head, he should anoint the shoulders," etc. (Vsm. 100).

adhyayanam dānam.[12] In contrast, the *Maitrī Upaniṣad* uses the term *skandha* in the sense of a "mass" of smoke.[13] A similar usage of the word is found in the Pāli canon: the *sutta* also use the word *khandha* to refer to a "mass" of fire and of water (*aggikkhandha* and *udakakkhandha*).[14] This usage is widespread in Pāli literature, for we find constant references to the "mass of suffering" (*dukkhakkhandha*).[15]

The word *khandha* is also used in Theravāda literature to refer to the concept of "division," in the sense of a variety of constituent groups. The *Dīghanikāya*, for example, alludes to four *khandha*: morality (*sīla*), concentration (*samādhi*), wisdom (*paññā*) and release (*vimutti*).[16] The same source mentions another association of three *khandha* which corresponds to the previous grouping less release.[17]

In both pre-Buddhist and Buddhist literature, the number of meanings associated with the term *khandha* is striking. However, the most important usage of the term in Pāli canonical literature is in the sense of the *pañcakkhandhā*, "the five aggregates." The importance of this meaning is evidenced by the fact that Nyānātiloka's *Buddhist Dictionary* provides only the definition referring to the five aggregates.[18] It also must be stressed that this particular definition of the term is non-existent in currently available pre-Buddhist literature, whether Upaniṣadic or Vedic.

The Five Aggregates and the *Dhammacakkappavattanasutta*

The number of appearances of the term *pañcakkhandhā* in the *sutta* and the fact that the five aggregates are discussed in the first discourse of

12 "There are three branches of duty. The first is sacrifice, study of the Vedas and alms-giving. The second is austerity. The third is a 'student of dharma' (*brahmacārin*) dwelling in the house of a teacher, settling himself permanently in the house of a teacher." *Trayo dharmaskandhā yajñodhyayanaṁ dānamiti prathamaḥ, tapa eko dvitīyaḥ, brahmacāryācāryakulavāsī tṛtīyotyantamātmānamācāryakulevasādayan* (Siromani Uttamur T. Viraraghavacharya, ed., *Chandogyopanishadbhashya* [Tirupati: Sri Venkatesvara Oriental Institute, 1952], ii, 23).

13 J.A.B. Buitenen, trans., *Maitrāyaṇīya Upaniṣad: A Critical Essay. With Text, Translation and Commentary* (The Hague: Mouton, 1962), vii, 11.

14 Respectively, M. ii, 34 and S. iv, 179.

15 Vin. i, 1; S. ii, 95; S. iii, 14; A. i, 77; A. v, 184; etc.

16 D. iii, 229.

17 D. i, 206.

18 Nyānātiloka, *Buddhist Dictionary*, pp. 76-80.

the Buddha—the *Dhammacakkappavattanasutta*—would indicate their intrinsic Buddhist character. A careful reading of the Buddha's first discourse, however, casts some doubt on this assumption. Before preaching his first sermon, the Buddha's doctrine was unfathomable to people of that day and age. Yet he only briefly referred to the *pañcakkhandhā* in that discourse. This implies that their intricate connotations were already understood by those to whom the discourse was addressed. For example, in summarizing the various reasons for unhappiness, the Buddha concluded "in brief, the five clinging-aggregates lead to suffering,"[19] without elaborating on the term *pañcakkhandhā* any further. Neither of the two texts that contain commentaries on the *Dhammacakkappavattanasutta*, the *Sāratthappakāsinī* or the *Samantapasādika*, shed light on this matter. Therefore, the term *pañcupādānakkhandhā* (basically endowed with the same connotation as *pañcakkhandhā* as we will soon see) seems to have been a term in current use.

The absence of a definition of the Buddhist sense of the word *khandha* in pre-Buddhist literature leads us to three possible hypotheses: (1) the term existed then but was not recorded in the pre-Buddhist philosophical treatises available to us (or might have been incorporated in some of the Ājīvaka speculative works, sources which have not yet been discovered, if they exist); (2) the word *khandha* might have been a philosophical innovation introduced by the Buddha but, for literary reasons, the compilers of the Pāli canon decided not to include the detailed explanation of the term in the *Dhammacakkappavattanasutta* even though the Buddha might have explained it then; or (3) the *Dhammacakkappavattanasutta* was not composed at the beginning of the Buddha's ministry, but later in his career (or even after his death) when the Buddhist meaning of the term *pañcakkhandhā* had been established and was familiar to those within the tradition. The hypothesis that a well-developed doctrine was projected back into an earlier time to gain special authority is quite popular among Western scholars. It is also possible, however, that the abundant references to the term found in later discourses might have prompted the compilers to suppress its explanation here, so as to shape the first discourse of the Buddha into a concise and thorough summary of the entire doctrine.

Initially, the first hypothesis seems the most plausible, since a forerunner of the Buddhist *khandha* is found in early *Brāhmaṇa* and

19 *Saṅkhittena pañcūpādānakkhandhā dukkhā* (S. v, 421).

Upaniṣad, where five factors also compose the major divisions of the individual. The *Taittirīya Upaniṣad*[20] elaborates a division of the individual (*puruṣaḥ*) into five different selves (*ātmā*)—the self made of food (*annarasamayaḥ*), the self made of organic activities (*ātmāprāṇamayaḥ*), the self made of the mind (*ātmāmanomayaḥ*), the self made of cognition (*ātmāvijñānamayaḥ*), and the self made of bliss (*ātmānandamayaḥ*)—all of which are relatively similar to the five Pāli *khandha*. The *rūpakkhandha* could correspond to the "self made of food" since the *Dīghanikāya* describes *rūpa* as "being made of the four great elements which consist of gross food."[21] The *saññākkhandha* and the *viññāṇākkhandha* could respectively be associated with the self made of mind and the self made of consciousness. The *saṅkhārakkhandha*, as K. N. Jayatilleke has pointed out,[22] could also be related to the self made of organic activities since the *saṅkhārakkhandha* is described in the *Majjhimanikāya* as including the "in and out breathing,"[23] while the self made of organic activities resembles the Upaniṣadic meaning of *prāṇa*, the vital breath.[24] Only *vedanākkhandha* and the self made of bliss seem not to correspond. As with the Buddhist *pañcakkhandhā*, these five Upaniṣadic factors are united only during one's lifespan; at the moment of death, they separate.[25] Stressing the similarity between the Buddhist and Upaniṣadic interpretation of the components of the individual, Stcherbatsky said,

> This difference [between the Buddhist and Upaniṣadic aggregates] bears witness of the enormous progress achieved by Indian philosophy during the time between the primitive Upaniṣads and the rise of Buddhism. In the Buddhist system we have a division of mental faculties into feeling [*vedanā*], concept [*saññā*], will [*saṅkhāra*] and pure sensation [*viññāṇa*], in which modern

20 Swāmī Gambhīrānanda, trans., *Eight Upaniṣads; With the Commentary of Śaṅkharācārya* (Calcutta: Advaita Ashrama, 1986), 1:223-397.

21 *Tiṭṭh' atevāyaṁ Poṭṭhapāda oḷāriko attā rūpi cātummahābhūtiko kabaliṅkārāhārabhakkho* (D. i, 186).

22 K.N. Jayatilleke, *The Early Buddhist Theory of Knowledge* (Delhi: Motilal Banarsidass, 1980), p. 221.

23 *Assāsapassāsā ... kāyasaṅkhāro* (M. i, 301).

24 Bṛihadāraṇyaka Upaniṣad 3.9.26; Kaṭha Upaniṣad, 2.2.5. Extracted from R.E. Robert Ernest, trans., *The Thirteen Principal Upanishads* (Delhi: Oxford University Press, 1985).

25 Th. Stcherbatsky, *The Central Conception of Buddhism and the Meaning of the Word "Dharma"* (Delhi: Motilal Banarsidass, 1970), p. 61.

> psychology would not have much to change. In the Upaniṣads it is a very primitive attempt, giving breath, speech, sense of vision, sense of audition and intellect as elements. But one point of similarity remains: the last, and evidently, the most important element is in both cases *manas*. The macrocosm, or the Universal Soul, is likewise analyzed by the Upaniṣads into five component elements. In the number of the Buddhist *skandha* and in the position of *manas* (= *vijñāna*) among them we probably have the survival of an old tradition.[26]

As Stcherbatsky suggested, the term *pañcakkhandhā* might have been either a synonym for, or a popular term referring to, these five brāhmanic factors. Yet the context in which *pañcakkhandhā* is used in the *Dhammacakkappavattanasutta* implies connotations such as impermanence and no-self, both of which are incongruent with the brāhmanic tradition. If the concept of *khandha* had been one referring to the earlier brāhmanic division of the personality, the Buddha would not have attached so much importance to the difference in meaning implied by his own use of the term. This leads us to consider the second and third hypotheses as more probable—namely, that the Buddhist meaning attributed to *khandha* represented an innovation in Indian philosophy. It is impossible, however, to ascertain whether the *Dhammacakkappavattanasutta* originally included a detailed discussion on the *pañcakkhandhā*, subsequently suppressed for literary reasons, or whether the concept of *pañcakkhandhā* was later included in the first discourse of the Buddha. But we do have sufficient grounds to assert that the term *pañcakkhandhā* is a philosophical innovation on the part of the Buddhists.

Pañcakkhandhā and *Pañcupādānakkhandhā*

So far, the terms *pañcakkhandhā* and *pañcupādānakkhandhā* have been used almost interchangeably. The only, but crucial, difference between these two forms of aggregates is that the group of the *pañcupādāna-kkhandhā* is potentially subject to biases (*āsava*) and clinging (*upādāna*), while the other is not. With regard to clarifying the meaning and the interrelation of the *pañcakkhandhā* by establishing a correlation with the theory of dependent origination, only a study of the *pañcupādāna-kkhandhā* would be relevant; those *khandha* not involved in the

26 Stcherbatsky, *Central Conception of Buddhism*, p. 61.

multiplication of misery and the binding to the wheel of birth and rebirth are not related to the *paṭiccasamuppāda*. Yet this study focusses on both the *pañcakkhandhā* and the *pañcupādānakkhandhā*, for the simple reason that our primary goal is to establish the function and clarify the interrelation between each of the aggregates. Since the aggregates of one group function in exactly the same manner as those of the other group—with the slight nuance that aggregates of the *pañc-upādānakkhandhā*-group are still objects of clinging—this comprehensive approach is the most appropriate to achieve our aim.

The distinction, however, between the two sets of *khandha* ought to be clarified. The *Atthasālinī* explains the word *ādāna* (*pañca* + *upa* + *ādāna* + *khandhā*) by suggesting that it means "to catch hold of strongly," and that its prefix *upa* merely adds an emphasis, just as in the words despair (*upāyasa*) and denounced (*upakkuṭṭha*).[27] The *Khandhā-sutta* of the *Saṁyuttanikāya* explicitly defines these two sets of "aggregates" without, however, comparing them:

> And what, monks, are the five aggregates? Whatever matter, sensation, recognition, karmic activities, and consciousness, be it past, present, or future, internal or external, gross or subtle, inferior or superior, far or near, these are called matter, sensation, recognition, karmic activities and consciousness aggregates. ... And what, monks, are the five clinging-aggregates? Whatever matter, sensation, recognition, karmic activities, and consciousness, be it past, present, or future, internal or external, gross or subtle, inferior or superior, far or near, that are subject to cankers [*āsava*: biases], subject to clinging, these are called matter, sensation, recognition, karmic activities and consciousness "clinging-aggregates.[28]

27 *Upādānan ti daḷhagahaṇaṁ, daḷhattho hi ettha upasaddo upāyāsa-upakkuṭṭhādīsu viya* (Dhs. 385).

28 *Yaṁ kiñci bhikkhave rūpam (vedanā, saññā, saṅkhārā, viññāṇaṁ) atītānāgatapaccu-ppannaṁ ajjhattaṁ vā bahiddhā vā oḷārikaṁ vā sukhumaṁ vā hīnaṁ vā paṇītaṁ vā yaṁ dūre santike vā ayaṁ vuccati rūpakkhandho—vedanākkhandha, saññākkhandha, saṅkhārakkhandha, viññāṇakkhandha. ... Yaṁ kiñci bhikkhave rūpam (vedanā, saññā, saṅkhārā, viññāṇaṁ) atītānāgatapaccuppannaṁ ajjhattaṁ vā bahiddhā vā oḷārikaṁ vā sukhumaṁ vā hīnaṁ vā paṇītaṁ vā yaṁ dūre santike vā sāsavam upādānīyaṁ, ayaṁ vuccati rūpupādānakkhandho—vedanupādānakkhandha, saññupādānakkhandha, saṅkhārupādānakkhandha, viññāṇupādānakkhandha* (S. iii, 47-48).

In his article "*Khandha* and *upādānakkhandha*," Bhikkhu Bodhi points out that "the fact that a differentiation is drawn between the two sets with the phrase *sāsava upādāniya* implies that a genuine difference in range does exist: that there are, in other words, aggregates of each sort which are *anāsava anupādāniya*."[29] This implies that certain aggregates are neither subject to biases (*āsava*) nor clinging (*upādāna*). I will borrow Bodhi's expression and refer to this particular set of aggregates as "the bare aggregates." Bodhi also points out that, since each of these *pañcupādānakkhandhā* is either an individual instance of matter, sensation, recognition, karmic activities or consciousness, we can postulate that they are all included among the *pañcakkhandhā* themselves.[30] For example, any matter (*rūpa*) belonging to the *pañcupādānakkhandhā* automatically belongs to the *pañcakkhandhā*. *Pañcakkhandhā* is therefore a generic term that includes both the *pañcupādānakkhandhā* and the "bare aggregates," those aggregates which are not subject to clinging.

The word *pañcupādānakkhandhā* is often translated as the "clinging aggregates," in the sense of "the aggregates that are clinging." However, according to the *sutta* literature, "clinging" can be divided into four categories: "clinging to sensual pleasures, clinging to wrong views, clinging to rites and rituals, and clinging to the theory of self."[31] In fact, "clinging to sensual pleasures" is classified under the mental factor of greed (*lobha*), and the three other forms of clinging under the mental factor of wrong views (*diṭṭhi*);[32] and both these mental factors belong exclusively to the *saṅkhārakkhandha*. Accordingly, we cannot possibly state that all the five aggregates are "clinging," for only the *saṅkhārakkhandha* is directly responsible for this activity. Therefore, this translation of *pañcupādānakkhandhā* as "the aggregates that are clinging" is misleading.

---

29 Bhikkhu Bodhi, "*Khandha* and *Upādānakkhandha*;" *Pali Buddhist Review* 1(1) (1976): 94. Note that the hyphenated spelling of "clinging-aggregates" is used to refer to the *pañcupādānakkhandhā* since it leaves the expression in its original compounded form; whereas "clinging aggregates" is used to express a specific interpretation (*karmadhāraya*) of the compound which would then mean the "aggregates that are clinging."

30 Bodhi, "*Khandha* and *Upādānakkhandha*," p. 94.

31 *Cattāro 'me āvuso upādānā: kāmupādānaṁ diṭṭhupādānaṁ sīlabbatupādānaṁ attavādupādānaṁ* (M. i, 51; also at M. i, 66; D. ii, 58, iii, 230; S. ii, 3).

32 Dhs. 212-13.

A more accurate translation of the term *pañcupādānakkhandhā* would be "the five aggregates which are the object of clinging." Since, by definition, a totally liberated person (an *arahant* or a buddha) does not generate any form of clinging, we could say that by extension this definition of the *pañcupādānakkhandhā* indirectly associates the five "clinging-aggregates" with the ordinary people (*puthujjana*) caught up in the wheel of *saṁsāra*, and the five "bare aggregates" with those who have escaped the cycle of birth and rebirth and have attained enlightenment. It is important to stress that these totally liberated "persons" generate neither craving nor aversion.

It would seem, therefore, that the concept of *pañcupādāna-kkhandhā* would not apply to liberated persons since none of their aggregates can possibly be the object of their own clinging which is, in theory, non-existent. In defining the five clinging-aggregates as those "that a person clings to as his personality,"[33] David Kalupahana supports this theory. By definition, upon realizing the state of stream-entry (*sotāpanna*), one eradicates all the different types of "personality beliefs" (*sakkāyadiṭṭhi*) and no longer perceives the aggregates as one's own self. According to this reasoning, enlightened persons who are alive on this mundane plane are not characterized by the five clinging-aggregates (*pañcupādānakkhandhā*), but rather by the "bare aggregates" which are beyond biases and clinging, and are not perceived as "one's own."

It would be wrong, however, to establish a parallel between the five "bare aggregates" and the aggregates of *arahant* and buddhas, as the *Saṃyuttanikāya* explicitly denies any such correlation:

> An *arahant*, friend Koṭṭhita, should examine these five clinging-aggregates with method as being impermanent, suffering, sick, as a swelling, as a dart, as ill-health, as alien, transitory, void and selfless. For the *arahant*, friend, there is nothing further to be done, nor is there return to upheaving of what is done. Nevertheless, these things, if practised and enlarged, conduce to a happy state [*diṭṭhadhammasukhavihāra*] and to mindfulness and thorough understanding.[34]

---

33 David J. Kalupahana, *The Principles of Buddhist Psychology* (Albany: State University of New York Press, 1987), p. 17.

34 *Arahatā pi kho āvuso Koṭṭhita ime pañcupādānakkhandhe aniccato dukkhato rogato gaṇḍato sallato aghato ābādhato parato palokato saññato anattato yoniso manasi kattabbā. Natthi khvāvuso arahato uttarikaraṇīyaṁ katassa vā paṭiccayo. Api ca kho*

This passage states that even *arahant* possess the five "clinging-aggregates" although, by definition, they do not generate clinging nor do they entertain any form of "personality beliefs." It therefore contradicts Kalupahana's definition of the clinging-aggregates as those to which an individual clings as one's own personality.

Where, then, can we find these "bare aggregates"? In his article, Bodhi suggests that the "bare aggregates" can be found only in "the happy state" (*diṭṭhadhammasukhavihāra*), which he interprets as the "fruit of arahantship in which the world disappears and Nibbāna remains."[35] As with many Pāli words, the term *diṭṭhadhammasukhavihāra* has several shades of meaning. Literally, it simply means "abiding in bliss owing to the *dhamma* being observed," yet it is often translated as "a pleasant abiding here and now." In the *Devadaha Sutta* of the *Saṁyuttanikāya*, for example, it seems extremely difficult to read anything more into the term than this peaceful abiding. But elsewhere, it is clearly used to refer to the absorptions (*jhāna*) themselves,[36] as well as to the attainment of the fruits of arahantship (*arahattaphalasamāpatti*).[37] In private correspondence, Bhikkhu Bodhi explained that the correlation between *diṭṭhadhammasukhavihāra* and the *arahattaphalasamāpatti* is supported by the fact that "insight" into the aggregates as impermanent, suffering, etc. is not required for entering into the absorptions, while it does lead to the attainment of fruition.[38] Therefore, in this particular context, Bhikkhu Bodhi's interpretation of *diṭṭhadhammasukhavihāra* as the fruits of arahantship seems convincing, especially since the *Visuddhimagga* itself states that noble persons attain fruition "for the purpose of abiding in bliss here and now."[39] Before proceeding any further, however, we need to clarify what is meant by "fruit of arahantship" in order to grasp the distinction between "clinging-aggregates" and "bare aggregates."

---

ime dhammā bhāvitā bahulīkatā diṭṭhadhammasukhavihārāya ceva saṁvattanti satisampajaññāya cāti (S. iii, 168; translation inspired by F.L. Woodward, trans., *The Book of the Kindred Sayings* [*Saṁyuttanikāya*] [London: P.T.S., 1917-1922], 3:144).

35 Bodhi, "*Khandha* and *Upādānakkhandha*," p. 94.

36 M. i, 40-41; iii, 4.

37 SA. ii, 239.

38 Refer to Chapter 23 of the *Visuddhimagga* for a complete description of the practices required for entering into the *jhāna*. For a more elaborate discussion on *jhāna*, see Winston Lee King's *Theravāda Meditation: The Buddhist Transformation of Yoga* (University Park: Pennsylvania University Press, 1980).

39 *Kasmā samāpajjantī ti diṭṭhadhammasukhavihārattham* (Vsm. 700).

Theravāda Buddhism claims that four levels of realization (the "fruits of the path," *maggaphala*) are attained before reaching final *nibbāna*: stream-entry (*sotāpanna*), or the fruits of one who falls in the stream—the person attaining this fruit will attain final *nibbāna* within seven lives at the most; once-return (*sakādāgāmī*); non-return (*anāgāmī*); and arahantship (*arahant*). At the moment of entering the path of any of these four stages, the person leaves behind the defilements and the five aggregates that are consequent upon wrong views.[40] At that very moment, all the phenomena, except for mind-produced materiality (*cittasamuṭṭhānaṁ rūpaṁ*) are wholesome (*kusala*).[41] This implies that the five aggregates, which are a mere classification of the different elements (*dhamma*) of an individual experiencing this state, are free from biases and clinging at that specific time; none of the aggregates present is the result of wrong views.[42] It also seems that when someone reaps the fruit of any one of these four paths, one temporarily "surveys" *nibbāna*. According to Buddhaghosa, at the end of the fruition, the consciousness re-enters the life continuum,[43] and the person proceeds to review *nibbāna* in the following manner: "this is the state that I surveyed as an object."[44] The passage from one level of realization to another is also called a change of lineage (*gotrabhū*), for one has (temporarily) eradicated the external signs of karmic activities (*saṅkhāra*) and becomes intent on the pursuit

40 *Sotāpattimaggakkhaṇe [sakadāgāmimaggakkhaṇe, anāgāmīmaggakkhaṇe, arahatta-maggakkhaṇe] dassanaṭṭhena sammādiṭṭhi micchādiṭṭhiya vuṭṭhāti, tadanuvattakakilesehi ca khandhehi ca vuṭṭhāti* (Ps. i, 71).

41 *Sotāpattimaggakkhaṇe jātā dhammā ṭhapetvā cittasamuṭṭhānām rūpaṁ sabbe 'va kusalā honti* (Ps. i, 116).

42 Ps. i, 71. Strictly speaking, both path (*magga*) and fruit (*phala*) are specific *citta*, states of consciousness. In the cognitive series of the path, the *maggacitta* occurs for onc mental moment, which destroys the defilements to be eliminated by that particular path. The *maggacitta* is followed immediately by two or three mind-moments of *phalacitta*, which experience the bliss of liberation accomplished by the *magga*. Thereafter, the mental process returns to the *bhavaṅga*. For a more elaborate discussion on the presence of the four mental aggregates while one is experiencing the fruits of the path, see the *Visuddhimagga*, Chapters 14 and 23.

43 *Phalapariyosāne pan'assa cittaṁ bhavaṅgaṁ otarati* (Vsm. 676).

44 *Ayaṁ me dhammo ārammaṇato paṭividdho ti amantaṁ nibbānaṁ paccavekkhati* (Vsm. 676). *Nibbāna* is often classified as one of the five objects of thoughts *dhammā-rammaṇa*. See Shwe Zan Aung, trans., *Compendium of Philosophy (Abhidhammattha-saṅgaha)* (London: P.T.S., 1967), p. 3.

of *nibbāna*.[45] Although one may have undergone a change of lineage and surveyed *nibbāna*, however, as long as arahantship has not been attained, one has not reached the final goal. As the *Atthasālinī* says:

> Although a *gotrabhū* has seen *nibbāna*, he is like one who came to see the king for a specific purpose. Having seen the king riding on an elephant on a certain road, and being asked whether he had seen the king or not, he replies that he had not, for he had not seen the king for the specific purpose he had come. In the same manner, although a person might have seen *nibbāna*, he cannot be said to have "insight" (*dassana*) because the impurities to be forsaken have not been eradicated yet.[46]

Those experiencing any of these four fruits of the path are temporarily surveying *nibbāna* as an object, and dwell in a state where their four mental aggregates cannot be perceived by those who still have certain types of biases and clinging. It is in this state that the "bare aggregates" can be found, for those dwelling in it, whether they are mere stream-enterers or *arahant*, are temporarily free of biases and clinging[47] as long as the time their "supramundane" experience lasts. Afterwards, they will assume the five clinging-aggregates again. The *arahant*, however, can induce this state of "surveying" by the mere contemplation of their five clinging-aggregates as suffering, impermanent, selfless and so on. A passage of the *Saṁyuttanikāya* even states that *arahant* involved in the practice of contemplating the breath (*ānāpānasati*) may also attain the state of *diṭṭhe dhamme sukhavihāra*,[48] the fruit of arahantship.

---

45 *Bahiddhāsaṅkhāranimittaṁ abhibhuyyitvā nirodhaṁ nibbānaṁ pakkhandatīti gotrabhū* (Ps. i, 66).

46 *So hi paṭhamaṁ nibbānaṁ dassanato dassanan ti vutto. Gotrabhū pana kiṁ cāpi paṭhamataraṁ nibbānam passati? Yathā pana rañño santikaṁ kenacid eva karaṇiyena āgato puriso dūrato va rathikāya carantaṁ hitthikkhandhagataṁ rājānaṁ disvā pi 'diṭṭho te rājā ti' puṭṭho disvā kattabbakiccassa akatattā 'na passāmī ti' āha, evameva nibbānaṁ disvā kattabbassa kiccassa kilesappahānassābhāvā na dassanan ti vuccati* (DhsA. i, 43).

47 *Sabbe [dhammā] 'va kusalā honti* (Ps. i. 116).

48 *Ye ca kho te bhikkhave bhikkhū arahanto khīṇāsavā vusitavanto katakaraṇīyā ohitabhārā anuppattasadaṭṭhāparikkhīṇabhavasaṁyujanā sammadaññā vimuttā. Tesam ānāpānasatisamādhi bhāvito bahulīkato diṭṭheva dhamme sukhavihārāya ceva saṁvattati satisampajaññāya ca* (S. v, 326).

The passage of the *Saṁyuttanikāya* cited above alludes to the fact that *arahant* can still be characterized by the *pañcupādānakkhandhā*. Buddhaghosa clarifies the difference between *pañcupādānakkhandhā* and the "bare aggregates" in his commentary on the *Dhammasaṅgaṇi*, the *Atthasālinī*:

> Although the aggregates of the arahat [*sic*] who has destroyed the cankers [*āsava*: biases] become conditions for clinging in others, when they say, for example, "Our senior uncle the Thera! Our junior uncle the Thera!," the noble paths, fruits, and Nibbāna [the *navalokuttaradhammā*; see p. 28] are not grasped, misapprehended, or clung to. Just as a red-hot iron ball does not provide a resting-place for flies to settle, so the noble paths, fruits or Nibbāna [*navalokuttaradhammā*], due to their abundant spiritual sublimity, do not provide a condition for grasping through craving, conceit, and wrong views.[49]

This implies that, although those who do not generate any more clinging (the *arahant*) have totally eradicated the biases, they still possess the five clinging-aggregates in the sense that their five aggregates still constitute a ground for clinging in others. As a result, these aggregates are still clinging-aggregates. However, *arahant* do have the possibility of dwelling in a supramundane state of consciousness that "cannot be apprehended by a mind defiled with the biases and clinging due to their sublime purity, a purity flowing from the absolute purity of their object, *nibbāna*."[50] Therefore, the aggregates can only exist as "bare aggregates" in beings dwelling in this state of consciousness which is neither accessible to, nor perceptible by, those who are still subject to clinging.

In order to shed light on this state of consciousness where "bare aggregates" are present, we need to review certain elements of Theravāda doctrine: the thirty-one levels of existence and the transcendental realm (*lokuttara*). This will offer an explanation as to

49 ... *khīṇāsavassa khandhā amhākam Mātulathero amhākaṁ Cullapituthero ti vadantānaṁ paresaṁ upādānassa paccayā honti, maggaphalanibbānāni pana agahitāni aparāmaṭṭhāni anupādiṇṇān' eva. Tāni hi yathā divasasantatto ayoguḷo makkhikānaṁ abhinisīdanassa paccayo na hoti evam evaṁ tejussadattā taṇhāmānadiṭṭhivasena gahaṇassa paccayā na hontī ti. Tena vuttaṁ: ime dhammā anupādiṇṇa-anupādānīyā ti* (DhsA. 347). Translation taken from Bodhi's "*Khandha* and *Upādānakkhandha*," p. 96.

50 Bodhi, "*Khandha* and *Upādānakkhandha*," p. 96; see also Dhs. 196, 213, 248, 258.

why the material aggregate cannot possibly be included as one of the "bare aggregates." According to the *Sāratthappakāsinī*, a commentary on the *Saṁyuttanikāya*, the material aggregate (*rūpa*) is only present in the *kāmāvacara* (realm of sensuality), while the remaining four aggregates (*vedanā, saññā, saṅkhāra* and *viññāṇa*) can be found in any of the four divisions: *kāmāvacara, rūpāvacara, arūpāvacara* and *lokuttara*.[51] The first three realms (*āvacara*) comprise the thirty-one planes of existence constituting the mundane realms, whereas the fourth (*lokuttara*) includes the supramundane (*nibbāna*). The *kāmāvacara* is characterized by craving towards objects such as form, sound, odour, taste, touch and idea. This realm includes eleven planes of existence: the six celestial realms (*sagga*),[52] the human realm (*manussaloka*), and the four states of misery (*apāya*).[53] The material realm (*rūpāvacara*) is characterized by the four absorptions (*jhāna*) and corresponds to the sixteen material heavenly planes, while the immaterial realm (*arūpāvacara*) is characterized by the four attainments (*samāpatti*) and corresponds to the four immaterial planes.[54] In two of the latter only the four mental aggregates can exist—they are devoid of material bodies.

The transcendental realm (*lokuttara*), on the other hand, refers to a sphere that is beyond or above (*uttara*) the mundane worlds (*loka*) and the three realms of existence; in other words, it refers to *nibbāna*. However, the word *lokuttara* is often used to refer to the nine supramundane elements (*navalokuttaradhammā*). In such a context, the word is used to designate the four paths and their respective fruits as well as *nibbāna*.[55] The four paths are those that lead to the realization of the states of stream-entry, once-return, non-return and *arahant*; the fruits are the realizations themselves in which a sight of *nibbāna* is also

---

51 *Rūpakkhandho kāmāvacaro cattāro khandhā catubhūmakā* [*sic*] (SA. ii, 270). The term *catubhūmakā* should be read as *catubhūmika*; an enumeration of these four *bhūmika* is given in Buddhaghosa's *Visuddhimagga* (Vsm. 452, 475, 493).

52 The six celestial realms of the *kāmāvacara* are: *catumahārājikadeva, tāvatiṁsa, yāma, tusita, nimmānarati, paranimmitavasavatti.*

53 These four states include hell (*nirayaloka*), the animal kingdom (*tiracchānayoniloka*), the ghost realm (*petaloka*), and the demon world (*asuranikāyaloka*).

54 These planes are: *ākāsānañcayatanūpagadeva, viññāṇañcāyatanūpagadeva, ākiñcaññāyatanūpagadeva, nevasaññānāsaṇṇāyatanūpagadeva*. Only beings who have experienced the four attainments can be reborn in these planes.

55 *Katamo lokuttaro vimokkho? Cattāro ca ariyamaggā cattāri ca sāmaññaphalāni nibbānañ ca. Ayaṁ lokuttaro vimokkho* (Ps. ii, 40).

implied. According to the *Paṭisambhidāmagga*,[56] although the term *lokuttara* implies a certain dissociation and a crossing over from the world, it does not seem that the term refers to a totally transcendental experience, for the individual only dwells temporarily in the fruition states, and these states are still characterized by the four mental aggregates. However, it is impossible to detect any of the five aggregates within *nibbāna* without residue (*nirupādisesa nibbāna*) for that state is defined as the full extinction of the five aggregates (*khandhaparinibbāna*).[57] When the word *lokuttara*, then, refers exclusively to *nibbāna* without residue and not the four paths and their fruits, the term *loka* means the five aggregates, while *uttara* means beyond or above.[58]

The *Sāratthappakāsinī* says that the material aggregate is only present in the realm of sensuality, and the remaining four aggregates can be found in any of the four divisions. Although the fourth division consists of the transcendental realm (*lokuttara*), it has to be understood as the first eight constituents of the nine supramundane elements (*navalokuttaradhammā*), where *nibbāna* without residue is excluded, for none of the aggregates can be present in that state. It is in the transcendental realm that the four mental aggregates (*vedanā, saññā, saṅkhāra* and *viññāṇa*) cannot be approached as objects of clinging (or as *pañcupādānakkhandhā*). This is so because, on the one hand, liberated individuals are totally free from the biases and clinging and, on the other hand, their four mental aggregates function on a different level of consciousness from those of ordinary people, since their mental aggregates have *nibbāna* as their object (*nibbānārammaṇā*).[59] Therefore, this level of consciousness cannot be apprehended by the common people.

Since the material aggregate exists only in its grosser form in the realm of sensuality, it always remains a clinging-aggregate in the sense that it is a potential object of clinging for beings dwelling in the sensual sphere. Therefore, the material aggregate can never be classified under the terminology of "bare aggregate," for it is always associated (at least potentially) with clinging. As Buddhaghosa stated in the *Visuddhimagga*,

56 Ps. ii, 166-67.

57 It., 41. A more elaborate discussion of *nibbāna* without residue is offered on p. 55.

58 Mahā Thera Nārada, trans., *A Manual of Abhidhamma: Abhidhammatthasaṅgaha by Anuruddha* (Rangoon: Printed by the Buddha Sasana Council, 1970), p. 11.

59 Ps. i, 116.

the four mental aggregates (*vedanā, saññā, saṅkhāra* and *viññāṇa*) can be free from biases while the material aggregate (*rūpa*) cannot.[60] Technically, matter always falls into the category of the clinging-aggregates (*pañcupādānakkhandhā*), but when seen in the global perspective of the four other "bare aggregates" (*vedanā, saññā, saṅkhāra* or *viññāṇa* in the fruition states), it is classified as part of the "bare" *pañcakkhandhā* simply for purposes of classification (*rāsaṭṭhena*).[61]

The term *pañcakkhandhā*, then, is all inclusive. While the term *pañcupādānakkhandhā* refers only to those aggregates that are potential objects of clinging, the term "bare aggregates" cannot refer to that which could potentially become objects of clinging. Now that this distinction has been established, we shall analyze each of the *khandha* to discover what their respective functions are, and how they relate to the doctrine of dependent origination.

60 *Ettha ca yathā vedanādayo anāsavā pi atthi, na evaṁ rūpaṁ* (Vsm. 478).

61 *Yasmā pan'assa rāsaṭṭhena khandhabhāvo yujjati, tasmā khandhesu vuttaṁ; yasmā rāsaṭṭhena ca sāsavaṭṭhena ca upādānakkhandhabhāvo yujjati, tasmā upādānakkhandhesu vuttaṁ. Vedanādayo pana anāsavā va khandhesu vuttā, sāsavā upādānakkhandhesu. Upādānakkhandhā ti c'ettha upādānagocarā khandhā upādānakkhandhā ti evam attho daṭṭhabbo. Idha pana sabbe p'ete ekajjham katvā khandhā ti adhippetā* (Vsm. 478). "Because *rūpa* can be described as a [bare] aggregate on account of its 'totalness,' it is classified amongst the [bare] aggregates. Because it can be described as a clinging-aggregate (*upādānakkhandha*) on account of its 'totalness' and its association with clinging, it is classified amongst the clinging-aggregates. But *vedanā, saññā, saṅkhāra* and *viññāṇa* are classified as [bare] aggregates when they are free from clinging, and as clinging-aggregates (*pañcupādānakkhandhā*) when objects of clinging. The term *upādānakkhandha* should be understood as referring to aggregates that are subject to clinging. On the other hand, all the aggregates ('bare aggregates' and clinging-aggregates) taken together are encompassed by the expression 'five aggregates' (*pañcakkhandhā*)."

Chapter 2

The *Rūpakkhandha*

At first glance, the *sutta* literature defines the *rūpakkhandha*—the material aggregate—in a concise and clear manner. "What is this material 'clinging-aggregate'? The four primary elements (*mahābhūta*) and secondary matter (*upādārūpa*). The four primary elements consist of earth, water, fire and air."[1] The problem with this definition, however, is that nowhere in the *nikāya* is there a clarification as to the nature of the *upādārūpa* ("secondary elements"). The *sutta* simply offer a general definition of matter stating that all matter is either past, present or future, internal or external, gross or subtle, small or large, far or near.[2]

In this chapter, I will first examine whether the general concept of *rūpa* can be correlated with the *rūpakkhandha* and then establish a correlation between the *rūpakkhandha* and some of the links of the *paṭiccasamuppāda*. Later abhidhammic and commentarial literature will help clarify what is meant by primary elements and secondary elements. All the elements comprised in the terminology of *rūpa* will then be classified in order to help us deepen our understanding of the different categories of matter (e.g., internal, external; gross, subtle; far, near, etc.). With an understanding of these classifications as well as the threefold classification mentioned in the *sutta* literature itself, we will then be in a position to establish a classification of all the material elements and to gain insight into the meaning of "matter," as well as to correlate the *rūpakkhandha* to some of the links of the *paṭiccasamuppāda*.

According to Y. Karunadasa's study, *Buddhist Analysis of Matter*, four major meanings can be ascribed to the term *rūpa*: *rūpa* in the sense of generic matter, *rūpa* in the sense of what is visible, *rūpa* in the sense of the *rūpadhātu* (*rūpaloka* or *rūpāvacara*; see p. 28) and finally, *rūpa* in

1 *Katamo c'āvuso rūpupādānakkhandho: cattāri ca mahābhūtāni catunnañ ca mahābhūtānaṁ upādāya rūpaṁ. Katame c'āvuso cattāro mahābhūtā: paṭhavīdhātu āpodhāru tejodhātu vāyodhātu* (M. i, 185; a similar passage is also found in M. i, 53 and S. ii, 3-4; iii, 59).

2 *Atītanāgatapaccupannaṁ ajjhattaṁ vā bahiddhā vā oḷārikaṁ vā sukhumaṁ vā hīnaṁ vā panītaṁ vā yaṁ dūre santike vā, sabbaṁ rūpaṁ* (S. iv, 382).

the sense of four *rūpajjhāna* or the four absorptions (*jhāna*). As Karunadasa remarked, "These four may be represented as the generic, specific, cosmological and the psychological meanings of the term."[3] Mrs. Carolyn Rhys Davids,[4] Surendranath Dasgupta[5] and S.Z. Aung[6] argue that not all of the elements that constitute "generic matter" are part of the *rūpakkhandha*. Karunadasa claims, however, that they have misinterpreted a passage from the *Yamaka*.[7] The passage reads,

> Is matter the material aggregate? Pleasant matter (*piyarūpaṁ*) and agreeable matter (*sātarūpaṁ*) are *rūpa*, but do not belong to the material aggregate; whereas the material aggregate is both matter and the material aggregate. What is neither the material aggregate nor matter? Pleasant matter (*piyarūpaṁ*) and agreeable matter (*sātarūpaṁ*) do not belong to the material aggregate but are matter; everything except matter and the material aggregate is neither matter nor the material aggregate.[8]

According to this, everything that comes under the heading of *rūpa*, except pleasant (*piyarūpa*) and agreeable matter (*sātarūpa*), belongs to the *rūpakkhandha*. Both Rhys Davids and Dasgupta agree with Aung's interpretation of this passage, in which Aung explains the terms *piya-rūpa* and *sātarūpa* as the eighty-one worldly classes of consciousness and their concomitants that are attractive and pleasant.[9] These eighty-one classes of consciousness do not, according to Aung, belong to the *rūpa-kkhandha*, which is made up solely of twenty-seven material qualities (the four primary elements and the twenty-three secondary elements). This interpretation suggests that the *Yamaka*'s definition of the term *rūpa* is not limited to matter, but also includes mental states (the eighty-

---

3 Y. Karunadasa, *Buddhist Analysis of Matter* (Colombo: Department of Cultural Affairs, 1967), p. 1.

4 Ymk. i, xi.

5 Surendranath Dasgupta, *A History of Indian Philosophy* (Delhi: Motilal Banarsidass, 1975), 1:94.

6 Shwe Zan Aung, trans., *Compendium of Philosophy (Abhidhammatthasaṅgaha)* (London: P.T.S., 1967), p. 273.

7 Karunadasa, *Buddhist Analysis of Matter*, pp. 4-5.

8 *Rūpaṁ rūpakkhandho ti? Piyarūpaṁ sātarūpaṁ rūpaṁ, na rūpakkhandho; rūpakkhandho rūpaṁ ceva rūpakkhandho ca. ... Na rūpaṁ na rūpakkhandho ti? ... Piyarūpaṁ sātarūpaṁ na rūpakkhandho, rūpaṁ; rūpañ ca rūpakkhandhañ ca ṭhapetvā avasesā na ceva rūpaṁ na ca rūpakkhandho* (Ymk. i, 16-17).

9 Aung, *Compendium of Philosophy*, p. 273.

one classes of consciousness). However, this particular interpretation is based, it would seem, on speculation as it is not supported by any textual evidence. Karunadasa has pointed out[10] a further weakness in this interpretation, since elsewhere in the abhidhammic literature we find a definition of *piyarūpa* and *sātarūpa* which includes the six internal and external sense-doors,[11] all of which are included in the *rūpakkhandha.*[12] There seems to be a contradiction between the *Yamaka,* which asserts that *piyarūpa* and *sātarūpa* do not belong to the *rūpakkhandha,* and the *Vibhaṅga,* which implicitly includes *piyarūpa* and *sātarūpa* in the *rūpakkhandha* since the six sense-doors, which are part of the *rūpakkhandha,* are included in the definition of these two terms. However, Karunadasa indicates that the two seemingly contradictory statements of the *Yamaka* and the *Vibhaṅga* are not mutually exclusive because the former belongs to a method of exposition particular to the *Yamaka*—a method that cannot be used to define the *rūpakkhandha.*[13] The *Yamaka* passage, therefore, is not relevant to a discussion of the similarity between *rūpa* and the *rūpakkhandha.*

In the *Visuddhimagga,* Buddhaghosa defines *rūpa* (in Karunadasa's sense of "generic matter") as the four primary elements and the matter derived from them.[14] As we saw on. 31, this is the standard definition of the *rūpakkhandha.* Here, Buddhaghosa not only applies the definition of the *rūpakkhandha* to the concept of *rūpa,* but also urges his reader to refer to his previous discussion on the *rūpakkhandha* in order to clarify the meaning of *rūpa.*[15] On the basis of this statement by as established an authority as Buddhaghosa, we may proceed with the assumption that, at least traditionally, the *rūpa-*

10 Karunadasa, *Buddhist Analysis of Matter,* p. 5.

11 In order to avoid confusion, we will, from now on, refer to the "internal sense-doors" as "sense-organs" (eye, ear, nose, tongue, body, mind), and the "external sense-doors" as the "sense-objects" (forms, sounds, smells, tastes, touches, thoughts).

12 *Kiṅ ca loke piyarūpaṁ sātarūpaṁ? Cakkhuṁ loke piyarūpaṁ sātarūpaṁ etth'esā taṇhā uppajjamānā uppajjati, ettha nivisamānā nivisati. Sotaṁ ... pe ... ghānaṁ ... jivhā ... kāyo ... mano ... rūpā ... saddā ... gandhā ... rasā ... phoṭṭhabbā ... dhammā loke piyarūpaṁ sātarūpaṁ etth'esā taṇhā uppajjamānā uppajjati, ettha nivisamānā nivisati* (Vbh. 101-102).

13 Explaining Karunadasa's argument is not necessary. However, those desiring further clarification can refer to Karunadasa's *Buddhist Analysis of Matter,* pp. 5-8.

14 *Rūpan ti cattāri mahābhūtāni catunnañ ca mahābhūtānaṁ upādāya rūpaṁ* (Vsm. 558).

15 *Tesaṁ vibhāgo Khandhaniddese vutto yevā ti* (Vsm. 558).

kkhandha has not been seen as different from *rūpa* in the sense of "generic matter."

While most Indian philosophical systems claim that there are five primary elements, the Buddhist and Jain traditions postulate only four. These two traditions, however, do not consider space (*ākāsa*) to be a primary element. The Theravāda school, however, incorporates space into its list of "secondary elements" (*upādārūpa*).[16]

The Four Primary Material Elements (*Mahābhūta*)

In a discussion with his son,[17] the Buddha concisely explains the four primary elements and their particular qualities. The earth element (*paṭhavīdhātu*) is described as whatever is hard and solid (*kakkhalaṁ kharigattaṁ*), such as the hair, nails, teeth, and other parts of the body. The water element (*āpodhātu*) is characterized by liquid (*āpogataṁ*), as in the case of blood, tears and saliva. The Buddha describes the fire element (*tejodhātu*) as that which is hot, like the heat that digests food. And finally the air element (*vāyadhātu*) is characterized by motion, like the different gases in the stomach and the abdomen.[18] According to a different source, the first three primary elements (earth, fire and air) also share the fundamental characteristic of solidity (*paṭigha*)[19] in the sense that there is bound to be an impact, a shock, when two of these material particles collide. This quality of solidity (Skr. *pratighāta*) is defined in the *Abhidharmakośa* as "l'impénétrabilité, le heurt ou résistance (*pratighāta*), l'obstacle qu'un *rūpa* oppose à ce que son lieu soit occupé par un autre *rūpa*."[20]

Buddhaghosa, in the commentary on the *Dhammasaṅgaṇi* and the *Visuddhimagga*, offers us a more extensive definition of these four primary elements. According to the commentator, the earth element is

---

16 See p. 39.

17 *Mahārāhulovādasuttaṁ* (M. i, 420); a similar description is found in the *Mahāhatthipadopamasutta* (M. i, 185).

18 Strangely enough, a discussion of the *ākāsadhātu* follows the description of these four elements just as if it belonged to primary matter. However, as we mentioned, the *ākāsadhātu* is not included in the Buddhist list of primary elements, but belongs to secondary matter.

19 Implied by Dhs. 147. For a further discussion on the term *paṭigha*, please refer to p. 41.

20 La Vallée Poussin, *Abhidharmakośa*, 1:24-25.

so called because it "is spread out,"[21] and it is the platform that supports the other three elements.[22] In commentarial literature, the earth element is literally perceived as a support for the other three primary elements, just as the earth is a support for mountains and trees.[23] According to Buddhaghosa, the water element is thus termed because of its characteristic of flowing (*appoti*), gliding (*āpiyati*) and satisfying (*appāyati*). The validity of the definition is questionable, however, for the Theravāda commentarial literature tends to define words through the use of terms that share the same etymology. For example, the earth element (*paṭhavī*) is described as *patthaṭattā*, and matter (*rūpa*) is often characterized by the verb *ruppati*.[24] These apparently false etymological interpretations could, in fact, simply be mnemonic devices that were never intended to be linguistically accurate. As for the definition of the water element, however, we know that the verb *appoti* is derived from the root *āp*, while *āpiyati* and *appāyati* seem to be connected to the Sanskrit root *ṛ*—which is not etymologically linked to *āpo*. However, the *Dhammasaṅgaṇi* uses the terms *sineha* and *bhandana* (which have no apparent or real etymological link with *āpo*) to define the water element.[25] These two words support Buddhaghosa's previous definition by implying that the water element is endowed with the characteristic of liquidity (*sineha*) and binding (*bhandana*). The fire element is defined by Buddhaghosa as that which possesses the characteristic of temperature (*teja*)[26] but, as with the water element, the *Dhammasaṅgaṇi* and the *Atthasālinī* offer a definition that does not restrict itself to providing a cognate word: "the fire element has the quality of heat (*usmā* or *uṇhā*)."[27] The air element represents the most

---

21 *Patthaṭattā pathavī* [*sic*] (Vsm. 364). The word *paṭhavī* may have been misspelled; on the other hand, this "error" may have been a conscious alteration on the part of Buddhaghosa in order to indicate the etymological derivation of *paṭhavī* from *patthaṭa*.

22 *Tattha kakkhaḷattalakkhaṇā paṭhavīdhātu patiṭṭhānarasā sampaṭicchanapaccupaṭṭhānā* (DhsA. 332).

23 *Tarupabbatādīnaṁ pakatipaṭhavī viya sahajātarūpānaṁ patiṭṭhānabhāvena pakkhāyati, upaṭṭhātī ti vuttaṁ hoti*. Anuruddha, *Abhidhammatthasaṅgaha*, p. 110.

24 The reader may wish to refer to the discussion on p. 46.

25 *Kataman taṁ rūpaṁ āpodhātu? Yaṁ āpo āpogataṁ sineho sinehagataṁ bandhanattaṁ* (Dhs. 177).

26 "It heats therefore it is called fire-element." *Tejatī ti tejo* (Vsm. 364).

27 *Yaṁ tejo tejogataṁ usmā usmāgataṁ usmaṁ usumāgataṁ* (Dhs. 177); a similar definition is found in DhsA. 332.

dynamic of the four primary elements in that it is primarily characterized by mobility and fluctuation.[28]

It is of crucial importance that none of the four primary elements can exist without the presence of the other three. Fire, for example, is not merely composed of the fire element, nor does water consist solely of the water element. The primary elements cannot exist independently of one another;[29] all four are present in every material particle. The *Paramatthamañjūsā*, a commentary on the *Visuddhimagga*, expands upon this point:

> ... likewise their [the four primary elements] undemonstrability, since they are not found inside or outside of each other for support. For if these elements were found inside each other, they would not each perform their particular functions, owing to mutual frustration. And if they were found outside each other, they would be already resolved (separate), and that being so, any description of them as unresolved (inseparable) would be meaningless. So although their standing place is undemonstrable, still each one assists the other by its particular function—the functions of establishing, etc., whereby each becomes a condition for the others as conascence condition and so on.[30]

Karunadasa stresses that all four primary elements appear in equal quantity in every manifestation of matter.[31] What renders different manifestations of matter distinct is not the quantitative, but rather the qualitative or "capability" (*sāmatthiya*) proportion of the primary elements. The difference between water and fire does not reside in the quantity of the fire element or water element found therein, but rather in the intensity of these two elements.

The last aspect of the primary elements that I would like to mention is their deceptiveness. According to the Theravāda tradition, these four primary elements and their respective qualities are inherent in every material particle. Matter is composed of nothing else, yet we not only perceive material particles as warm or cold, stable or moving,

---

28 *Yaṁ vāyo vāyogataṁ chambhitattaṁ thambhitattaṁ* (Dhs. 177).

29 *Na ca taṁ nissāya na tiṭṭhantī ti* (Vsm. 367).

30 *Paramatthamañjūsā*, 363. Quoted from Ven. Ñāṇamoli, trans., *The Path of Purification (Visuddhimagga) by Bhadantācariya Buddhaghosa* (Kandy: B.P.S., 1979), p. 400, n. 38.

31 Karunadasa, *Buddhist Analysis of Matter*, p. 26. The *Abhidharmakośa* supports this thesis by maintaining that "les grands éléments (*mahābhūtas*) sont, entre eux, *sahabhūhetu*" (La Vallée Poussin, *Abhidharmakośa*, 1:248-49).

hard or soft or spread or coagulated, but also as imbued with other qualities, such as colour. The primary elements, then, appear in a variety of forms apparently unrelated to their own qualities. Buddhaghosa explains this by resorting to one of his favourite methods of clarification: he makes a play on the word *mahābhūta* by comparing the four primary elements to a great magician:

> Just as a magician (*mahābhūta*) turns water that is not crystal into crystal, and turns a clod that is not gold into gold, and shows them, and being himself neither a spirit or a bird, shows himself as a spirit or a bird so too, being themselves [the four *mahābhūta*] not blue-black, they turn themselves into blue-black derived materiality [secondary elements], being themselves not yellow ... not red ... not white, they turn themselves into white derived materiality [secondary elements] and show that. In this way they are primary elements (*mahābhūta*) in being like the great creatures (*mahābhūta*) of a magician.[32]

Thus, these primary elements are the foundations which support the secondary elements.

The Secondary Material Elements (*Upādārūpa*)

The difference between primary and secondary elements is adumbrated in the *sutta* literature itself,[33] yet no specific description of the secondary elements is found in the *nikāya*. Although the *Abhidhamma-piṭaka* has elaborated a scheme of twenty-three secondary elements,[34] I have found neither such an elaboration, nor even a passing mention

32 *Yathā māyākāro amaṇiṁ yeva udakaṁ maṇiṁ katvā dasseti, asuvaṇṇaṁ yeva leḍḍuṁ suvaṇṇam katvā dasseti;—yathā ca, sayaṁ neva yakkho na yakkhī samāno, yakkhabhāvam pi yakkhibhāvam pi dasseti, evam eva sayaṁ anīlan' eva hutvā nīlaṁ upādārūpaṁ dassenti, apītāni alohitāni anodātān' eva hutvā odātaṁ upādārūpaṁ dassentī ti māyākāramahābhūtasāmaññato mahābhūtāni.* Vsm. 366-67. Translation from Ñāṇamoli, *The Path of Purification*, p. 98. A similar passage is found in DhsA. 299.

33 Such as in M. i, 53, 185; S. ii, 3-4, 59.

34 Dhs. 167. Some commentarial literature recognizes a twenty-fourth "secondary matter," the heart-basis (*hadayavatthu*). The heart-basis seems to be a post-canonical development since it is only mentioned in literature compiled during or after Buddhaghosa. To my knowledge, this element is not mentioned in the *sutta* literature. Since the mainstream canonical literature does not list this last element, I will not include it in the discussion of matter.

of the exact meaning of the secondary elements in the *sutta*. However, one passage found in a few instances in the *sutta* offers us a hint as to the nature of these secondary elements: "the four primary elements and the matter derived (*upādāṇaya rūpaṁ*) from them are called *rūpa*."[35] The *P.T.S Dictionary*[36] renders the term *upādāya* as "derived" and "secondary," thereby implying a prior substratum from which it could be "derived" (the primary elements). The *Atthasālinī* explains what is meant by the "matter derived" from the four great elements: "matter which is dependent on, is derived from, and is still attached to the four great elements. What is known as 'all matter' consists of the four great elements and the twenty-three derived material 'things' shown in due order."[37] These two references indicate that the secondary elements are always dependent on, and therefore secondary to, the four primary elements.

The list of the twenty-three secondary elements is given in the *Vibhaṅga*[38] and the *Dhammasaṅgaṇi*. The elements can be grouped into seven different categories, as indicated in Table 3.

Discussing every one of the twenty-three secondary elements would be far too tedious. Two points concerning them, however, merit some discussion. The first is the exclusion of bodily impressions (*phoṭṭhabbāyatana*) from the list of the various elements that constitute secondary matter. Since touch is one of the sense-organs, it would be natural to expect its respective sense-object to be included in the enumeration. The reason for its exclusion lies in the fact that this particular sense-object is constituted by three of the primary elements earth, fire and wind.[39] According to the Theravāda tradition, these three primary elements can be known by the tactile sense-door.[40] We

---

35 *Cattāri ca mahābhūtāni catunnaṁ ca mahābhūtānaṁ upādāya rūpaṁ, idaṁ vuccat' āvuso rūpaṁ.* Found in M. i, 53, 185; S. ii, 3-4, 59.

36 T.W. Rhys Davids and William Stede, *The Pāli Text Society Pāli-English Dictionary* (London: P.T.S., 1979).

37 *Cattāri mahābhūtāni upādāya nissāya amuñcitvā pavattarūpan ti attho. Idaṁ vuccati sabbaṁ rūpan ti, idaṁ cattāri mahābhūtāni padapaṭispāṭiyā niddiṭṭhāni tevīsati upādārūpānī ti sattavīsatipabhedaṁ sabbaṁ rūpaṁ nāma* (DhsA. 300).

38 Vbh. 1ff.

39 Phoṭṭhabbadhātu pana pathavī-tejo-vāyo-vasena tayo dhammā ti sankhaṁ gacchati. Vsm. 488. Similar statements are found in Dhs. 143, 179; Vbh. 72.

40 Not all Buddhist traditions, however, agree on this point. The *Abhidharmakośa*, for example, maintains that all the four primary elements are tangible: "*Le tangible est de onze espèces. Onze choses sont des choses tangibles* (spraṣṭavyadravya)*: les quatre grands éléments (*mahābhūta*), le doux, le rude, le lourd, le léger, le froid, la faim et la soif*" (La Vallée Poussin, *Abhidharmakośa*, 1:18).

Table 3
The Twenty-three Secondary Elements (*upādārūpa*)

A	**The first five sense-organs (internal sense-doors):**	
1.	*cakkhāyatana*	(organ of sight)
2.	*sotāyatana*	(organ of hearing)
3.	*ghānāyatana*	(organ of smell)
4.	*jivhāyatana*	(organ of taste)
5.	*kāyāyatana*	(organ of touch)
B	**The first four sense-objects (external sense-doors):**	
6.	*rūpāyatana*	(the visible)
7.	*saddāyatana*	(sound)
8.	*gandhāyatana*	(smell)
9.	*rasāyatana*	(taste)
C	**The three faculties:**	
10.	*itthindriya*	(faculty of femininity)
11.	*purisindriya*	(faculty of masculinity)
12.	*rūpajīvitindriya*	(material faculty of life)
D	**The two modes of self-expression:**	
13.	*kāyaviññatti*	(bodily expression)
14.	*vacīviññatti*	(vocal expression)
E	**The three characteristics of matter:**	
15.	*lahutā*	(lightness)
16.	*mudutā*	(elasticity)
17.	*kammaññatā*	(adaptability)
F	**The four phases of matter:**	
18.	*upacaya*	(growth)
19.	*santati*	(continuity)
20.	*jaratā*	(decay)
21.	*aniccatā*	(impermanence)
G	**The two unclassified elements:**	
22.	*ākāsadhātu*	(space-element)
23.	*āhāra*	(food)

cannot say, therefore, that the Theravāda tradition excludes the bodily impressions from its list of the different elements that constitute secondary matter, since it is implicitly included by the presence of the first three primary elements.

The second problem related to this enumeration is that Buddhism admits six sense-organs, the sixth being the mental organ (*mano*). However, we have seen that only the first five sense-organs are discussed and that the mental organ as well as its respective object, the mental object (*dhammāyatana*), are not included in the list of elements that constitute secondary matter. The reason for this exclusion is not, as David Kalupahana has suggested, that the mental organ and its respective object (*dhammāyatana*) belong to the *viññāṇakkhandha* rather than to the *rūpakkhandha*.[41] Kalupahana's interpretation is most likely grounded in the theories of the Sarvāstivāda, Sautrāntika and Yogācāra systems, according to which the mental organ (Skr.: *dharmāyatana*) is not part of the *rūpaskandha* (Pāli: *rūpakkhandha*). According to the Theravāda tradition, however, while it is true that the mental organ belongs to the *viññāṇakkhandha*,[42] its respective object, the mental object, belongs to the *rūpakkhandha* itself. Since the range of the mental object is extremely wide, it does not limit itself to secondary matter. The mental object includes one primary element as well as fifteen of the elements that constitute secondary matter (numbers ten to twenty-three in the above list), which are collectively termed *dhammāyatanapariyāpannarūpa*.[43] Therefore, since the mental object is composed of these sixteen elements of matter, it clearly does belong to the *rupakkhandha* rather than to the *viññāṇakkhandha*.

The Three Divisions of Matter

According to the *Saṅgītisutta* of the *Dīghanikāya*, matter is divided into three dual categories: visible and "resisting"; invisible and "resisting";

41 Kalupahana, *The Principles of Buddhist Psychology*, p. 29.

42 However, as mentioned in n. 34 on p. 37, post-canonical literature has incorporated a twenty-fourth element into the list of the elements that constitute secondary matter: the heart-basis (*hadayavatthu*). This twenty-fourth element is recognized by Theravāda scholasticism as the physical basis for the mental organ (VsmA. 449-50). The term *hadaya* itself, not as belonging to the secondary matter category, is also sometimes used as a synonym of *mano* and *manoviññāṇa* (Vbh. 87, 88, 144).

43 Dhs. 179; Vbh. 14, 72.

and, finally, invisible and "unresisting."[44] This threefold division occurs only once in the *nikāya* literature, and no explanation is given for it. The commentary on this particular *sutta* does not shed much light on the topic either.[45] The *Dhammasaṅgaṇi*, however, clarifies the meaning of the terms. According to this abhidhammic text, the term visible (*sanidassanaṁ*) is restricted to what is visible (*rūpāyatana*)—the only material element which can actually be perceived by the eye.[46] All the other elements of matter (primary or secondary) are considered *anidassanaṁ*, for they are invisible.[47] This statement may seem to conflict with the *sutta* definition of the primary elements (see p. 34) according to which the earth element finds expression in, for instance, hair, nails, etc., and the water element in blood, tears, and so on—all of which are visible. The *Abhidharmakośa* resolves this apparent contradiction by claiming that although all four primary elements are invisible, we can actually see them in partial manifestations, for their visibility is understood from the perspective of common usage. In reality, the elements themselves are invisible:

> Dans l'usage commun, ce qu'on désigne par le mot "terre," c'est de la couleur et de la figure; de même pour l'eau et le feu; le vent, c'est ou bien l'élément vent, ou bien de la couleur et de la figure. En effet, on parle de "vent noir," "vent circulaire"; mais ce qu'on appelle "vent" dans le monde, c'est aussi l'élément vent.[48]

The elements classified under "resisting" (*sappaṭighaṁ*) are the five sense-organs and their respective objects, for they can actually or potentially come in contact with one another.[49] We notice that bodily impression (*phoṭṭhabbāyatana*) is included in the list of resisting

---

44 *Tividhena rūpa-saṁgaho. Sanidassana-sappaṭighaṁ rūpaṁ, anidassana-sappaṭighaṁ rūpaṁ, anidassana-appaṭghaṁ rūpaṁ* (D. iii, 217).

45 DA. 997.

46 *Kataman taṁ rūpaṁ sanidassanaṁ? Rūpāyatanaṁ—idan taṁ rūpaṁ sanidassanaṁ* (Dhs. 146).

47 *Katamaṁ taṁ rūpaṁ anidassanaṁ? Cakkhāyatanaṁ ... pe ... kabaḷiṅkāro āhāro—idan taṁ rūpaṁ anidassanaṁ* (Dhs. 146. See also Kvu. 331ff.).

48 La Vallée Poussin, *Abhidharmakośa* 1:23-24.

49 *Kataman taṁ rūpaṁ sappaṭighaṁ? Cakkhāyatanaṁ, sotāyatanaṁ, ghānāyatanaṁ, jivhāyatanaṁ, kāyāyatanaṁ, rūpāyatanaṁ, saddāyatanaṁ, gandhāyatanaṁ, rasāyatanaṁ, phoṭṭhabbāyatanaṁ -idan taṁ rūpaṁ sappaṭighaṁ* (Dhs. 147).

elements while not being explicitly part of the enumeration of the twenty-seven elements of *rūpa*—the four primary elements and the twenty-three elements that constitute secondary matter. Although bodily impression does not seem to be a constituent of the list, it is implicitly included, for the three primary elements of earth, fire and air do in fact constitute bodily impression. Bodily impression is probably excluded out of a desire to avoid duplication: since the first three primary elements constitute bodily impression, there is no need to mention this element again in the enumeration. Therefore, when the *Dhammasangaṇi* says that bodily impression is resisting (*sappaṭighaṁ*), the first three elements of earth, fire and air are intended. The unresisting elements (*appaṭighaṁ*), on the other hand, are all those which are not resisting:[50] water and all the fourteen elements that follow, including femininity (*itthindriya*). Therefore, the classification of visible and resisting (*sanidissanaṁ; sappaṭighaṁ*) refers only to what is visible, while that of invisible and resisting (*anidassanaṁ; sappaṭighaṁ*) designates all the sense-organs and the sense-objects (with the exception of the *rūpāyatana* and the inclusion of the first three primary elements as bodily impression). And, finally, that of invisible and unresisting (*anidassanaṁ; appaṭighaṁ*) stands for all the remaining elements, i.e. water, femininity, masculinity, faculty of life, bodily expression, vocal expression, lightness, elasticity, adaptability, growth, continuity, decay, impermanence, space and food.

To summarize the implication of the classification of matter in the *Saṅgītisutta*, we can say that the twenty-seven material elements are invisible (*anidassanaṁ*) except, of course, *rūpāyatana* (the visible) which is visible (*sanidassanaṁ*) by definition. The first five sense-organs and their respective objects, which include the first three primary elements as bodily impression, are resisting (*sapaṭighaṁ*) and invisible (*anidassanaṁ*), while all the other elements are non-resisting (*apaṭighaṁ*) and invisible (*anidassanaṁ*). The reason for this first division of the material elements will become apparent at the conclusion of a discussion of the various categories of matter.

50 We become more and more aware of inherent tautologies in etymologically grounded definitions.

Further Classifications of Matter

All the elements of matter can be further classified, as we have seen, according to different categories such as past/present/future, internal/external, gross/subtle, small/large, and far/near. In this section, we will briefly look at the implications of three of these categories, namely (1) internal and external (*ajjhatta* and *bahiddhā*), (2) gross and subtle (*oḷārika* and *sukhuma*) and (3) far and near (*dūre* and *santike*).

The first category establishes a distinction between internal or personal (*ajjhatta*) and external or foreign (*bahiddhā*) elements. This first distinction will prove to be of great import for correlating the five aggregates with the *paṭiccasamuppāda*. This classification is not restricted to the material aggregate, but is also applicable to the other four *khandha*,[51] for the distinction between external and internal lies simply in the fact that internal elements are those which "belong" to the individual while the external elements are those which "belong" to other individuals.[52] The first five sense-organs are the only material elements which are internal.[53] According to the same source, the external material elements (see Table 4) include the four primary elements (literally the sphere of the tangible [*phoṭṭhabbāyatana*] and the water element), the four sense-objects enumerated under the twenty-seven elements of *rūpa*, and all the following elements that constitute secondary matter.

The two following categories, gross and subtle, and far and near are used, as Karunadasa points out,[54] as a method for distinguishing the elements constituting mental object[55] from the other elements of *rūpa*. According to Buddhaghosa, the meanings of "far" and "near" are not at all linked, as we would expect, to the notion of spatial proximity, but rather to the capacity of being perceived.

---

51 Dhs. 187.

52 *Katame dhammā ajjhattā? Ye dhammā tesaṁ tesaṁ sattānaṁ ajjhattaṁ paccattaṁ niyatā paṭipuggalikā upādiṇṇā rūpā vedanā saññā saṅkhārā viññāṇaṁ—ime dhammā ajjhattā. Katame dhammā bahiddhā? Ye dhammā tesaṁ tesaṁ parasattānaṁ parapuggalānaṁ ajjhattaṁ paccattaṁ niyatā paṭipuggalikā ... pe ... viññāṇaṁ—ime dhammā bahiddhā* (Dhs. 187-88).

53 Dhs. 154ff.

54 Karunadasa, *Buddhist Analysis of Matter*, p. 38.

55 See p. 40.

Table 4
The External Material Elements

paṭhavī	earth element	(part of bodily impression)
tejo	fire element	(part of bodily impression)
vāyo	air element	(part of bodily impression)
āpo	water element	
rūpa	the visible	
sadda	sound	
gandha	smell	
rasa	taste	
itthindriya	faculty of femininity	
purisindriya	faculty of masculinity	
rūpajīvitindriya	material faculty of life	
kāyaviññatti	bodily expression	
vacīviññatti	vocal expression	
lahutā	lightness	
mudutā	elasticity	
kammaññatā	adaptability	
upacaya	growth	
santati	continuity	
jaratā	decay	
aniccatā	impermanence	
ākāsadhātu	space-element	
āhāra	food	

> Gross [*oḷārikaṁ*] means thick, that which may be seized by impact of the sensitive surface, because it has become the basis and the object of thought. Subtle [*sukhuma*] should be understood as the contradictory of what has been said. Remote: (an object may be) far [*dūre*] even though it stands near. This is when there is a difficulty of cognizing, because it is not to be seized by way of impact [*ghaṭṭana*]. The other term near [*santike*] (may apply to an object) though it stands far. This is when there is ease of cognizing, because it may be seized by way of an impact [*ghaṭṭana*].[56]

Karunadasa, in turn, comments that:

56 Pe Tin Maung, trans., *The Expositor (Atthasālinī)* (London: P.T.S., 1976), p. 438.

Table 5
Classification of the Twenty-seven Material Elements

Only the five previously discussed categories are listed. If an element possesses a certain quality, a "Y" is given under that particular quality. If an "N" is given, this element is characterized by the opposite quality.

Opposite qualities

mahābhūta	-------------------->	*upādārūpa*
paṭigha (sappaṭigha)	-------------------->	*appaṭigha*
ajjhatta	-------------------->	*bahiddhā*
oḷārika	-------------------->	*sukhuma*
santike	-------------------->	*dūre*

	mahābhūta (primary elements)	*paṭigha* (resisting)	*ajjhatta* (internal)	*oḷārika* (gross)	*santike* (near)
1. *paṭhavī*	Y	Y	N	Y	Y
2. *tejo*	Y	Y	N	Y	Y
3. *vāyo*	Y	Y	N	Y	Y
4. *āpo*	Y	N	N	N	N
5. *cakkhu*	N	Y	Y	Y	Y
6. *sota*	N	Y	Y	Y	Y
7. *ghāna*	N	Y	Y	Y	Y
8. *jivhā*	N	Y	Y	Y	Y
9. *kāya*	N	Y	Y	Y	Y
10. *rūpa*	N	Y	N	Y	Y
11. *sadda*	N	Y	N	Y	Y
12. *gandha*	N	Y	N	Y	Y
13. *rasa*	N	Y	N	Y	Y
14. *itthindriya*	N	N	N	N	N
15. *purisindriya*	N	N	N	N	N
16. *rūpajīvitindriya*	N	N	N	N	N
17. *kāyaviññatti*	N	N	N	N	N
18. *vacīviññatti*	N	N	N	N	N
19. *lahutā*	N	N	N	N	N
20. *mudutā*	N	N	N	N	N
21. *kammaññatā*	N	N	N	N	N
22. *upacaya*	N	N	N	N	N
23. *santati*	N	N	N	N	N
24. *jaratā*	N	N	N	N	N
25. *aniccatā*	N	N	N	N	N
26. *ākāsadhātu*	N	N	N	N	N
27. *āhāra*	N	N	N	N	N

> because of their being thus easily known (*gahanassa sukarattā*), they are styled *santike* (proximate). For this self-same reason they are also called *oḷārika*. The *dhammāyatana-rūpa* [elements constituting mental object] cannot be known through the medium of any of the first five sense-organs; their existence is known by a process of inference. In this sense they are not easily known (*duppariññeyya*). Hence they are described as *dūre* (far). For this self-same reason they are also called *sukhuma* (subtle).[57]

Therefore, the material elements constituting mental objects are described as far and subtle because they are not easily perceptible. Buddhaghosa's definition of far and subtle revolves around the concept of lack of impact (*ghaṭṭana*), for there is no direct contact between the first five sense-organs and the mental objects. The concept of lacking an impact is similar to that of unresisting (*appaṭigham*; see p. 42) and, therefore, it is no surprise to learn that the fifteen material elements classified as far and subtle refer to the exact same elements that are classified as unresisting, i.e., those that constitute mental objects.

Implications of the Previous Classifications

Many scholars, including F.L. Woodward,[58] S.Z. Aung[59] and S. Dasgupta,[60] have been puzzled by a certain canonical definition stating that *rūpa* has a definite "subjective" element: *Rūpaṁ ruppati* (or literally: "*rūpa* affects"). Although I agree with Woodward that *ruppati* cannot be considered as the proper etymology for the word *rūpa*, I feel that this particular definition sheds light on the nature of matter, since matter is not simply an objective reality independent of the perception of the individual.

The distinctions that we have covered so far between the different kinds of "matter" emphasize the deep empirical sense that characterizes Buddhism. It seems that Theravāda Buddhism stresses that for something to be present for someone, it needs to be perceived. Unless there is perception of the object (be it perception of the object itself or perception of its mere conceptualization), it is absolutely

57 Karunadasa, *Buddhist Analysis of Matter*, p. 38.

58 F.L. Woodward, trans., *The Book of the Kindred Sayings (Saṁyuttanikāya)* (London: P.T.S., 1917-22), 3:73.

59 Aung, *Compendium of Philosophy*, p. 273.

60 Dasgupta, *A History of Indian Philosophy*, 1:94.

meaningless for that person—it is absent. Absence does not deny the absolute reality of the object when unperceived by a subject, but stresses that the object is of no significance to such a subject. Understanding this, we can now make sense of the distinctions between the different kinds of matter.

The division of matter into internal and external has strong implications for this study, for it also establishes a distinction between matter endowed with ontological reality independent of its being perceived, and matter whose reality is dependent on a potential perception. The elements of matter in the internal classification are the five sense-organs (vision, audition, smell, taste and touch), and they are endowed with reality whether or not they are perceived. These five sense-organs are also dependent on the primary elements, which constitute their foundation. The four primary elements, therefore, are also endowed with the same reality. The category "external" refers to the material elements whose reality is dependent on a potential perception. It is easy to understand why four of the sense-objects (visible forms, sounds, smells and tastes) are included in this division, for they can all potentially be perceived by an individual.

The inclusion in this division of the four primary elements and the last fourteen elements that constitute secondary matter may seem problematic at first. Furthermore, the exclusion of bodily impressions and of mental objects (*dhammāyatana*) from the "external" category would seem equally odd. We must recall, however, that bodily impression is made up of the first three great elements (earth, fire and air). Although all the four great elements have a reality independent of potential perception, they become factors in the bodily impression only when they can be perceived by an individual, that is, only when there can be an actual contact between an individual and the first three elements. In other words, these three great elements are not always bodily impression, although the bodily impression itself is always composed of them.

As for the mental objects, they are only apparently left out since they are described by the fifteen elements: the fourth primary element (water) and the last fourteen elements that constitute secondary matter (water, femininity, masculinity, faculty of life, bodily expression, vocal expression, lightness, elasticity, adaptability, growth, continuity, decay, impermanence, space and food). The same reasoning employed above regarding the bodily impression is applicable to the mental object: the mental object is always composed of one or more of the fifteen elements given above.

With respect to the *paṭiccasamuppāda*, the most important of the various divisions of matter is that between internal (objective) and external (subjective) matter. The first refers to material reality (as well as our five sense-organs) existing independently of the potential perception of it, and the second to the form that matter takes in order to be apprehended by the senses. In other words, this twofold division can be expressed as (1) the five sense-organs as well as the four primary elements, and (2) the six sense-objects. The first four sense-objects are explicitly listed in the Pāli canon as categories of matter, while the last two (bodily impression and mental object) are implicitly included by, respectively: (1) the first three primary elements, and (2) the water element and the last fourteen elements that constitute secondary matter. It is these six sense-objects that constitute the "subjective" aspect of matter—subjective in the sense that they can potentially be perceived by, and affect (*ruppati*), the individual.

Correlation between the *Rūpakkhandha* and the *Paṭiccasamuppāda*

There is a direct relation between the *rūpakkhandha* and the fifth and sixth links of the chain of dependent origination: the six sense-doors (*saḷāyatanā*) and contact (*phassa*). The six sense-doors (*saḷāyatanā*) are usually understood in terms of "internal" and "external"—respectively, the six sense-organs and the six sense-objects. However, it is widely understood that in the formula of the *paṭiccasamuppāda* itself, the term *saḷāyatanā* includes only the six sense-doors and not their respective objects.[61] The *sutta*, abhidhammic and commentarial literature support this view.[62] There is, therefore, a direct correlation with the six sense-doors link of the *paṭiccasamuppāda* and the five sense-organs that partly constitute the *rūpakkhandha*. The problem that we face, however, is that the six sense-doors include six sense-organs, whereas the *rūpa-*

---

61 Karunadasa, *Buddhist Analysis of Matter*, p. 79; Bhikkhu Ñāṇamoli, trans., *The Guide (Nettippakaraṇaṁ)* (London: P.T.S., 1977), p. 48, n. 164/5; Nyānātiloka, *Buddhist Dictionary*, p. 25, 123.

62 *Katamañca bhikkhave saḷāyatanaṁ. Cakkhāyatanaṁ sotāyatanaṁ ghānāyatanaṁ jivhāyatanaṁ kāyātanamaṁ manāyatanam. Idam vuccati bhikkhave saḷāyatanam* (S. ii, 3). *Tattha katamaṁ nāmarūpapaccayā saḷāyatanaṁ? Cakkhāyatanaṁ ... pe ... manāyatanaṁ; idaṁ vuccati nāmarūpapaccayā saḷāyatanaṁ* (Vbh. 164. See also a similar interpretation in Vsm. 565).

kkhandha only admits five of them by excluding the mental organ from its list, the latter belonging to the *viññānakkhandha*. However, the mental sense-organ has already been implicitly introduced into the chain of dependent origination by the two preceding links, *viññāṇa* and *nāma-rūpa*,[63] and, as we will now see, the following link, contact (*phassa*), explicitly requires the presence of the mental organ.

Contact is usually defined as the meeting of consciousness (*viññāṇa*), a sense-organ (*indriya*) and an external stimulus (*visaya*).[64] In keeping with this understanding, contact not only requires the presence of a consciousness,[65] but also of the sense-organs and the sense-objects. The sense-objects are presumably excluded from the six sense-doors link as it seems to be an explanation of our personal bondage to misery; since sense-objects, when unperceived, have no influence on our binding to *saṁsāra*, it is understandable that they are not included. However, they are included in the link of contact, for here, by *actually* being perceived, they have a direct influence on the individual. There is a further correlation between the sense-objects discussed in the *rūpakkhandha* and those of contact. In the *rūpa-kkhandha* the sense-objects are potential objects of perception, while here, because of the congregation of consciousness, sense-organs and sense-objects, they are actual objects of perception. The conjunction of these three implies that contact is bare sensory experience, devoid of any subjective inclinations. Contact therefore refers to bare percept. It is important, however, to note the difference between contact and the sense-objects. While the latter can *potentially* be perceived, the former is *actually* perceived.

In our discussion of the *rūpakkhandha*, we have seen that, when divided into the categories of sense-organs and sense-objects, matter can be correlated to two links of the *paṭiccasamuppāda*—namely the six sense-doors (*saḷāyatanā*) and contact (*phassa*). The sense-organs (except the mental organ) belong to the six sense-doors, while the sense-objects along with the mental organ are included in contact. When these sense-objects are actually perceived, they constitute, along

63 The exact interrelation among *viññāṇa, nāmarūpa, mano* and the other sense-organs and the following links of the chain will be explained in the chapter on *viññāṇa*.

64 *Cakkhuñ c'āvuso paṭicca rūpe ca uppajjati cakkhuviññāṇaṁ tiṇṇaṁ saṅgati phasso* (M. i, 111. A similar passage is found in S. iv, 32).

65 As we will see in the chapter on *viññāṇa*, there are six types of consciousness, one of which is the *manoviññāṇa*.

with consciousness and the sense-organs, "contact"—which I would describe as bare sensory experience, devoid of any subjective inclination. This experience can potentially turn into a sensation (*vedanā*),[66] the aggregate discussed in the next chapter.

66 *Phassapaccayā vedanā* (M. ii, 32); stated slightly differently at M. iii, 242. See also M. iii, 17 and its commentary MA. iv, 78.

Chapter 3

The *Vedanākkhandha*

The whole of the *rūpakkhandha*, as we saw in the previous chapter, is contained by "the six sense-organs" (*saḷāyatana*) and contact (*phassa*). According to the formula of the *paṭiccasamuppāda*, *phassa* is a necessary condition for the arising of *vedanā* (sensation). The principal difference between contact and *vedanā* should be noted carefully: the former is the mere perception of external stimuli—a perception devoid of any subjective interpretation; the latter, however, has a definite subjective content, for it must either be pleasant, unpleasant or neutral.[1] It is this subjectivity that differentiates *vedanā* from contact.

According to the *Yamaka*, there is no distinction between the terms *vedanā* and *vedanākkhandha*,[2] and nowhere in the canon is such a distinction elaborated. The *Majjhimanikāya* explains the meaning of the term *vedanā* by "*vedeti vedetīti kho āvuso, tasmā vedanā ti vuccati*":[3] "it is called 'sensation' because one 'senses.' " Here again, a Pāli text defines a term through the use of etymologically related terms, thus hindering a clear understanding. However, the *Pāli Text Society Dictionary* agrees with the canonical statement holding that the word *vedanā* is derived from the root *"ved"* or the verb *"vedeti,"* both meaning "to know" or "to experience." If the word *vedanā* is indeed related to *vedeti*, the implication is that *vedanā* means either physical or mental experience.

Several divisions of *vedanā* into categories ranging in number from two to one hundred and eight can be found in the Pāli Canon.[4]

---

1 *Katamā pan' ayye sukhā vedanā, katamā dukkhā vedanā, katamā adukkhamasukhā vedanā ti. Yaṁ kho āvuso Visākha kāyikaṁ vā cetasikaṁ vā sukhaṁ sātaṁ vedayitaṁ ayaṁ sukhā vedanā ...* (M. i, 302).

2 *Vedanā vedanākkhandho ti? Āmantā* (Ymk. 17).

3 M. i, 293.

4 "Oh, Ānanda, according to one classification, *vedanā* are classified in two, according to another, in three, according to another, in five, to another, in six, according to another, in eighteen, to another, in thirty-six, to another, in one hundred and eight." *Dve p'Ānanda vedanā vuttā mayā pariyāyena tisso pi vedanā vuttā mayā pariyāyena, pañca pi vedanā vuttā mayā pariyāyena, cha pi vedanā vuttā mayā pariyāyena, aṭṭhādasa pi vedanā vuttā mayā pariyāyena, chattiṁsāpi vedanā vuttā mayā pariyāyena, aṭṭhasataṁ vedanāsatam pi vuttaṁ mayā pariyāyena* (M. i, 398; also at S. iv, 224).

Of these, the most important classifications group *vedanā* into categories of three, five and six. The *Majjhimanikāya* clarifies the threefold division of *vedanā* into pleasant, painful and neither pleasant nor painful. By further distinguishing these three sorts of *vedanā* between those experienced either on the body or in the mind, we arrive at a sixfold division.[5] The *Saṁyuttanikāya* elaborates a similar classification[6] which takes into consideration whether the *vedanā* is mental or physical in nature. This classification is usually known as the *pañcindriyā*, where the five *indriya* refer to the five types of *vedanā*; these are not to be confused with the five moral strengths (*pañcabalā*) of the same name (*pañcindriyā*).[7] As *pañcindriyā*, *vedanā* are divided into five groups: the first two refer to pleasant (*sukhindriyā*) and painful (*dukkhindriyā*) bodily *vedanā*, the third and fourth are pleasant (*somanassindriyā*) and painful (*domanassindriyā*) mental *vedanā*, and finally the fifth consists of neither pleasant nor painful (*upekkhindriyā*) bodily and mental *vedanā*.[8] *Vedanā* are also grouped into six divisions based on the

5 M. i, 302.

6 S. v, 210.

7 Almost no difference is found between the five faculties, *pañcindriyā*, and the five strengths, *pañcabalā*; both refer to the exact same qualities. The only semantic nuance found in the texts is one pertaining to the quality and opposite quality of each of the *indriya*. The faculties of (1) faith, (2) effort, (3) mindfulness, (4) concentration and (5) wisdom, respectively, have as qualities and opposite qualities: (1) determination and disbelief, (2) energy and idleness, (3) establishing and negligence, (4) calmness and agitation and (5) knowledge and ignorance (Ps. iii, 22-23). These pairs of qualities play a critical role in the distinction between *bala* and *indriya* because the meaning of these two terms is defined in reference to these qualities and opposite qualities. The *Săratthappakāsinī* seems to derive its interpretation of *indriya* from the word *inda*, meaning ruler [*Indra* in Sanskrit refers to the wrathful god who held a powerful position in the vedic pantheon, hence the Pāli meaning] since each of the five faculties is regarded as the controlling factor, a ruler of its respective quality (SA. iii, 247). For example, the faculty of faith is considered an *indriya* because of its perfect control over the characteristic of determination. The same source explains the use of *bala*, or strength, because it is unshakable by the opposite faculty. The *bala* of faith is so-called because its steadiness when confronted with its opposite quality, disbelief (SA. iii, 247). The *Paṭisambhidāmagga* commentary gives a very similar definition, with the distinction that the author has replaced the word *inda* by *adhipati*, which also means "ruler" (PsA. iii, 618-19). The *Paṭisambhidāmagga* commentary's definition is copied verbatim in the *Visuddhimagga* (Vsm. xxii, 37). Although the nuance identified in the commentaries is worth noting, it does not indicate any major distinction between *indriya* and *bala*.

8 S. v, 210-11.

particular sense-organ (*āyatana*) through which the *vedanā* is "perceived."[9] The first five sense-organs—eye, ear, nose, tongue and body—are physical, while the sixth sense-organ—the mind—is mental. Although there is a clear distinction between mental and physical *vedanā*, this arrangement from the *Majjhimanikāya*—with its predominance of bodily *vedanā*—implicitly underscores the aggregate's physical aspect. Since only the *vedanā* triggered by the sixth sense-organ (the mental organ) has a stronger mental content, it is logical to assume that most of the *vedanā* are physically based. However, it is important to stress that even those *vedanā* related to the five physical sense-organs do have a mental function, for *vedanā* is different from mere percept in that a certain interpretation of the stimuli must have taken place. *Vedanā*, as stated previously, are always either pleasant, unpleasant or neutral, a characteristic that differentiates them from objective percept. Therefore, my use of the term "sensation" as a translation for *vedanā* does not, it should be stressed, refer to an anoetic sentience, or a bare experience devoid of personal inclinations.

In order to understand the role that *vedanā* plays within the theory of dependent origination, it is of crucial importance to examine the states which are deprived of *vedanā*, for these attainments have been the objectives of most Theravāda Buddhist practitioners. They are also those that are attained when any link of the *paṭiccasamuppāda* is deactivated. In the next pages we will therefore clarify the distinctions with two types of *nibbāna* and with a state that resembles it—*saññā-vedayitanirodha*.

The Eradication of *Vedanā*

Pāli texts repeatedly refer to a state beyond sensation or, more literally, a state characterized by the eradication of *saññā* and *vedanā* (*saññā-vedayitanirodha*), which Buddhaghosa and Dhammapāla have compared to *nibbāna*. An understanding of the nature of this state will have a

9 *Cha vedanākāya veditabbā ti iti ... paṭicca vuttaṁ? Cakkhuñ ca paṭicca rūpe ca uppajjati cakkhuviññāṇaṁ, tiṇṇaṁ saṁgati phasso, phassapaccayā vedanā; sotañ ca paṭicca sadde ca uppajjati sotaviṇṇāṇaṁ; ghānañ ca paṭicca gandhe ca uppajjati ghānaviṇṇāṇanaṁ; jivhañ ca paṭicca rase ca uppajjati jivhāviṇṇāṇaṁ; kāyañ ca paṭicca phoṭṭhabbe ca uppajjati kāyaviṇṇāṇaṁ; manañ ca paṭicca dhamme ca uppajjati manoviññāṇaṁ, tiṇṇaṁ saṁgati phasso, phassapaccayā vedanā. Cha vedanākāya veditabbā ti iti yan taṁ vuttaṁ idam etaṁ paṭicca vuttaṁ. Idaṁ pañcamaṁ chakkaṁ* (M. iii, 281).

direct impact on our understanding of Buddhist soteriology and of *nibbāna* itself. I begin my investigation of *saññāvedayitanirodha* by examining the textual evidence describing it, and then looking at some modern interpretations of the state.

Since *nibbāna*, according to the Theravāda tradition, is possessed of a single nature, without division,[10] there is a certain irony to the heated debates among scholars as to its exact nature. Some equate *nibbāna* with the state of consciousness attained by Siddhattha Gotama at the age of thirty-five under the Bodhi tree; this state is also experienced upon attaining arahanthood.[11] Others perceive *nibbāna* as a state that can be attained only upon death,[12] since it is often described as a condition beyond mind and matter (*nāmarūpa*), transcending the five aggregates. A third group interprets *nibbāna* as being synonymous with the mental state known as *saññāvedayitanirodha* (literally "the cessation of recognition and of sensation"). The last interpretation falls somewhere between the first two, for it is clearly described as an experience beyond mind and matter but wherein the experiencer continues to live after exiting the trance. (It is worth noting, however, that the experiencer is clinically dead during the trance.)

A Bhāradvāja *brāhmaṇa* once asked the Buddha: "How can one untangle this mess?"[13] Considering the tradition's seemingly conflicting opinions regarding the true interpretation of *nibbāna*, this is a question we could ask too! I will look at subtle distinctions between these *apparently* different states. An examination of the distinction between the *nibbāna* that the Buddha attained at the age of thirty-five and the *nibbāna* he entered into at the time of death, followed by a study of traditional and academic controversies associated with *saññāvedayitanirodha*, will shed light on the question of whether the interpretation of

---

10 AbhS. vi,14.

11 Th. Stcherbatsky represents the followers of this perspective: "Buddha and *Nirvāṇa* are different names for the same thing" (Th. Stcherbatsky, *The Conception of Buddhist Nirvāṇa* [Varanasi: Bharatiya Vidya Prakashan, 1968], p. 79).

12 As Louis de La Vallée Poussin stated in one of his lectures at Manchester College: "It may therefore be safely maintained that *Nirvāṇa* is annihilation" (*The Way to Nirvana: Six Lectures on Ancient Buddhism as a Discipline of Salvation* [Cambridge: Cambridge University Press, 1979], p. 117).

13 *Anto jaṭā bahi jaṭā jaṭāya jaṭitā pajā: taṃ taṃ Gotama pucchāmi: ko imaṃ vijaṭaye jaṭan ti*. S. i, 13; 165. Also quoted in Buddhaghosa's introduction to his *Visuddhimagga* (Vsm. 1).

saññāvedayitanirodha is consistent throughout the tradition, and on the role of *vedanā* in the attainment of the Buddhist ideal.

Most Buddhist schools hold that the historical Buddha experienced enlightenment under the Bodhi tree at the age of thirty-five and, according to certain scholars,[14] reached *nibbāna* simultaneously. According to others, however, he only entered into *nibbāna* when he passed away at the age of eighty. These two perspectives on *nibbāna* are not, however, mutually exclusive; there are said to be two types of *nibbāna*, namely *sopādisesa* (with residue) and *nirupādisesa* or *anupādisesa* (without residue).

According to Pāli texts, *nibbāna* has a single nature and is thus without division or distinction. But for analytical purposes, and in order to describe the attainment of *nibbāna*, the concept can be divided into two categories: with residue and without residue.[15] This apparent paradox is thoroughly explained by Buddhaghosa in the *Visuddhimagga*:

> But this [single goal, *nibbāna*] is firstly called *with result of past clinging left* (*sopādisesa*) since it is made known together with the [aggregates resulting from the past] clinging still remaining [during the *arahant*'s life], being thus made known in terms of the stilling of defilement and the remaining [result of the past] clinging that are present in one who has reached it by means of development. But [secondly, it is called *without result of past clinging left (nirupādisesa)*] since after the last consciousness of the *arahant*, who has abandoned arousing [future aggregates] and so prevented *kamma* from giving result in a future [existence], there is no further arising of aggregates of existence, and those already arisen haven disappeared. So the [result of past] clinging that remained is non-existent; and it is in terms of this non-existence,

14 "Aussi bien quand le Bouddha est parvenu du même coup à la Clairvoyance et au Nirvâna, c'est un cri de triomphe et d'allégresse qui s'échappe de ses lèvres à l'idée qu'il a enfin brisé les chaînes du Destin et s'est pour toujours libéré de la prison corporelle" (A. Foucher, *La Vie du Bouddha d'après les textes et les monuments de l'Inde* [Paris: J. Maisonneuve, 1987], p. 326).

15 *Tad etaṁ [nibbānaṁ] sabhāvato ekavidham pi, saupādisesanibbānadhātu anupādisesanibbānadhātu ceti duvidhaṁ hoti kāraṇapariyāyena* (Abhs. vi, 14). The text further classifies *nibbāna* into three modes: void, signless and absolute content. This division, however, does not influence our discussion. See S.Z. Aung's translation of the *Abhiddhammatthasaṅgaha* entitled *Compendium of Philosophy* (London: P.T.S., 1979), p. 166.

> in the sense that "there is no [result of past] clinging here, that the [same goal is called] *without result of past clinging left.*"[16]

The *Itivuttaka*—upon which the previous passage of the *Visuddhimagga* probably bases its interpretation—mentions that one who has attained *nibbāna* with residue continues to possess the five senses and to experience both pleasant and painful sensations,[17] while the attainment of *nibbāna* without residue is characterized by the eradication of all becomings (*bhava*),[18] implying that no emergence from this state is possible.

On the other hand, the state of *sopādisesa nibbāna*, as the words themselves imply, is *nibbāna* with residue in the sense that subtle *kamma* still remain. These *kamma* are not strong enough to propel the *arahant* into another rebirth, but merely sufficient to maintain the life process. Liberated persons cease to produce further *kamma*, for the *kamma*-process (*kammabhava*) has been eradicated. They have eradicated all *kamma*-results (*kammavipāka*) that may lead to another life, but must still reap some subtle *kamma*-results in this life. It is these *kamma*-results that maintain both the regeneration of the five aggregates and the *kamma*-process itself. Therefore, *nibbāna* with residue could be correlated to a state of mind that alters our perception of the world, or rather, enables us to really perceive the world as it is (*yathābhūta*).

Nirupādisesa nibbāna, on the other hand, is "*nibbāna* without residue" in the sense that all *kamma* have been completely eradicated and, consequently, no fuel remains to perpetuate life. *Nibbāna* without residue is usually referred to as a total extinction of the five aggregates (*khandhaparinibbāna*). The state of *nibbāna* without residue is beyond mind and matter and no different from the state of *nibbāna* that the Buddha attained at the moment of death.

Correlations are often made between the terms *nirupādisesa nibbāna* (without residue) and *parinibbāna*, and between *sopādisesa*

---

16 Ñāṇamoli, *The Path of Purification*, pp. 580-81. This subject is further elaborated in the *Itivuttaka* (38-41) as well as in Kamaleswar Bhattacharya's article, "*Upadhi, upādi* et *upādāna* dans le canon bouddhique pāli," in *Mélanges d'indianisme à la mémoire de Louis Renou* (Paris: Publications de l'institut de civilisation indienne, 1967), pp. 81-97.

17 *Disesā nibbānadhātu* (It. 38).

18 *Anupādisesā pana samparāyikā yamhi nirujjhanti bhavāni sabbaso* (It. 38).

nibbāna and "plain" *nibbāna*. However, there is no sound textual justification for such an identification. In the *sutta* literature the term *parinibbāna* is restricted to the passing away of *arahant*—the attainment of *nibbāna* without residue. Yet the substantive in these particular passages functions as an elegant or polite term for an *arahant*'s death rather than entering into *nibbāna* without residue itself. We often find the verb form *parinibbāyati* being used to mean the attainment of arahantship itself without implying the passing away of the *arahant* at that particular moment.[19] Furthermore, commentarial literature mentions two kinds of *parinibbāna*: (1) *kilesaparinibbāna*, the extinction of defilements which is equated with *nibbāna* with residue, and (2) *khandhaparinibbāna*, or the extinction of the aggregates—the passing away of the *arahant*, *nibbāna* without residue. As Peter Masefield pointed out in his article "The Nibbāna-Parinibbāna Controversy,"[20] not even the past participle *parinibbuta* refers exclusively to the state of *nibbāna* without residue.[21] Because of its dubious significance, I prefer not to use the term *parinibbāna*. The concepts of without residue (*nirupādisesa*) and with residue (*sopādisesa*) are the precise technical terms that refer respectively to the total eradication of the aggregates at the time of the death of the *arahant*, and to the state attained by a living *arahant*.

The State of *Saññāvedayitanirodha*

Although the distinction between these first two kinds of *nibbāna* is clear, the problem associated with the state of *saññāvedayitanirodha* is not so simple. Pāli texts repeatedly refer to this state beyond sensation—a state characterized by the eradication of recognition and sensation (*saññā* and *vedanā*) which Buddhaghosa and Dhammapāla compare to *nibbāna*. In order to better understand this mysterious state,

19 See M. i, 67.

20 Peter Masefield, "The Nibbāna-Parinibbāna Controversy," *Religion* 9 (Autumn 1979): 216.

21 See the two following references. *Sukhaṁ vā yadi va dukkhaṁ adukkhamasukhaṁ sahā ajjhattañ ca bahiddhā ca yaṁ kiñci atthi veditaṁ etaṁ 'dukkhan' ti ñatvāna mosadhammaṁ palokinaṁ phussa phussa vayaṁ passaṁ evaṁ tattha virajjati vedanānaṁ khayā bhikkhu nicchāto parinibbuto ti* (Sn. 144). *Samāhito sampajāno sato buddhassa sāvako vedanā capajānāti vedanānañca sambhavaṁ. Yattha cetā nirujjhanti maggañca khayagāminam vedanānaṁ khayā bhikkhu nicchāto parinibbuto ti* (S. iv, 204; similar passage at S. v, 57).

I will now examine pertinent textual evidence, and respond to some modern interpretations.

The life of Siddhattha Gotama just prior to his enlightenment, as portrayed in the *Ariyapariyesanasutta*, offers numerous references to "trancelike" states. According to this text, the *bodhisattva* visited many saints who were engaged in different types of penance, the most eminent being Āḷārakālāma and Uddaka Rāmaputta. Gotama first approached Āḷārakālāma and mastered the third attainment (the stage of *ākiñcāyatanasamādhi*) which was the highest known to his teacher. When he realized this state did not correspond to final liberation, he left Āḷārakālāma and went to study under Uddaka Rāmaputta. With the latter, he quickly mastered the fourth attainment (*nevasaññānāsaññā samādhi*)—again, the highest he could learn from him. The *bodhisattva* did not regard this condition as final liberation either and thus left to pursue his goal independently.[22] Only then did he finally experience *nibbāna*[23] and become a *buddha*. The text states explicitly that Gotama had attained all the eight stages—the four absorptions and the four attainments—and that he attained an even higher state: *nibbāna*. In this same *sutta*, Gotama is portrayed as instructing the monks, not only as to how to attain each of these eight absorptions, but also how to reach a state higher than these eight. This state is called *saññāvedayita-nirodha*,[24] the eradication of recognition and sensation. At first glance this state seems to be the same as *nibbāna*. As La Vallée Poussin says:

> Ils [les bouddhistes] pensent que ce neuvième [recueillement] a été découvert par le Bouddha; ils le nomment, non pas recueillement d'inconscience ("sans *saṁjñā*"), mais recueillement de destruction de la conscience et de la sensation ("*saṁjñā-vedayitanirodha*") ou, plus simplement, recueillement de la destruction (*nirodhasamāpatti*); ils lui donnent un caractère nettement bouddhique en le définissant comme une prise de contact avec le *Nirvāṇa* (ou avec une entité semblable au *Nirvāṇa*).[25]

---

22 *Nāyaṁ dhammo nibbidāya, na virāgāya na nirodhāya na upasamāya na abhiññāya na sambodhāya na nibbānāya saṁvattati* (M. i, 165).

23 M. i, 167.

24 M. i, 174-75.

25 Louis de La Vallée Poussin, "Musīla et Nārada; Le chemin du nirvāṇa," in *Mélanges chinois et bouddhiques* (Bruxelles: Institut Belge des Hautes Études Chinoises, 1937), p. 212.

Yet many modern scholars, such as Rune Johansson, hold that *saññā-vedayitanirodha* is different from *nibbāna*:

> ... *saññāvedayitanirodha* is not included and it is not identified [in Pāli texts] with *nibbāna*. There are texts that would seem to imply a very close relationship, but they are exceptions. *Nirodha* is frequently mentioned as an aid to the attainment of nibbāna; but nibbāna can be attained on the other levels just as well, even without meditation [the author probably means the practice of the *jhāna* and *samāpatti*]; what is important is the destruction of the obsessions.[26]

Yet the *Ariyapariyesanasutta* depicts the Buddha teaching his disciples how to successively reach the eight absorptions, the same eight that he had himself attained, and how to experience *saññāvedayitanirodha*. According to this text, the Buddha establishes a parallel between the various attainments his disciples achieve, and his own. From a rhetorical perspective, then, it would be strange for the ninth attainment of the Buddha—*nibbāna*—to be described as radically different from the ninth attainment of his disciples, *saññāvedayitanirodha*. Theoretically, there should not be any major difference between the two, especially since *saññāvedayitanirodha* is described in the same way that *nibbāna* often is. Both are described as "crossing over the entanglement of the the world," and as being out of reach of the Evil One (Māra).[27]

If the correlation between *saññāvedayitanirodha* and *nibbāna* were based solely on this hypothesis, of course, it would not stand on firm ground. However, the correlation finds strong support in the commentarial literature—texts that Johansson may have overlooked. For example, in a chapter devoted to the discussion of *saññāvedayitanirodha*, the *Visuddhimagga* states that certain monks enter into this "trance" thinking: "Let us dwell in bliss by being without consciousness here and now and reaching the cessation that is nibbāna."[28] A few pages later, the same text reiterates that *saññāvedayitanirodha* is "an attainment which a noble one may cultivate; the peace it gives is reckoned as

26 Rune E.A. Johansson, *The Psychology of Nirvana* (London: George Allen and Unwin, 1969), pp. 49-50.

27 M. i, 175.

28 *Ditth' eva dhamme acittakā hutvā nirodhaṁ nibbānaṁ patvā sukhaṁ viharissāmā ti samāpajjanti* (Vsm. 705); translation from Ñāṇamoli, *The Path of Purification*, p. 828.

nibbāna here and now."[29] The commentary of the *Visuddhimagga* goes even further by introducing a vague correlation between the term *saññāvedayitanirodha* and *nibbāna* without residue: *Nibbānaṁ patvā ti anupādisesanibbānaṁ patvā viya.*[30] It is noteworthy that the commentator's introduction of the particle *viya* suggests similarity rather than identity. The passage should therefore be translated thus: "[in this particular context of the *Visuddhimagga*, the expression] 'attaining *nibbāna*' means attaining [a state] similar to *nibbāna* without residue." Dhammapāla established no more than a correlation between *saññāvedayitanirodha* and *nibbāna* without residue (*anupādisesanibbāna*); he did not establish a one-to-one correlation between the two terms, but only stated that they are "similar."[31] However, Buddhaghosa mentions that the mind of one who has emerged from *saññāvedayitanirodha* tends towards *nibbāna*.[32] This suggests that the "trance" is a kind of adumbration of *nibbāna* that bends the mind towards achieving *nibbāna* itself rather than being a state resembling it.

Although commentarial literature vaguely links *saññāvedayita-nirodha* with *nibbāna* without residue, this equation is often questioned by scholars. For example, David Kalupahana stated that "scholars more conversant [than William James] with the Buddhist tradition go to the extent of equating the state of cessation (*saññāvedayitanirodha*) with freedom (*nibbāna*)."[33] According to Kalupahana, these two states cannot, in any way, be equated. There seems, however, to be a flaw in Kalupahana's argument against correlating *saññāvedayitanirodha* with *nibbāna*. While he correctly points out that the former ought to be experienced by the body (*kāyena sacchikaraṇīyā*),[34] his preceding remark is misleading; Kalupahana argues that the *Ariyapariyesanasutta*, in which the Buddha refused to equate freedom with the state of cessation, should serve as a corrective to this misidentification by James

29 *Iti santaṁ samāpattiṁ imaṁ ariyasevitaṁ, ditth' eva dhamme nibbānaṁ iti sankhaṁ upāgataṁ*. Vsm. 709; translation from Ñāṇamoli, *The Path of Purification*, p. 833.

30 VsmA. 902.

31 Vasubandhu, in his *Abhidharmakośa*, seems to have been as careful as Dhammapāla in his definition of *saññāvedayitanirodha*: he stated only that it is similar (*sadṛśa*) to *nibbāna* (AbhK. ii, 44).

32 *Vuṭṭhitassa kin ninnaṁ cittaṁ hotī ti nibbānaninnaṁ* (Vsm. 708).

33 Kalupahana, *The Principles of Buddhist Psychology*, p. 76.

34 Which is interpreted by the commentator as arising simultaneously with the mental body (*nāma*). *Kāyena ti sahajātā-nāma-kāyena* (D.A. iii, 1023).

and others.[35] A careful reading of the *Ariyapariyesanasutta*, however, shows that the Buddha never refused to equate *nibbāna* with *saññā-vedayitanirodha*. What we do find in this particular text is simply a statement that none of the eight absorptions can be equated with *nibbāna*:

> This *dhamma* [the teaching of Āḷāra Kālāma] does not lead to disregard, nor to dispassion, nor to cessation, nor to tranquillity, nor to super-knowledge, nor to awakening, nor to *nibbāna*, but only as far as reaching the plane of "no-thing."[36]

Kalupahana seems to have mistakenly associated *saññāvedayitanirodha* with the four absorptions and the four attainments, perhaps because it is sometimes described as the ninth absorption[37] or because it is one of the eight deliverances (*vimokkhā*).[38] It is important to recall, however, that *saññāvedayitanirodha* is not usually even mentioned along with the eight absorptions except when it is described as being higher than any of them. Moreover, the *Ariyapariyesanasutta* does not mention the attainment of *saññāvedayitanirodha* in this specific passage,[39] and taking it for granted as implied is risky. It is, therefore, far from clear that the Buddha refused to equate *saññāvedayitanirodha* with *nibbāna*.

Saññāvedayitanirodha is known as a state beyond mind and matter, as is *nibbāna* without residue. However, one notable difference between the two is that the latter can only be experienced after death, while the former requires that one be alive. Alive, yes, but not apparently so. For all intents and purposes, one dwelling in *saññā-vedayitanirodha* exhibits the same features as a deceased person, with the slight exceptions that life (*āyu*) and bodily heat are still present, and

35 Kalupahana, *The Principles of Buddhist Psychology*, p. 94.

36 *Nāyaṁ [Āḷārakālāmassa] dhammo nibbidāya na virāgāya na nirodhāya na upasamāya na abhiññāya na sambodhāya na nibbānāya saṁvattati, yāvad-eva ākiñcaññāyatanūpa-pattiyā ti* (M. i, 165); translation inspired by I.B. Horner, trans., *The Collection of the Middle Length Sayings (*Majjhimanikāya*)* (London: P.T.S., 1959), 1:209. The same is said about the teaching of Uddaka Rāmaputta with the slight nuance that this latter leads no further than to the state of "neither-perception-nor-non-perception" (see M. i, 166).

37 For example, the *Dīghanikāya* describes nine successive "cessations," which consist of the four absorptions, the four attainments and *saññāvedayitanirodha* (D. iii, 266).

38 A. iv, 306.

39 That is, M. i, 166-67.

that the sense-organs are purified.[40] Thus the experiencer is technically but not actually dead.

We saw earlier that *nirupādisesa nibbāna* is sometimes defined as the total extinction of the five aggregates. *Nibbāna* without residue is also comparable to *saññāvedayitanirodha* in that the five aggregates are almost completely deactivated and become temporarily latent. As the name *saññāvedayitanirodha* implies, this state is devoid of *saññā* and *vedanā*. Without the existence of these two aggregates, neither of the two remaining mental aggregates (*saṅkhāra* and *viññāṇa*) can be present in their active form. According to the *paṭiccasamuppāda*, *saṅkhāra* is necessary for the arising of the *viññāṇa*, which has the potential to turn into *vedanā*. Thus, if *vedanā* is eradicated, there can be no *saṅkhāra*, for the three links of the *paṭiccasamuppāda* that follow *vedanā (taṇhā, upādāna* and *bhava*) are members of the *saṅkhārakkhandha*.[41] Furthermore, in the absence of *saṅkhāra*, *viññāṇa* cannot arise. This argument is implicitly supported by the *Visuddhimagga* in its definition of *saññāvedayitanirodha*: "What is the attainment of cessation [*saññā-vedayitanirodha*]? It is the disappearance of consciousness (*citta*) and its mental factors (*cetasika*) owing to their progressive eradication."[42] Noteworthy is that *abhidhamma* literature synonymously interchanges the terms *citta* and *viññāṇa*,[43] while *cetasika* comprises not only *vedanā* and *saññā*, as we would expect from *saññāvedayitanirodha*, but also the fifty factors that constitute *saṅkhāra*. It follows that since *saññāvedayita-nirodha* is devoid of *citta* and *cetasika*, it is therefore devoid of *viññāṇa, vedanā, saññā* and *saṅkhāra* as well. Only the remaining aggregate, the *rūpakkhandha*, must continue to be present, for the body remains alive and must be sustained by the material faculty of life (*rūpajīvitindriya*), one of the twenty-three elements that constitute secondary matter. Therefore, *saññāvedayitanirodha* is not simply a "more radical negation

---

40 *Āyu aparikkhīṇo, usmā avūpasantā, indriyāni vippasannāni* (M. i, 296).

41 See my article on "A Brief Survey of the Relation between the *Paṭiccasamuppāda* and the *Pañcakkhandhā*", in K.I. Koppedrayer, ed., *Contact Between Cultures: South Asia* (Lewiston: Edwin Mellen Press, 1992), p. 237.

42 *Tattha kā nirodhasamāpattī ti yā anupubbanirodhavasena cittacetasikānaṁ dhammānaṁ appavatti* (Vsm. 702).

43 Nyānātiloka, *Buddhist Dictionary*, p. 37.

of apperceptions [*saññā*]," as Tilmann Vetter suggests,[44] but a radical negation of all four mental aggregates. In this sense, neither can it be equated, as Winston King advances,[45] with the fruits of the paths, for these are still characterized by the four mental aggregates, while *saññā-vedayitanirodha* is completely devoid of them.

It is said that while in the state of *saññāvedayitanirodha*, the body is entirely protected from injury. Pāli texts offer the startling example of Mahānāga, who was dwelling in this trance when the house in which he was temporarily living caught fire. The blaze persisted until the villagers put it out; Mahānāga, meanwhile, was oblivious. After all, without the four mental aggregates, he could not possibly have been aware of anything! It is said that only the house burned; the monk was left untouched by the flames. It is interesting to note that when describing the villagers' attempt to quench the fire with water, Buddhaghosa employed the causative form (*nibbāpetvā*), which shares the same etymology as *nibbāna*. Emerging from *saññāvedayitanirodha*, Mahānāga made a pun ("I am discovered!").[46] While in the trance, Mahānāga's own fire (i.e., his five aggregates) was temporarily quenched; after he emerged from *saññāvedayitanirodha* and realized that the villagers were trying to extinguish the fire, he exclaimed "I (meaning the five aggregates metaphorically associated with the fire) am discovered," thus stressing the crucial polarity between fire and water, the five aggregates and *nibbāna*. He then flew away.

Unfortunately, the sensational (albeit deprived of sensation) state of *saññāvedayitanirodha* is not available to just anyone. According to the *Visuddhimagga*, only the non-returner and the *arahant* who have

---

44 "Probably in a period already dominated by the method of discriminating insight some persons wished to make use of this wasteland and discovered in the cessation of apperceptions and feelings [*saññāvedayitanirodha*] a state (or rather a name) not yet touched by any criticism. 'Neither apperception nor non-apperception' [the fourth *samāpatti*] now becomes the last but one stage and its description is to be understood as a middle-way formulation allowing for a more radical negation of apperceptions" (Tilmann Vetter, *The Ideas and Meditative Practices of Early Buddhism* [Leiden: E.J. Brill, 1988] p. 68).

45 *Saññāvedayitanirodha* "is the maximum possible temporal extension of those nibbāna realizations contained in Path and fruition awareness as well as the experiential ultimate, *nibbāna* itself, tasted in one's present existence" (Winston Lee King, *Theravāda Meditation: The Buddhist Transformation of Yoga* [University Park: Pennsylvania University Press, 1980], p. 104).

46 Vsm. 706.

successively passed through the eight absorptions can enter it.[47] This point is extremely important, for many scholars argue that equating *saññāvedayitanirodha* with *nibbāna* is impossible since, according to the Theravāda tradition, *nibbāna* can be experienced only by means of wisdom (*paññā*) and discriminative insight (*vipassanā*), while the eight absorptions can be attained simply by practising concentration (*samatha*). However, the fact that it is compulsory to be either a non-returner or an *arahant* in order to experience *saññāvedayitanirodha* implies that a certain amount of wisdom and discriminative insight have been acquired. In fact, only those who have perfected these two qualities could be capable of experiencing the state of *saññāvedayita-nirodha*.[48] As Winston King emphasizes, "only those who have attained the Path can attain cessation. It cannot be repeated too often that cessation is an integral blending of the two [insight (*vipassanā*) and concentration (*samatha*)]."[49] Therefore, non-returners and *arahant* who have reached the goal (*sopādhisesanibbāna*) but have not followed the path of the absorptions cannot reach this state.

Paul J. Griffiths disagrees with this position so strongly that he devotes an entire book to refuting it. According to Griffiths, only the path of discriminative insight leads to *nibbāna*, and only the path of concentration leads to the absorptions and to *saññāvedayitanirodha*. The two are distinct and thus can never be blended, as King suggests, in order to attain either goal. Griffiths claims that Buddhaghosa and other commentators wrongly attempt to reconcile these two paths by correlating *saññāvedayitanirodha* with *nibbāna* without residue and by stating that in order to experience cessation, one must have already perfected wisdom through discriminative insight to the level of non-returner. His disagreement with Buddhaghosa is so intense that he

---

47 *Ke taṁ samāpajjanti, ke na samāpajjantī ti sabbe pi puthujjanā sotāpannā sakadāgāmino, sukkhavipassakā ca anāgāmino arahanto na samāpajjanti. Aṭṭha samāpattilābhino pana anāgāmino khīṇāsavā ca samāpajjanti: dvīhi balehi samannāgatattā tayo ca saṅkhārānaṁ paṭippassaddhiyā soḷasahi ñāṇacariyāhi, navahi samādhicariyāhi vasībhāvatā paññā nirodhasamāpattiyā ñāṇaṁ ti hi vuttaṁ* (Vsm. 702). The reader might want to refer to the section of the *Visuddhimagga* (pp. 702-709) which explains how one can enter *saññāvedayitanirodha*, what the requirements are and how one emerges from that state, etc.

48 See A. iii, 192; Vsm. 705.

49 King, *Theravāda Meditation*, p. 108.

comes close to accusing him of heresy.[50] Griffiths' statement is rather fierce, and I do not feel his arguments bear out the charge.

Griffiths presents two major arguments against the identification of *saññāvedayitanirodha* and *nibbāna*. The first is based on the following statement from the *Visuddhimagga*: "Why do they attain *nirodha*? ... they attain it thinking: 'let us live happily [*sukhaṁ*] by being mindless in this very moment and having attained cessation which is *nibbāna*'."[51] According to Griffiths,

> it is unclear how a condition in which no mental events occur can possess affective tone as appears to be suggested [by Buddhaghosa]. Presumably it would be more accurate to describe the attainment of cessation as a condition which is free from both happiness and sadness and indeed from all affective tone whatever.[52]

The remark is accurate; *saññāvedayitanirodha* is a state where none of the mental aggregates function, making it impossible to experience either pleasant or unpleasant sensations. However, Griffiths' reference does not give proper consideration to Dhammapāla's commentary to the *Visuddhimagga*. According to Dhammapāla, the word happiness (*sukhaṁ*) in this particular passage simply means the absence of suffering.[53] The commentator believes that this is what Buddhaghosa intended when he said that those wishing to attain cessation do so in order to "live happily." The first noble truth postulates the universality of suffering. Suffering does not merely result from unpleasant sensations, physical or mental, but is inherent in all compounded phenomena (*saṅkhāra*)—all psycho-physical phenomena of existence, all five aggregates. These are characterized by constant change. They arise and pass away; they are transitory (*anicca*). Because of this inherent instability, they are subject to suffering.[54] Moreover, suffering is often

50 Paul J. Griffiths, *On Being Mindless: Buddhist Meditation and the Mind-Body Problem* (Illinois: Open Court, 1986), p. 29. See p. 66 below for Griffiths' actual charge.

51 *Kasmā samāpajjantī ti ... ditth' eva dhamme acittakā hutvā nirodhaṁ nibbānaṁ patvā sukhaṁ viharissāmā ti samāpajjanti* (Vsm. 705).

52 Griffiths, *On Being Mindless*, p. 29.

53 *Sukhaṁ ti niddukkhaṁ* (VsmA. 1673.22).

54 As stated in the *Saṁyuttanikāya*: "What do you think, monks: is *rūpa* permanent or impermanent?" "Impermanent, Sir." "And that which is impermanent, is it suffering or pleasant?" "Suffering, Sir." *Taṁ kiṁ maññatha bhikkhave rūpaṁ niccaṃ vā*

directly correlated with the five clinging-aggregates (*saṅkhittena pañc-upādānakkhandhā pi dukkhā*). Although the state of *saññāvedayita-nirodha*, defined as being beyond any of the four mental aggregates, can certainly not be characterized by pleasant and unpleasant sensations, it can be understood as a "pleasant" experience in Dhammapāla's sense, for it transcends the suffering that is inherent in all types of sensations.

Griffiths' second argument is that Buddhaghosa's identification of *nibbāna* with *saññāvedayitanirodha* "seems to approach uneasily close to a standard Buddhist heresy ... for it ... encourages some version of the annihilation view."[55] In the Theravāda tradition, the annihilation view (*ucchedadiṭṭhi*) is defined as the belief (held by non-Buddhists, of course) that there is an unchanging self that remains constant throughout life and which, at the time of death, simply disappears. Of course, Buddhism categorically rejects the view that there is a permanent entity which is identified with the five aggregates:[56] the tradition denies the truth of this presupposition altogether by affirming that there is merely a sequence of similar events that are causally related, but that this similarity can in no way be perceived as identity. Furthermore, Buddhism also repudiates the view that there is absolutely no existence after death,[57] but rather that there exists a continuum from one life to another, wherein the last consciousness of the present life (*cuticitta*) engenders the first consciousness of the next (*paṭisandhi-viññāṇa*). The only possible way to exit this cycle of birth, death and rebirth is to eradicate all karmic activities (*saṅkhāra*) during the lifetime and to attain *nibbāna*; otherwise the saṃsāric cycle is perpetuated. This being standard Buddhist doctrine, I do not see how Griffiths can make a statement such as "many Buddhist texts, especially those which discuss the question of the nature of *nibbāna*, do in fact read as though they embrace just this 'annihilation view.' "[58] It is true that *nibbāna* is most often described using negative terms, but reaching the goal is often the

---

aniccaṁ vāti. Aniccam bhante. Yam panāniccaṁ dukkhaṁ vā taṁ sukhaṁ vā ti. Dukkham bhante (S. iii, 67). The same mode of questioning is used for the four other mental aggregates.

55 Griffiths, *On Being Mindless*, p. 29.

56 *Rūpaṁ vedayitaṁ saññaṁ viññāṇaṁ yañca saṅkhataṁ n' eso aham asmi* (S. i, 112).

57 Such as portrayed in D. i, 55.

58 Griffiths, *On Being Mindless*, p. 29.

result of many lives of practice;[59] this very point indicates that there is some sort of continuum from one existence to another, a view that the nihilists would reject. "However this may be," as Griffiths continues, "it certainly seems as though this text of Buddhaghosa's, identifying the attainment of cessation with *nibbāna,* is one of those that encourages some version of the 'annihilation view.' "[60] It is not the association of *saññāvedayitanirodha* with *nibbāna* which should be considered in this light, but *nibbāna per se*, as it is the latter (or at least *nibbāna* without residue) which is described as being beyond the five aggregates[61]—a statement resembling the annihilation view in the sense that all constituents of the individual are destroyed, but contradicting it in that there is still something left (perfect bliss; *paramaṁ sukhaṁ*), and that something existed prior to the attainment.

The Theravāda commentarial tradition has established a vague relationship between *saññāvedayitanirodha* and *nibbāna* without residue, in the sense that in the particular passage of the *Visuddhimagga* referred to earlier, Buddhaghosa does not seem to be making a straightforward doctrinal statement that *saññāvedayitanirodha* is *nibbāna.* He simply states that certain monks enter this trance thinking: "let us dwell in bliss by being without consciousness here and now and reaching the cessation that is *nibbāna*."[62] The rhetorical device of placing the statement in the mouths of others is not typical of Buddhaghosa when writing in a strictly analytical manner and when supporting a doctrinal point. Perhaps the statement is meant to be understood metaphorically. Hence the commentator, Dhammapala, rushes in to prevent misunderstanding by explaining that "reaching the cessation that is *nibbāna*" means "as though reaching *nibbāna* without residue."

---

59 For example, the *Jātaka* offers the biographies of hundreds of the previous lives of the *bodhisattva* on his way to enlightenment.

60 Griffiths, *On Being Mindless*, p. 29.

61 "But [secondly, it is called *without result of past clinging left (nirupādisesa)*] since after the last consciousness of the Arahant, who has abandoned arousing [future aggregates] and so prevented kamma from giving result in a future [existence], there is no further arising of aggregates of existence, and those already arisen have disappeared. So the [result of past] clinging that remained is non-existent; and it is in terms of this non-existence, in the sense that there is no [result of past] clinging here, that the [same goal is called] *without result of past clinging left*" (Ñāṇamoli, *The Path of Purification*, pp. 580-81).

62 Vsm. 705.

However, according to Pāli sources, there is a major distinction between *saññāvedayitanirodha* and *nibbāna*. On the one hand, *nibbāna* is not merely a meditative state, but a phenomenon which exists by itself (*sabhāvadhamma*). As an ontological phenomenon, *nibbāna* differs from all other *dhamma* in that it is unconditioned, unborn,[63] undying,[64] etc. It is realized by practitioners when they attain the paths and fruits, but its existence is by no means dependent on anyone's attainment. *Nibbāna* exists and remains as such whether or not it is realized. On the other hand, *saññāvedayitanirodha* is not a phenomenon which exists by itself since it has no individual essence and it is produced (*nipphanna*). For the simple reason that it has no individual essence, according to the *Visuddhimagga*, it is not classifiable as formed or unformed, mundane or supramundane.[65] According to Pāli literature, *nibbāna* is a real phenomenon (*dhamma*), base (*āyatana*), and element (*dhātu*), while *saññāvedayitanirodha* is not. The latter is simply the cessation of mental factors reached through the procedure described in the *Visuddhimagga*.[66] In the light of these canonical definitions of *saññāvedayitanirodha* and *nibbāna*, the equation of these two states becomes almost impossible.

Finally, a few words must be said with regard to a final hypothesis, put forward by Louis de la Vallée Poussin[67] regarding *saññāvedayitanirodha* and its place within Buddhism. In his article, de La Vallée Poussin explores the debt of Buddhism to the ancient form of *Saṁkhyā-yoga* where the practice of complete withdrawal of the senses was the only means of achieving cessation of the mental activities (*cittavṛttinirodha*), which was in turn the only means of attaining liberation (*kaivalya*). He argues that the early Buddhists wanted to show that having incorporated every kind of practice into their system, they had reached an attainment higher than any of those associated with

---

63 Dhs. 2; Sn. 362; It. 87; Ud. 80, etc.

64 Vsm. 507.

65 *Nirodhasamāpattisaṅkhatā asaṅkhatā ti ādi pucchāyaṁ pana saṅkhatā ti pi asaṅkhatā ti pi lokiyā ti pi lokuttarā ti pi na vattabbā. Kasmā? Sabhāvato n' atthitāya* (Vsm. 709). A similar statement regarding the mundane and supramundane classification of *saññāvedayitanirodha* is found in the *Kathavatthu*, p. 516.

66 Vsm. 705ff.

67 Louis de La Vallée Poussin, "Le Nirvāṇa d'après Āryadeva," in *Mélanges chinois et bouddhiques* (Bruxelles: Institut Belge des Hautes Études Chinoises, 1932), 1:127-35.

other practices.[68] Therefore integrating *saññāvedayitanirodha* into the Buddhist tradition may have been simply the result of an attempt to make Buddhism appear superior to rival practices.

As mere scholars with limited resources at our disposition, it may be impossible to determine with certainty whether *nibbāna* and *saññā-vedayitanirodha* are truly one and the same; but we can be sure of the existence of profound controversies on the subject! I have argued, however, that Kalupahana and Griffiths, both of whom challenge the commentarial correlation between the two terms, fail to provide adequate support for their positions. Nor do the Pāli texts seem to be in total accord on this matter: the *sutta* literature does not explicitly equate *saññāvedayitanirodha* with *nibbāna*, the *abhiddhamma* seems to stress the difference between these two stages, and the commentarial and sub-commentarial literature imply a similarity between them. Yet, one point seems clear: *nibbāna* and *saññāvedayitanirodha* both share a "blissful feeling"[69] (which itself may again be interpreted in various ways). The peace generated by *saññāvedayitanirodha* "is reckoned as *nibbāna* here and now"[70] for it shares *nibbāna*'s peaceful quality. However, *saññāvedayitanirodha* cannot be identical to *nibbāna*, for it has no individual essence (*sabhava*) and it is produced (*nipphanna*). It could simply be a kind of blissful foretaste of the *nibbāna* element without residue, but on this matter as well, the texts remain unclear. One certain thing, however, is that *saññāvedayitanirodha* is a state where the four mental aggregates are temporarily deactivated.

The State of *Vedanākkhaya*

Now that we have discussed *saññāvedayitanirodha*, we also ought to mention another kind of elimination of sensation. This, however, is not termed eradication (*nirodha*), but rather destruction (*khaya*), and refers to a slightly different state. We find passages including this term in the *Suttanipāta*:

68 This hypothesis of "appropriation" was also advanced by Martin Wiltshire regarding other Buddhist doctrines. See *Ascetic Figures Before and in Early Buddhism: The Emergence of Gautama as the Buddha* (New York: Mouton de Gruyter, 1990).

69 Blissful in the sense that it is devoid of sensation rather than being characterized by a pleasant feeling.

70 VsmA. 833.

> Whatever sensations one experiences, pleasant, unpleasant or neutral, inside or outside, they should be understood as suffering, as illusory, as destined for destruction. Realizing that whenever there is contact, sensations pass away [as soon as they arise], one is free from passion, has destroyed the sensations and is fully liberated (*parinibbuto*).[71]

Similar passages are found in the *Saṁyuttanikāya*:

> A disciple of the Buddha, with concentration, awareness and constant thorough understanding of impermanence [*sampajāno*] knows with wisdom the sensations, their arising, their cessation and the path leading to their destruction. One who has reached the destruction of sensation is freed from craving, is fully liberated (*parinibbuto*).[72]

According to the texts, people "destroying sensations" are fully liberated, yet nowhere is it stated, as it is with the state of *saññā-vedayitanirodha*, that in order to undertake this practice and attain the goal, one must have previously attained the eight absorptions. Therefore, a difference seems to be implied between the state of destruction of sensations (*vedanākkhaya*) and *saññāvedayitanirodha*. Moreover, people who have accomplished the state of destruction of sensations are still alive and interact with the world, whereas those dwelling in the state of *saññāvedayitanirodha* are characterized by a complete alienation from experience.

As was pointed out by Padmasiri de Silva,[73] the state of destruction of sensations (*vedanākkhaya*) does not imply the destruction of all sensations. According to the *Saṁyuttanikāya*, *vedanā* can be classified into eight types. The first four are caused by bodily disturbances such as those originating from bile (*pitta*), phlegm (*semha*),

71 *Sukhaṁ vā yadi va dukkhaṁ adukkhamasukhaṁ sahā ajjhattañ ca bahiddhā ca yaṁ kiñci atthi veditaṁ etaṁ 'dukkhan' ti ñatvāna mosadhammaṁ palokinaṁ phussa vayaṁ passaṁ evaṁ tattha virajjati vedanānaṁ khayā bhikkhu nicchāto parinibbhuto ti* (Sn. 738-39).

72 *Samāhito sampajāno sato buddhassa sāvako | vedanā capajānāti vedanānañca sambhavaṁ | yattha vetā nirujjhanti maggañca khayagāminam | vedanānaṁ khayā bhikkhu nicchāto parinibbuto ti ||* (S. iv, 204. Another similar passage is at S. v, 57).

73 Padmasiri de Silva, "Kamma and vedanānupassanā," in *The Importance of Vedanā and Sampajañña* (Igatpuri: Vipassanā Research Institute, 1990), n.p. (paragraph 11 of the article).

wind (*vata*), and a combination of them all (*sannipātika*). The fifth originates from climatic conditions (*utupariṇāmajā*). The sixth arises from disagreeable things coming together (*visamaparihārajā*) such as sitting too long or an improper combination of food. The seventh is caused by injuries and external attacks (*opakkamika*), such as being bitten by a snake. And finally, the eighth type of *vedanā* is caused by the ripening of one's own *kamma* (*kammavipākajāni vedayitāni*).[74] Of all these types, it is only the last, those sensations generated by past *kamma*, that are destroyed when the expression *vedānākkhayā* is used. The other seven types of *vedanā* are still functioning. When one has attained the state of destruction of sensations, one still functions normally, but no *vedanā* arises because of past *kamma*. Furthermore, those *vedanā* that arise do not lead to the production of any new *kamma*, for those who have attained this state are, as stated in the two passages quoted above, fully liberated (*parinibbuto*). This attainment of full liberation, as long as one is alive, is no different from *nibbāna* with residue,[75] for it can be considered a state of mind, or more accurately, the state of a purified mind.

Vedanā as Bifurcation Point

The place that *vedanā* occupies in Buddhist soteriology is crucial, since *vedanā* constitutes the bifurcation point from which diverge the road leading to the multiplication of unhappiness and the road leading to the eradication of misery.[76] Because of the Buddhist pivotal theory of dependent origination (*paṭiccasamuppāda*), *vedanā* is often misunderstood as not only being the basis for, but also as inevitably leading to, craving. However, if we carefully examine the Great Discourse on Causation (*Mahānidānasutta*) where each of the twelve links of the theory of dependent origination is explained, we do not find any textual

74 S. iv, 230.

75 *Arahattapattito paṭṭhāya kilesavaṭṭassa khepitattā sa-upādisesena carimacittanirodhena khandhavaṭṭassa khepitattā anupādisesena cā ti dvīhi pi parinibbānehi parinibbutā anupādāno viya padīpo apaṇṇattikabhāvaṁ gatā* (DhA. ii, 163).

76 *Vedanāya kho Vaccha aññāṇā vedanāsamudaye aññāṇā vedanānirodhe aññāṇā vedanānirodhagāminiyāpaṭipadāya aññāṇā. Evam imāni anekavihitāni diṭṭhigatāni loke uppajanti.* "Vaccha, it is from the lack of knowledge in reference to the arising of sensations, to the eradication of sensations and to the path leading to the eradication of sensations that various wrong views regarding the universe arise" (S. iii, 258). Wrong views are said to bind one to misery.

evidence stating that *vedanā* necessarily leads to craving. All that is said is:

> "With sensation as condition, there is craving. This, Ānanda, should be understood in this way. If there were no sensation at all, of any kind, anywhere—i.e., no sensation arising from eye-contact, no sensation arising from ear-contact, no sensation arising from nose-contact, no sensation arising from tongue-contact, no sensation arising from body-contact, and no sensation arising of mind-contact—then, no sensation would be present; with the cessation of sensation, would craving be discerned?" "Definitely not, *bhante*." "Therefore, Ānanda, sensation is the cause, source, origin and condition for craving."[77]

This passage explicitly states that *vedanā* is a condition for craving, and that if no *vedanā* is found, craving cannot arise. But it does not state that *vedanā* is the only causal factor involved in the production of craving. The fact that craving cannot be produced without the presence of a *vedanā* does not imply that craving is necessarily produced when a *vedanā* is present. As Kalupahana noted:

While it is true, and this is actually the position held by the Buddha, that pleasant sensations *could* give rise to craving and lust, and unpleasant sensations (*dukkhā vedanā*) can be the cause of aversion and hatred (*dosa*), the causal relation is not a one-to-one relation.[78]

---

77 *"'Vedanāpaccayā taṇhā ti' iti kho pan' etaṁ vuttaṁ, tad Ānanda iminā p'etaṁ pariyāyena veditabbaṁ yathā vedanāpaccayā taṇhā. Vedanā va hi Ānanda nābhavissa sabbena sabbaṁ sabbatthā sabbaṁ kassaci kimhici, seyyathīdaṁ cakkhu-samphassajā vedanā, sota-samphassajā vedanā, ghāna-samphassajā vedanā, jivhā-samphassajā vedanā, kāya-samphassajā vedanā, mano-samphassajā vedanā, sabbaso vedanāya asati vedanā-nirodhā api nu kho taṇhā paññāyethāti? No h'etaṁ bhante'. 'Tasmā ih'Āmanda (sic) es'eva hetu etaṁ nidānaṁ esa samudayo esa paccayo taṇhāya, yadidaṁ vedanā'"* (D. ii, 58). A similar passage is repeated for each of the twelve links.

78 Kalupahana, *The Principles of Buddhist Psychology*, p. 46. Th. Stcherbatsky supports this view by saying that the "*pratītyasamutpāda* can hardly be called causation in the sense in which it is usually understood. It really means dependently co-ordinated-origination or dependent existence. According to it every momentary entity springs into existence in co-ordination with other moments. Its formula is '*asmin sati idam bhavati*' there being this, there appears that! According to this, there could be neither *causa materialis*, nor *causa efficiens*. An entity is not really produced, it is simply co-ordinated" (*The Conception of Buddhist Nirvāṇa*, p. 9).

Vedanā itself is devoid of the connotation that many have read into the *paṭiccasamuppāda*; *vedanāpaccayā taṇhā* does not imply that *vedanā* is a sufficient condition for the arising of *taṇhā* (craving), but simply that it is a necessary condition. For example, when narrating his experience before he attained enlightenment, the Buddha mentioned to Aggivessana that while dwelling in jhānic ecstasy, he was not affected by the pleasurable *vedanā* that characterize such states,[79] and was not, therefore, generating craving. The Buddha was experiencing sensations, but was not producing any *kamma* or craving. A further example is found in the *Majjhimanikāya* where the Buddha is described as experiencing the arising and fading away of sensations.[80] Since a Buddha, by definition, is completely free from craving, the *vedanā* that arise within him cannot give rise to craving. Hence, *vedanā* itself is not a sufficient condition for the emergence of craving; rather, the perspective from which sensations are approached plays a crucial role in the emergence of craving. In fact, the *Majjhimanikāya* states that those *vedanā* approached as impermanent, sorrowful and subject to the vicissitudes of life (*vipariṇāmadhamma*) eradicate the tendency of reacting to sensations with greed,[81] which would ultimately generate craving.

Wholesome and Unwholesome *Vedanā*

This particular soteriological approach to sensations is further described in the *Saṁyuttanikāya* as leading away from craving and any other defilements. Describing a monk in contemplation, the Pāli sources say:

> He is aware of the *vedanā* thus: "there has arisen in me one of the five types of *vedanā*. Now this has its condition, its cause, its reasons, and has been conditioned. That this *vedanā* should arise without these is impossible." Thus he comes to know fully the *vedanā*, its arising and its ceasing: and, thereafter, when a *vedanā*

79 *Evarūpā pi kho me Aggivessanauppannā sukhā vedanā cittaṁ na pariyādāya tiṭṭhati.* Literally: Thus, Aggivessana, my mind was standing not having been overpowered by the pleasurable *vedanā* previously arisen (M. i, 247).

80 *Yampi, bhante, Bhagavato viditā vedanā uppajanti, viditā upaṭṭhahanti, viditā abbhatthaṁ gacchanti* (M. iii, 124).

81 M. iii, 218-20.

> arises, it comes to cease without remainder,—that also he fully knows.[82]

The *Majjhimanikāya* further states that a "certain kind" of *vedanā*—which kind may still be either pleasant, painful or neutral—is conducive to the development of unwholesome states (*akusalā dhammā*), while "another kind" of *vedanā* leads to the cultivation of wholesome states.[83] This passage does not reveal which kind of *vedanā* is conducive to either wholesome or unwholesome states, but its commentary, the *Papañcasūdanī*, clarifies this point. This source defines the sensations leading to the unwholesome states as belonging to the householder (*gehasitā*),[84] but makes no mention of those leading to the wholesome state. In another *sutta* of the *Majjhimanikāya*, however, unwholesome states are contrasted with those belonging to the renouncer (*nekkhamasitā*);[85] it seems that those belonging to the renouncer are conducive to wholesome states since their very quality lies in the way they are approached. They are perceived as "they really are," i.e., as painful and impermanent. This distinction between these two types of *vedanā* is not intrinsic to the *vedanā* themselves, but rather results from the way one approaches the *vedanā*. However, we have to be careful not to be misled by the terms. Although the words *gehasitā* and *nekkhamasitā* literally refer to the household life and that of renunciation respectively, they concern the mental disposition of a person rather than their outer dress or apparent condition. Nothing prevents a householder from attaining stages that certain monastics have failed to reach due to their lack of practice. As is stated in the

82 *So evam pajānāti. Uppannaṁ kho me idaṁ domanassindriyam* (and for all the other *indriya*). *Tañca kho sanimittaṁ sanidānam sasaṅkhāraṁ sappaccayaṁ. Taṁ vata animittam anidānam asaṅkhāram appaccayaṁ domanassindriyam uppajjissatīti netaṁ thānaṁ vijjati. So domanassindriyaṁ ca pajānāti domanassindriyasamudayañca pajānāti. Domanassindriyanirodhaṁ ca pajānāti. Yattha cuppannaṁ domanassindriyaṁ aparisesaṁ nirujjhati tañca pajānāti* (S. v, 14). I have taken the liberty of translating the term *indriya* as *vedanā* since the term *pañcindriyāni*, in this particular context, refers to the five types of *vedanā*. See p. 52 for a discussion of these five *indriya*.

83 *Idha' ekaccassa evarūpaṁ sukhaṁ vedanaṁ vediyatoakusalā dhammā abhivaḍḍhanti kusalā dhammā parihāyanti, idha pan'ekaccassa evarūpaṁ sukhaṁ vedanaṁ vediyato akusalā dhammāparihāyanti kusalā dhammā abhivaḍḍhanti.* ... The same is given in respect to painful and neutral *vedanā* (M. i, 475).

84 *Evarūpam sukhaṁ vedanaṁ pajahathā ti idaṁ cha gehasitasomanassavasena* (MA. ii, 187).

85 M. iii, 217ff.

Dhammapāda: "Even though one may be highly dressed—in other words, not wearing the simple monastic habit and therefore being a householder—if one is poised, calm, controlled and established in the holy life, having laid aside the rod towards all beings, this person is truly a *brahmaṇa*, a recluse, a *bhikkhu*."[86] This passage supports the popular adage *habitus non facit monachum* (clothes don't make the monk). The Pāli canon even apprises us of certain householders who had attained a higher development than certain monks. For example, Citta Gahapati, who remained a householder throughout his life, possessed a thorough understanding of the teaching of the Buddha[87] and had attained a stage that was superior to many who had become monastics.[88] Equally, there are cases of monks who remained as undeveloped at the mental level as an ordinary householder (*putthujana*). For example, the venerable Nanda was tormented by thoughts of his former wife,[89] and his mental state did not reflect the calm of the true renunciate, but rather the agitation of the householder. Therefore, we have to stress that the terms *nekkhamasitā* and *gehasitā* refer to ways of approaching the *vedanā* rather than to physical appearance and social status.

The *Papañcasūdanī* further interprets these two terms of *gehasitā* and *nekkhamasitā* as being similar to the terms *āmisā* and *nirāmisā*, also used to describe *vedanā*.[90] The *Satipaṭṭhānasutta*, a text essentially concerned with meditative practices, also uses these terms of *āmisā* and *nirāmisā vedanā*.[91] The term *āmisā* is derived from the Sanskrit *āmiṣa* or *āmis*, both meaning "raw flesh,"[92] and the word *nirāmisā* literally means "without raw flesh." We might easily say that the Buddhist meaning of the terms has been extended respectively to "non-vegetarian" and "impure" and to "vegetarian" and "pure." However, as Seyfort Ruegg established in his article "Ahimsa and Vegetarianism in

86 *Alaṅkato ce'pi samaṁ careyya santo danto niyato brahmacārī sabbesu bhūtesu nidhāya daṇḍaṁ so brāhmaṇo, so samaṇo, so bhikkhu* (Dh. 142).

87 A. i, 26.

88 Vsm. 442.

89 G.P. Malasekera, *Dictionary of Pāli Proper Names*, vol. 2 (London: P.T.S., 1974), p. 10.

90 MA. i, 278. The kinds of *vedanā* that the *Papañcasūdanī* is referring to are described in detail in the *Saḷāyatanavibhaṅgasutta* (M. iii, 219).

91 M. i, 59 also at A. iii, 411 and D. ii, 298.

92 V.S. Apte, *The Practical Sanskrit English Dictionary* (Kyoto: Rinsen Book Company, 1986), p. 346.

the History of Buddhism," the establishment of vegetarianism in Buddhism is closely connected to "a specific religious and philosophical teaching: the tathāgatagarbha doctrine,"[93] which was elaborated much later than the *Satipaṭṭhānasutta*. It seems that, at the time the *Satipaṭṭhāna* was composed, meat-eating was not yet perceived as "corrupting." We cannot therefore establish a relation between the meaning of these two words and the connotations implied by eating meat. However, it is very clear from this particular *sutta* that the *vedanā* represented as *nirāmisā* symbolize those *vedanā* which are not conducive to further defilements such as craving or aversion.

In this chapter, we have discussed the states of *saññāvedayitanirodha* and of *vedanākkhaya*. The former is a state comparable to *nibbāna* without residue, for none of the mental aggregates can be found therein. The latter is more comparable to *nibbāna* with residue, for the five aggregates of a person experiencing such a state are still functioning. We have also discussed many classifications of *vedanā* such as *nirāmisā, nekkhamasitā, āmisā* and *gehasitā*. We came to the conclusion that a certain means of approaching *vedanā* would transform them into *nirāmisā* or *nekkhammasitā vedanā*, which are of an inoffensive nature, while an alternative approach would transform *vedanā* into *āmisā* or *gehasitā vedanā*, which are endowed with a negative connotation since they will act as potential agents in the future arising of craving and aversion. The factor responsible for this particular approach to *vedanā* is the next aggregate: recognition (*saññā*). It is this third aggregate that will transform sensations into *nirāmisā* (*nekkhamasitā*) or *āmisā* (*gehasitā*), a transformation that will be either responsible for the generation or eradication of craving.

93 D. Seyfort Ruegg, "Ahimsa and Vegetarianism in the History of Buddhism," in *Buddhist Studies in Honour of W. Rahula*, ed. O.H. de A. Wijesekera (London: Gordon Fraser, 1980), pp. 236-37.

Chapter 4

The *Saññākkhandha*

As we saw in the previous chapter, *vedanā* is a necessary but not a sufficient condition for the arising of craving (*taṇhā*). Craving depends not only on the occurrence of sensation, but also on the occurrence of a particular type of *saññā*. My aim in this chapter is twofold: first, to circumscribe the meaning of the term *saññākkhandha* and second, to show how it contributes to the emergence of craving within the framework of the chain of dependent origination.

Like *vedanā*, *saññā* is usually defined with respect to the six sense-doors (*āyatana*) through which the faculty is applied. Thus, *saññā* is classified in terms of (1) visible object (*rūpasaññā*), (2) sound (*sadda-saññā*), (3) smell (*gandhasaññā*), (4) taste (*rasasaññā*), (5) touch (*phoṭṭhabbasaññā*), and (6) mental object (*dhammasaññā*).[1] Moreover, as with *vedanā*, the canonical definition of *saññā* does not shed much light on the meaning of the term since the verb used to define it (*sañjānāti*) refers to the root from which the term *saññā* is derived.[2] Fortunately, the *Saṁyuttanikāya* offers us a glimpse of what *saññā* could mean by expanding on the former definition: "It is called 'recognition' because it 'recognizes.' What does it 'recognize'? It 'recognizes' [regarding the organ of sight] such things as blue, yellow, red, white, etc. Because it 'recognizes', it is therefore called 'recognition.' "[3]

Words such as "to be conscious" and "consciousness"[4] or "to perceive" and "perception"[5] are often used to translate the term *saññā*. However, my translation is grounded in the belief that both "perception" and "consciousness" carry misleading connotations with

1 A. iii, 413.

2 *Sañjānātisañjānātīti kho avuso, tasmā saññā vuccati* (M. i, 293).

3 *Kiñca bhikkhave saññaṁ vadetha? Sañjānātīti kho bhikkhave tasmā saññā ti vuccati. Kiñ casañjānāti? Nīlam pi sañjānāti pītakam pi sañjānāti lohitakam pi sañjānāti odātam pi sañjānāti. Sañjānātīti kho bhikkhave tasmā saññā vuccati* (S. iii, 87).

4 As F.L. Woodward translated these two words in *The Book of the Kindred Sayings* (London: P.T.S., 1917-22), 3:74.

5 As I.B. Horner rendered them in *The Collection of the Middle Length Sayings*, 1:352.

regard to *saññā*. The word "recognition," on the other hand, tends to imply that the subject imposes certain categories upon the percept in order to classify it. The term "recognition" can definitely not be mistakenly ascribed to the concept of *viññāṇa*. To use our reference from the *Saṁyuttanikāya* as a supporting example for this decision, we may say that the words "to perceive" and "to be conscious of" would suggest that the blueness, yellowness or redness of the object is inherent in the object itself, whereas saying "to recognize" implies that the colour (which may not be exactly blue, yellow or red, if such pristine colours indeed exist) is "categorized" by being linked to previous labellings. In fact, the word blue names nothing but a concept, and different people form different concepts to describe the same sensation. For example, one person may call two colours with different tones blue, while another may recognize these colours as indigo and aquamarine. Both have an extremely similar sensory experience, yet their recognition differs. The classic dialogue between King Milinda and Nāgasena on the definition of a chariot further exemplifies this point.[6] Milinda is unable to define the chariot without referring to all its constituent parts. The chariot is a mere category, a mental conceptualization used by the *saññā* to order, to classify the various sensory experiences resulting from contact with the external object that we normally term chariot. This faculty of recognition leads to the formation of concepts, usually rendered in Pāli by the expression *paññattī*.[7] The *Aṅguttaranikāya* supports the analogy by elaborating on the result of *saññā*, saying that "*saññā* always results in a 'concept' [*vohāra*, expression of worldly usage]: whatever is conceptualized has previously been 'saññanized.' "[8] This is very similar to the Sanskrit equivalent of the term *saññā* (*saṁjñā*) which usually means "name," "technical term" or "notion."[9]

---

6 Mil. 27ff. This simile had already been used by the Therī Vajirā in her discussion with Māra. *Nayidha sattūpalabbhati. Yathā hi aṅgasambhārā. Hoti saddo ratho iti. Evaṁ khandhesu santesu. Hoti satti sammuti* (S. i, 135).

7 For further information on *paññattī*, refer to A.K. Warder's article on "The Concept of a Concept," *Journal of Indian Philosophy* (1971), especially p. 189.

8 *Katamo ca bhikkhave saññānaṁ vipāko? Vohāravepakkāham bhikkhave saññā vadāmi; yathā yathā naṁ sañjānāti, tathā tathā voharati 'evaṁ saññī ahosin' ti* (A. iii, 413-14).

9 Vasubandhu says that one is aware of blue (*nīlaṁ vijānāti*), but one ascribes the notion of blue to the perception (*nīlam iti saṁjānāti*). "La notion (saṁjñā) consiste dans la préhension des caractères" (La Vallée Poussin, *Abhidharmakośa*, 1:28).

The *Vibhaṅga* classifies *saññā* into three categories: wholesome (*kusala*), unwholesome (*akusala*) and neutral (*avyākata*).[10] Neither canonical nor commentarial literature sheds much light on these classifications. However, before establishing a correlation between *saññā* and the *paṭiccasamuppāda*, I will attempt to clarify what the text means by "unwholesome" and "wholesome" *saññā*.

Unwholesome *Saññā*

Like *vedanā*, *saññā* can also be perceived as an obstacle to spiritual progress. While the *Vibhaṅga* does not clarify what constitutes wholesome and unwholesome *saññā*, the *Suttanipāta* mentions that "one has not even the slightest *saññā* as regards to what is seen, heard or said; how can anyone in the world here doubt about such *brāhmaṇa*—i.e., one who has not even the slightest *saññā*—who does not hold a view (*diṭṭhi*)?"[11] This passage implies, first, that true *brāhmaṇa*[12] are free from the control of *saññā*; and second, that *saññā* is associated with the generation of views—these emerge from ignorance (*avijjā*)[13] and are therefore linked to craving and conducive to an unwholesome future.[14] By emancipating themselves from the hold of the *saññā*, these *brāhmaṇa* have automatically eradicated the possibility of the arising of new views and of craving. The *Suttanipāta* also states that "the destruction of sorrow follows from the eradication of *saññā*."[15] This

10 *Tividhena saññākkhandho: atthi kusalo, atthi akusalo, atthi avyākato* (Vbh. 28).

11 *Tassīdha diṭṭhe va sute mute vā pakappitā n'atthi aṇū pi saññā: taṁ brāhmaṇaṁ diṭṭhimanādiyānaṁ denīdha lokasmiṁ vikappayeyya* (Sn. 802).

12 In Buddhist terminology, the term *brāhmaṇa* is not limited to the members of a particular social group. Instead, the *sutta* literature defines a "true" *brāhmaṇa* as one who is established in *sīla, samādhi* and *paññā* (see *Kūṭadantasutta*, D. i, 127-49). *Brāhmaṇa* in the Buddhist sense is often employed as a synonym of *arahant*.

13 S. i, 145; ii, 153.

14 A. i, 22-23.

15 ... *saññāya uparodhanā evaṁ dukkhakkhayo hoti* (Sn. 732).

view is grounded in the fact that *saññā* is seen as the cause of "obsession"[16] (*papañca*), which hinders spiritual progress.[17]

A brief look at the word *papañca* will help us understand more thoroughly the negative aspect of *saññā*. The term *papañca* itself is problematic, for it seems to have been used differently in the *sutta*, abhidhammic and commentarial literatures. In the *sutta*, the term obsession seems interchangeable with wrong views (*diṭṭhi*). For example, the *Suttanipāta* clearly states that the ground of obsession lies in the belief that "I am the thinker."[18] The *Saṁyuttanikāya* goes even further by stating that most human beings approach reality with obsessions, but if one has removed the worldly things (*gehasitā*) which are the product of the mind, one moves towards renunciation (*nekkhammasitā*).[19] The *Sāratthappakāsini* vaguely explains the term *papañcasaññā*, as used in this particular passage, as the notion of obsession created by unwholesome *saññā*.[20] This leads us to a narrower

16 *Saññānidānā hi papañcasaṅkhā* (Sn. 874). The *Niddesa* equates *papañcā* and *papañcasaṅkhā*. *Papañcā yeva papañcasaṅkhā* (Nid. i, 280; 344). The term *papañca* literally means "proliferation" and may refer to the proliferation of thoughts that govern our behaviour without our being aware of it. This is why I translate the term as "obsession." However, as Richard Hayes notes, "the term '*prapañca*,' when used in the context of a Buddhist work is virtually devoid of any precise meaning. [The terms '*prapañca*' and '*dṛṣṭi*'] may be regarded as variables that are capable of being given a more or less precise meaning by the Buddhist who uses them. Despite being variables, they do have a constant feature, which is that every Buddhist uses these words to connote wrongful uses of the mind. So, whenever we encounter the terms in a given text, all we can know for sure is that they refer to mental habits that have to be got rid of if we are to attain the greatest good" (*Dignaga on the Intrepretation of Signs* [London: Kluwer Academic Publishers, 1988], p. 68, n. 35). For a detailed analysis of the term, however, the reader should refer to Bhikkhu Ñāṇananda's *Concept and Reality in Early Buddhist Thought* (Kandy: B.P.S., 1986), a work devoted entirely to the study of *papañca*.

17 M. 1, 65; S. i, 100; iv, 52, 71; A. ii, 161; iii, 393, etc.

18 *Mantā 'ham asmi* (Sn. 916).

19 This is a loose translation of the following verse: *Papañcasaññā itarītarā narā | papañcayantā upayanti saññino | manomayam gehasitañca sabbaṁ | panujja nekkhammasitam irīyati* || (S. iv, 71).

20 *Kilesasaññāya papañcasaññā nāma hutvā* (SA. ii, 382). It is interesting to note that the term *kilesa* is often associated with the mind-defiling passions. See Nyānātiloka, *Buddhist Dictionary*, p. 80.

interpretation of the term, where *papañca* is used, more or less, as a synonym for desire, wrong views and conceit.[21]

The *Pāli Text Society Dictionary* translates the compound *papañcasaññā* as idée fixe, a translation which renders the meaning of the term very adequately, for the *Papañcasūdanī* explains the term as "the faculty of recognition associated with the obsessions related to wrong views and craving."[22] However, clarifications on obsession are found in the *Majjhimanikāya* where the term is used as part of a small causal chain reflecting a psychological process:

> Visual consciousness arises on account of visual forms and the eye, the meeting of these three is contact (*phassa*). On account of contact there is a sensation (*vedanā*). What one senses (as a sensation), one recognizes (*sañjānāti*, from *saññā*). What one recognizes, one "thinks about" (*vitakka*).[23] What one thinks about, one is obsessed with. What obsesses one is the cause of the number of obsessions which assail a person with regard to past, present or future visual forms cognizable by the eye.[24]

According to this and other examples, contact is a necessary element for the arising of sensations, and sensations in turn are needed for the recognition to arise. However, recognition constitutes a further precondition for the appearance of "thinking about" and obsessions. This passage demonstrates that the *saññākkhandha* definitely follows *vedanākkhandha* and precedes obsessions.

The concept of obsession is also closely associated with desire. As one of the verses of the *Theragathā* reports: "one who follows [his] obsessions is [like] a deer delighting in obsessions who has failed to

---

21 *Taṇhādiṭṭhimānappabhedaṁ papañcaṁ* (SnA. II, 431). Similar at Nid. i, 280; 344-45 and Net. 37.

22 *Papañcasaññā ti taṇhādiṭṭhipapañcasampayuttā saññā* (MA. ii, 75).

23 On the term *vitakka*, see D. ii, 277. In his translation of the *Dīghanikāya*, Maurice Walshe supports the translation of the term as "thinking." See Walshe, *Thus Have I Heard* (London: Wisdom Publications, 1987), p. 587, n. 611.

24 *Cakkhuṇ c'āvuso paṭicca rūpe ca uppajjati cakkhuviññāṇaṁ tiṇṇaṁ saṅgati phasso, phassapaccayā vedanā, yaṁ vedeti taṁ sañjānāti, yaṁ sañjānāti taṁ vitakketi, yaṁ vitakketi taṁ papañceti, yaṁ papañceti tato nidānaṁ purisaṁ papañcasaṅkhā samudācaranti atītānāgatapaccuppannesu cakkhuviṇṇeyyesu rūpesu* (M. i, 111-12). Similar occurrences of the formula also appear at M. i, 259; S. iv, 67, etc.

attain *nibbāna*, the peace from bondage and the unsurpassable."[25] This metaphorical passage does not directly point to the association of obsession with craving. However, E.R. Sarathchandhra expands the image to arrive at the following: one ruled by his obsessions is comparable to a deer who follows a mirage thinking that it is a pool of water; the deer is thirsty and believes that the mirage (*papañca*) will quench its thirst, just as people seek happiness and are convinced that sensual pleasure will fulfil their desire.[26] Although obsession cannot be directly correlated with craving, it can be associated with the emergence of craving because, as the *Sakkapañhasutta* states, envy (*issā*) and avarice (*macchariya*), as well as desire (*chanda*[27]), have their origin in *papañcasaññā*.[28] Therefore, it would seem that both *saññā* and the more precise *papañcasaññā* are necessary conditions for the arousal of craving—the link of the *paṭiccasamuppāda* that follows *vedanā*.

However, it must be stressed that obsession and *papañcasaññā* are not elements of the *saññākkhandha* itself. As we have seen, the *saññākkhandha* is seen as the cause (or one of the causes) of obsessions,[29] but these are never said to be part of the *saññākkhandha*. Furthermore, the causal chain of the *Majjhimanikāya* mentioned above implies that *saññā* is a necessary condition for thinking about (*vitakka*), which in turn is responsible for obsessions. It is also worth noting that this same causal chain implicitly establishes a distinction between the *saññākkhandha* and the *saṅkhārakkhandha* since, as we will see later, thinking about is one of the members of the *saṅkhārakkhandha* and it would be illogical if obsessions, which follows thinking about, belonged to the *saññākkhandha*.[30]

According to the sixth book of the *Abhidhamma*, the *saññā-kkhandha* needs to be distinguished from recognition of views (*diṭṭhi-*

---

25 *Yo papañcam anuyutto papañcābhirato mago, cirādhāyī so nibbānaṁ yogakkhemaṁ anuttaraṁ* (Th. i, vs. 989).

26 E.R. Sarathchandra, *Buddhist Theory of Perception* (Colombo: Ceylon University Press, 1958), p. 10.

27 *Chanda* is equated in the commentary with craving (*taṇhā*).

28 D. ii, 277-78.

29 Sn. 874.

30 In fact, if we adopt the *sutta* hypothesis mentioned on p. 80 that *papañca* is a synonym of *diṭṭhi*, *papañca* is automatically classified under the *saṅkhārakkhandha* category, for *diṭṭhi* is explicitly described as one of the fifty elements that fall into the category of *saṅkhārakkhandha* (see p. 107).

saññā). Only the *Yamaka* refers to this nuance, while other texts, such as the *Dhammasaṅgaṇi*,[31] imply that the faculty of recognition, the fact of having recognized and the state of having perceived all belong to the *saññākkhandha*. The *Dhammasaṅgaṇi* does not seem to admit a distinction between the various *saññā*, while the *Yamaka* does. This apparent contradiction might be due primarily to a semantic misunderstanding of the term *diṭṭhisaññā*. The *Pāli Text Society Dictionary* translates the word *diṭṭhi* as "view, theory, belief, dogma" and stresses that unless preceded by the adjective *sammā*, it usually carries a negative connotation. To my knowledge, however, the compound *diṭṭhisaññā* is almost never used in the *sutta* literature and seems to be particular to the *Yamaka*.[32] The *Yamaka* commentary elucidates the term by equating it with the concept of *papañcasaññā*[33] which, as we have seen, is intimately related to craving.

This first distinction between the *saññākkhandha* and recognition of views (*diṭṭhisaññā*)—defined as *papañcasaññā* by the *Pañcappakaraṇatthakathā*—indicates that the *saññākkhandha* does not include obsessions and that craving is not inevitably generated by the *saññākkhandha* itself. In fact, obsessions—as well as recognition of views—would fall into the category of *saṅkhārakkhandha* and not of the *saññākkhandha*, for, as the *Nettipakaraṇa* states, "obsessions are craving, views, conceit and whatever *saṅkhāra* are activated by them."[34] The same text further supports this statement by saying that "whatever is obsession, whatever are the *saṅkhāra* and whatever are the delighting in the past, future and present, all these are the same."[35] The *Yamaka* does not classify recognition of views (and obsessions) as *saññākkhandha* because it belongs to the *saṅkhārakkhandha*. As noted previously, *saññā* is often seen as the cause of obsessions. The *saññākkhandha* is the ground for the development of obsessions (as views, *diṭṭhi*). I must stress, however, that obsession itself does not belong to

31 *Katamo tasmiṁ samye saññākkhandho hoti? Yā tasmiṁ samaye saññā sañjānā sañjānitattaṁ—ayaṁ tasmiṁ samaye saññākkhandho hoti* (Dhs. 17).

32 One occurrence of the term has been found in the *Mahāniddesa* of the *Khuddakanikāya* where it is equated to wrong views (Nid. 93).

33 *Saññāyamake tāva diṭṭhisaññā ti papañcasaññā ti ādīsu āgatā diṭṭhisaññā* (C.A.F. Rhys Davids, ed., *Pañcappakaraṇatthakathā*, *Journal of the P.T.S.* 6 (1910-12): 59.

34 *Papañcā nāma taṇhādiṭṭhimānā tadabhisaṅkhātā ca saṅkhārā* (Net. 37).

35 *Yo cāpi papañco, ye ca saṅkhārā yā ca atītānāgatapaccuppannassa abhinandana, idaṁ ekattaṁ* (Net. 38).

the *saññākkhandha*, for the latter is merely a function that triggers the arising of the former, which, in fact, partakes of the *saṅkhārakkhandha*.

Wholesome *Saññā*

Saññā is not always represented as a hindrance to salvation. The *Aṅguttaranikāya*, for example, provides us with an example of the positive value of *saññā*. Once, the closest disciple of the Buddha, Ānanda, came to report that the monk Girimānanda had been struck by a serious illness. The Buddha then told Ānanda to visit Girimānanda and recite "ten *saññā*" to the sick man; from this mere recitation, he says, "there are grounds to believe that the sickness will be allayed."[36] These ten *saññā* consisted of (1) the recognition of impermanence (*aniccasaññā*), (2) the recognition of selflessness (*anattasaññā*), (3) the recognition of unpleasantness (*asubhasaññā*), (4) the recognition of danger (*ādīnavasaññā*), (5) the recognition of abandoning (*pahāna-saññā*), (6) the recognition of dispassion (*virāgasaññā*), (7) the recognition of cessation (*nirodhasaññā*), (8) the recognition of disenchantment with the entire world (*sabbaloke anabhiratasaññā*), (9) the recognition of the impermanence in reference to all compounded things (*sabbe saṅkhāresu aniccasaññā*), and (10) the mindfulness of breathing (*ānapanasati*).

We may wonder why the Buddha thought that there were grounds to believe that the mere recitation of these ten recognitions might alleviate the suffering of Girimānanda. The *Asibandhakaputta-sutta*[37] demonstrates that the Buddha did not believe that the power of words could alter one's destiny; hence for him to say that the mere recitation of the ten *saññā* would improve Girimānanda's future seems incongruous. However, it is possible that he simply meant that hearing the ten *saññā* might encourage Girimānanda to develop these recognitions—this would result, if not in a cure for the sickness itself, in alleviating the unhappiness that caused it.

Just as there are two types of *vedanā*—*āmisā* and *nirāmisā*—we also find two kinds of *saññā*: those that lead to sorrow and unhappi-

36 *Sace kho tvaṁ Ānanda Girimānandassa bhikkhuno upasaṅkamitvā dasa saññā bhāseyyāsi, ṭhānaṁ kho pan' etaṁ vijjati, yaṁ Girimānandassa bhikkhuno dasasaññā sutvā so ābādho ṭhānaso paṭipassambheyya* (A. v, 108).

37 S. iv, 310.

ness[38] because of their generating of obsessions, and those that improve one's future by approaching reality through the three characteristics of existence (*anicca, anatta,* and *dukkha*)[39] and seven other perspectives which, taken all together, constitute the ten *saññā* enumerated in the *Girimānandasutta*. The *Girimānandasutta* is not the only text to refer to this wholesome aspect of *saññā*. For example, these wholesome *saññā* are classified in categories of seven in the *Dīgha-nikāya*, where it is said that they are conducive to [spiritual] prosperity,[40] in categories of six in the *Aṅguttaranikāya*, where they are qualified as integral constituents of knowledge (*vijjā*),[41] in categories of five, in the *Dīghanikāya*, where they are described as leading to the maturity of liberation,[42] and finally, in the *Aṅguttaranikāya*,[43] where they are described as being very fruitful, merging in and leading to the deathless (*nibbāna*).

To my knowledge, the whole Pāli canon along with its commentaries support the view that *saññā* can be wholesome when it is geared towards the recognition of elements essential for liberation. What is important to note is that three main elements are explicitly or

---

38 As mentioned in Sn. 732; 802.

39 *Dukkha* is indirectly implied by the reference to *asubha* and *ādīna*.

40 *Yāvakīvañ ca bhikkhave bhikkhū anicca-saññaṁ bhāvessanti, anatta-saññaṁ bhāvessanti, asubha-saññaṁ bhāvessanti, ādīnava-saññaṁ bhāvessanti, pahāna-saññaṁ bhāvessanti, virāga-saññaṁ bhāvessanti, nirodha-saññaṁ bhāvessanti, vuddhi yeva bhikkhave bhikkhūnaṁ pāṭikaṅkhā no parihāni* (D. ii, 79). The seven recognitions mentioned by this passage are those of impermanence, non-self, non-beautiful, danger, overcoming, dispassion and cessation. It seems clear that prosperity is used in the "spiritual" sense in this context for the Buddha is addressing a monastic audience.

41 *Cha yime bhikkhave dhammā vijjābhāgiyā. Katame cha? Aniccasaññā, anicce dukkhasaññā dukkhe anattasaññā, pahānasaññā, virāgasaññā, nirodhasaññā* (A. iii, 334). These six recognitions are: impermanence, suffering amidst what is impermanent, not-self amidst what is suffering, overcoming, dispassion and cessation.

42 *Pañca vimutti-paripācaniyā saññā. Aniccasaññā, anicce dukkhasaññā, dukkhe anatta-saññā, pahānasaññā, virāgasaññā*. These are the recognitions of impermanence, of suffering amidst impermanence, selflessness amidst suffering, overcoming and of dispassion (D. iii, 243).

43 *Pañc'imā bhikkhave saññā bhāvitā bahulīkatā mahapphalā honti mahānisaṁsā amatogadhā amatapariyosānā. Katamā pañca? Asubhasaññā maraṇasaññā ādīnava-saññā āhāre paṭikkūlasaññā sabbaloke anabhiratasaṇṇā* (A. iii, 79). These are the recognitions of unpleasantness, death, danger, unwholesomeness with regard to food and disenchantment with the whole world.

implicitly incorporated in all of these lists: the recognition of impermanence (*anicca*), of suffering (*dukkha*) and of selflessness (*anatta*). As hinted above, these three main elements constitute the basis for wisdom. In order to attain the goal, whether *nibbāna* with or without residue, or even *saññāvedayitanirodha*, what is definitely required by the practitioner is to have developed wisdom through *vipassanā*, insight, which in turn is cultivated by the awareness of impermanence, suffering and selflessness. As Buddhaghosa states in the *Visuddhimagga*, there are eighteen major kinds of *vipassanā*[44] and six of these eighteen are among the various enumerations of wholesome *saññā* seen above. These are impermanence, selflessness, suffering, dispassion, eradication and danger (*ādinava*). The cultivation of these wholesome *saññā* will not lead to the further generation of craving, but will help to develop wisdom through which one can break away from the cycle of life and death and the chain of dependent origination.

Wholesome *Saññā* and the *Saññākkhandha*

At this point, we may wonder whether or not this wholesome *saññā* does, in fact, belong to the *saññākkhandha*. Buddhaghosa argues in the *Visuddhimagga* that the function of *saññā* as one of the aggregates is simply to recognize objects as "blue," "yellow" and so forth. The *saññākkhandha*, according to this particular text, cannot lead to the penetration of the characteristics of existence: one could not, through the faculty of recognition, grasp at the deepest level the characteristics of impermanence, suffering and selflessness.[45] Buddhaghosa goes on to establish, through a metaphor, a radical difference between the *saññākkhandha* and wisdom (*paññā*). While the former merely recognizes the appearance of objects, the latter analyzes every object and perceives it as it is—that is, from a Buddhist point of view, as impermanent, painful and selfless. According to the *Visuddhimagga*, the *saññākkhandha* itself cannot deeply apprehend these three characteristics of existence. Yet, the discussion of the various

---

44 Vsm. 695. The eighteen contemplations (*anupassanā*) enumerated there are those of impermanence, suffering, selflessness, aversion, detachment, cessation, abandoning, destruction, vanishing, change, unconditioned, desirelessness, emptiness, higher wisdom regarding all phenomena, knowledge and vision of reality as it is (*yathābhūtañāṇadassana*), danger, reflecting and turning away. Those that are italicized are included in at least one of the enumerations of wholesome *saññā*.

45 Vsm. 437.

wholesome *saññā* indicates that there *can* be a recognition of impermanence (*aniccasaññā*), of suffering (*dukkhasaññā*) and of selflessness (*anattasaññā*). As evidenced by the *Sumaṅgalavilāsinī*,[46] there are "five *saññā* leading to liberation."[47] Also interesting to note is that three of these five *saññā* are contemplations of the three characteristics of existence.[48] The *Sumaṅgalavilāsinī* implies not only that the object of *saññā* can be the three characteristics of existence, but also that these very recognitions can lead to liberation through the development of wisdom.

The *Visuddhimagga*, as I have noted, claims that the primary function of the *saññākkhandha* is to interpret by means of a sign (*nimitta*).[49] The term *nimitta*, in this context, refers to the outward appearances of an object and excludes the more subtle attributes that characterize every phenomenon of existence. For example, a particular kind of deliverance described as signless (*animitta*) is interpreted in the *Atthasālinī* as being the result of the practice of the threefold contemplation.[50] By observing the three characteristics of existence, one attains the deliverance known as the "signless." The signs, in this context, are the beliefs in permanence, delight and self, which are all outward appearances not reflecting reality as it really is—as characterized by impermanence, suffering and selflessness. While the *saññākkhandha* itself is concerned with recognizing the outward appearances, the signs, the wholesome *saññā* apprehend the "signless." Therefore, since wholesome *saññā* do not apprehend signs, they cannot be classified as members of the *saññākkhandha*, for the latter only deals with appearances.

Correlation between *Saññā* and the *Paṭiccasamuppāda*

According to the *paṭiccasamuppāda*, *vedanā* is a necessary condition for the arising of the next link, craving. However, in the chapter on *vedanā*

---

46 DA. iii, 1033.

47 *Pañca vimutti-paripācaniyā saññā*. In this expression, the term "liberation" (*vimutti*) is explicitly correlated to the state of arahanthood.

48 DA. iii, 1033.

49 *Sañjānapaccayanimittakaraṇarasā* (Vsm. 462).

50 *Animittavipassanaṁ kathesi. Vipassanā hi niccanimittaṁ sukhanimittaṁ attanimittañ ca ugghāṭeti, tasmā animittā ti* (DhsA. 221).

we saw that not all sensations generate craving.[51] Depending on the response to a sensation, craving will either arise or not arise. *Saññā* is primarily responsible for the way in which the individual approaches sensations.

Whenever something is sensed, it is also recognized.[52] *Saññā* always accompanies and follows *vedanā*,[53] but depending on the particular orientation of the *saññā*, one may generate craving or start cultivating wisdom. The *saññākkhandha* lies between two links of the *paṭiccasamuppāda: vedanā* and *taṇhā*. We have just seen that it follows the *vedanākkhandha*, and the causal chain of p. 81 implies that it also precedes *taṇhā*. As we will see in the next chapter, *taṇhā* and the following two links of the *paṭiccasamuppāda* fall into the category of the *saṅkhārakkhandha*. That causal chain, then, places *saññā* between *vedanā* and thinking about (*vitakka*). Since thinking about belongs to the *saṅkhārakkhandha*, it is evident that the *saññākkhandhā* finds its place in between the *vedanākkhandha* and the *saṅkhārakkhandha*.

Saññā imposes categories on our sensations and classifies them. The texts usually give the example that a certain sensation is interpreted as "blue" or "yellow."[54] But this categorization goes much further by classifying sensations as "worth craving," and "worth hating." However, if the recognition that interprets the sensation is one of the positive *saññā*, no craving or aversion will be generated, for the recognition itself will signal that this particular sensation is not "worth craving for" since it is impermanent, suffering and selfless. Yet, if the sensation is interpreted by a recognition that leads to obsessions (similar to views, *diṭṭhi*), one will suffer under the illusion that this particular sensation is permanent, a source of pleasure or associated with the self. According to Buddhism, it is these particular views that are responsible for misperception of reality and bondage to *saṁsāra*, for they are grounds for craving.

As Buddhaghosa states in the *Visuddhimagga*, the *saññākkhandha* (necessarily associated with obsessions) has the function of interpreting by means of signs that are apprehended, like the blind men who

---

51 See pp. 71ff.

52 *Yaṁ vedeti taṁ sañjānāti* (M. i, 111-12). Similar occurrences also appear at M. i, 259; S. iv, 67, etc.

53 This is also evidenced by the causal chain described on p. 81.

54 S. iii, 87.

describe an elephant.[55] The comparison with the blind men probably refers to a story of the *Udāna*[56] where men blind from birth are asked to describe an elephant by touching only a certain part of the animal.[57] The blind men are all partially correct, but since their interpretation is based on their limited experiences, they cannot perceive the totality of the truth and the reality as it is (*yathābhūtañāṇadassana*).[58] However, if the unwholesome *saññā* were replaced by one or many of the various wholesome *saññā*, craving would not be generated, proper understanding of reality would arise and wisdom would be developed.

In this chapter, we have seen that the main function of the *saññākkhandha* is to recognize and interpret sensations through the imposition of categories. I have distinguished between two types of *saññā*. The wholesome *saññā* are recognitions of, in short, the three characteristics of existence. These do not belong to the *saññākkhandha* as such. The unwholesome *saññā*, on the other hand, are simply certain interpretations of reality that are not conducive to insight and that generate obsessions. The *saññākkhandha* is essentially constituted of these unwholesome *saññā*. Unless the *saññā* of an individual are governed by the wholesome *saññā*, that person is likely to generate craving, aversion, clinging and becoming, all of which fall under the next aggregate: *saṅkhāra*.

---

55 *Yathā gahitanimittavasena abhinivesakaraṇapaccupaṭṭhānā, hatthidassaka-andhā viya* (Vsm. 462).

56 Ud. 68-69. Although the simile found in the *Udāna* was used by the Buddha to explain to the king why different ascetics perceive the doctrine differently, Buddhaghosa has appropriated this parable and made it relevant to the function that *saññā* performs.

57 *Te ediso hatthī, n'ediso hatthī, n'ediso hatthī, ediso hatthī' ti aññamaññaṁ muṭṭhīhi saṁyujjhiṁsu* (Ud. 69).

58 Noteworthy is that knowledge and vision according to reality (*yathābhūtañāṇadassana*) is one of the eighteen major kinds of insight (*vipassanā*) mentioned in n. 44 on p. 85.

Chapter 5

The *Saṅkhārakkhandha*

My purpose in this chapter is, primarily, to uncover the basic meaning that links the various contexts in which the term appears; and, secondarily, to arrive at a precise interpretation of *saṅkhārakkhandha* and its function with respect to the theory of dependent origination. I will not attempt to find one English translation with which to render all the connotations of *saṅkhāra* since, as we saw above, such an undertaking would be doomed to failure. Rather, I will attempt to adduce an extensive (and, I hope, comprehensive) explanation of *saṅkhāra* that will provide an understanding of the general meaning of the word by stressing the simultaneous presence of its causal and effective dimensions. To achieve this task, I will first use the fivefold division to analyze the different contexts of the word. I will not discuss *saṅkhārakkhandha* within the scheme. Once the different contexts have been presented, and the meaning of the term within them has been clarified, I will proceed to discuss the general sense of the term *saṅkhāra*. Finally, I will examine the specific function of *saṅkhāra* as one of the *pañcakkhandhā*. This methodology will offer us both a general understanding of the term *saṅkhāra* and of the *saṅkhārakkhandha*.

Polysemy of the Term *Saṅkhāra*

In order to unravel the specific function of the *saṅkhārakkhandha*, I will first explore the meaning of the word *saṅkhāra* in its larger context. *Saṅkhāra* is one of the Pāli words most highly endowed with philosophical implications. Stcherbatsky remarks that "the word and conception *saṃskāra* performs a conspicuous part in all Indian philosophical systems. It usually means some latent mysterious power, which later on reveals itself in some potent fact."[1] In her introduction to the translation of the *Majjhimanikāya*,[2] I.B. Horner refers to a passage from the *Pāli Text Society Dictionary* in order to stress the semantic depth of the word *saṅkhāra*. It is "one of the most difficult terms in Buddhist metaphysics, in which the blending of the subjective-

---

1 Stcherbatsky, *The Central Conception of Buddhism*, p. 18.

2 Horner, *The Collection of the Middle Length Sayings*, 1: xxiv.

objective view of the world and of happening, peculiar to the East, is so complete, that it is almost impossible for Occidental terminology to get at the root of its meaning in a translation."[3] Mrs. Rhys Davids also expresses her bewilderment regarding the significance of the term:

> We are only at the threshold of its problems, and it is hence not strange if we find them as baffling as, let us say, our own confused usage of many psychological terms—feeling, will, mind—about which we ourselves greatly differ, would prove to an inquiring Buddhist. If I have not attempted to go into the crux of the *sankhāra-skandha* [*sic*], it is because neither the Manual [the *Dhammasaṅgaṇi*] nor its Commentary brings us any nearer to a satisfactory hypothesis.[4]

The exact meaning of this "mysterious power" still remains obscure. As Bandusena Madanayake points out in his doctoral thesis, "thirty scholars have put forward as many different meanings" for this single term.[5] One of the reasons for this diversity of translations might be the fact that within the Pāli language itself, *saṅkhāra* possesses many meanings. Surendranath Dasgupta explains the polysemy encountered in the Pāli canon by the fact that

> The Buddha was one of the ... earliest thinkers to introduce proper philosophical terms and phraseology with a distinct philosophical method and he had often to use the same word in more or less different senses. Some of the philosophical terms at least are therefore rather elastic when compared with the terms of precise and definite meaning which we find in later Sanskrit thought.[6]

Yet many scholars, such as Hans Wolfgang Schumann, suggest that the rather wide semantic field associated with the word *saṅkhāra* was nonexistent at the time of the Buddha. According to Schumann, this diversity of meanings resulted from the growth of exegesis on the earlier *sutta* literature and from the development of an intricate and systematic

---

3 Rhys Davids and Stede, *P.T.S. Pāli-English Dictionary*, p. 664.

4 C.A.F. Rhys Davids, trans., *Buddhist Psychology: An Inquiry into the Analysis and Theory of Mind in the Pāli Literature* (London: Luzac, 1924), p. lxxxi.

5 Bandu W. Madanayake, "The Study of Saṅkhāras in Early Buddhism" (Ph.D. diss., University of Toronto, 1987), p. 2.

6 Dasgupta, *A History of Indian Philosophy*, 1:86.

philosophical system that arose many centuries after the death of the Buddha.[7]

I.B. Horner divides *saṅkhāra* into four different categories, each having a different meaning. This classification consists of *saṅkhāra* (1) as one of the aggregates, (2) as one of the links of the *paṭicca-samuppāda*, (3) as a sort of activity associated with the body, speech and mind (*kāya, vacī* and *citta*) and finally (4) as properties when associated with the term life (*āyu*).[8] Schumann, in his thesis *Bedeutung und Bedeutungsentwicklung des Terminus Saṁkhāra im frühen Buddhismus*, elaborates a similar scheme by classifying the various interpretations of the term into four categories.[9] Using Horner's and Schumann's classifications as a starting point, I have developed a more extensive scheme consisting of five categories: (1) *saṅkhāra* as a *saṅkhata-dhamma*, as synonym of its cognate form *saṅkhata*, (2) as a *paccaya*, (3) as *āyu-saṅkhāra*, (4) as part of the compounded words *sasaṅkhāra* and *asaṅkhāra*, and finally, (5) as one of the five aggregates.

Saṅkhāra as *Saṅkhata*

Throughout the Pāli canon, the concept of *saṅkhāra* is closely associated with that of *saṅkhata*.[10] The usual definition of the term runs thus: "it is called *saṅkhāra* because it 'produces' *saṅkhata*."[11] Because the Pāli word for what I have translated as "to produce" is *abhisaṅkharoti*, a cognate of *saṅkhāra*, the deciphering of this definition is rendered more difficult. The *Atthasālinī* provides us with a description of *saṅkhata* that may clarify the above definition of *saṅkhāra*. "The *saṅkhata* are made, having been assembled by conditions, and whatever is not *saṅkhata* is *asaṅkhata*."[12] S.Z. Aung, in his appendix to the translation of the *Abhidhammattasaṅgaha*, emphasizes that, although the notion of being compounded is implied by the term *saṅkhata*, the idea of being conditioned and having been caused is the closest to the definition of

7 Hans Wolfgang Schumann, *Bedeutung und Bedeutungsentwicklung des Terminus Samkhāra im frühen Buddhismus* (Ph.D. diss., Bonn, Rheinishchen Friedrich-Wilhelms-Universität, 1957), pp. 84ff.

8 Horner, *The Collection of the Middle Length Sayings*, 1: xxiv-xxv.

9 Schumann, *Bedeutung und Bedeutungsentwhicklung des Terminus Saṁkhāra in frühen Buddhismus*, pp. 45ff.

10 Refer to p. 15 for a discussion of the *saṅkhata* and *asaṅkhata* groups.

11 *Saṅkhataṁ abhisaṅkharontīti bhikkhave tasmā saṅkhārā ti vuccanti* (S. iii, 87).

12 *Paccayehi samāgantvā katā ti saṅkhata, na saṅkhata ti asaṅkhatā* (DhsA. 47).

the term.[13] These conditions, or causes, that produce the *saṅkhata-dhamma* seem to be *saṅkhāra* as well.

Clearly, there is a definite relation between the two concepts (*viz.* *saṅkhāra* as a cause, and *saṅkhāra* as an effect, i.e., *saṅkhata-dhamma*), but the texts go so far as to suggest that there is no difference at all between them. In the *sutta* literature, there are a few instances where the first two characteristics of existence—impermanence and suffering—are used to qualify the term *saṅkhāra*. In these same passages, however, the third characteristic of existence, selflessness, is an attribute of *dhamma* rather than *saṅkhāra*:

Sabbe saṅkhārā aniccā ti;	All saṅkhāra are impermanent;
Sabbe saṅkhārā dukkhā ti;	All saṅkhāra are suffering;
Sabbe dhammā anattā ti.	All phenomena are selfless.[14]

I do not think that, here, the term *dhamma* is used in a different sense than *saṅkhāra*. If the Buddha had said "*sabbe saṅkhārā anattā,*" meaning that all the conditioned phenomena are substanceless, people might have wrongly inferred that the unconditioned phenomenon (*asaṅkhatadhamma*) must have a permanent entity (*atta*). The unconditioned phenomenon which, in the Theravāda tradition, is restricted to a unique component (*nibbāna*), is also devoid of any permanent entity (*atta*). In order to avoid the misunderstanding that *sabbe saṅkhārā anattā* could potentially imply, the term *saṅkhāra* is replaced by *dhamma* in this particular context. Moreover, by stating "*sabbe dhammā anattā,*" the text not only suggests that all the conditioned phenomena are *anatta*, but that the only unconditioned phenomemon—*nibbāna*—is *anatta* as well. The commentary on this passage also mentions that *saṅkhāra* is a synonym of *saṅkhata*, the latter referring to any element (*dhamma*) which has been conditioned.[15]

Therefore, we may affirm that *saṅkhāra*, as a *saṅkhata*, refers to all the principles of existence except *nibbāna* (and other *dhamma* considered by other traditions as *asaṅkhata*). Stcherbatsky presents an interesting theory as to why the conditioned phenomena are called *saṅkhāra*:

13 Aung, *Compendium of Philosophy*, p. 273.

14 S. i, 200; D. ii, 157; also Kvu. ii, 531.

15 *Tattha aniccā vata saṅkhārā ti ādisu vutta sabbe pi sappaccaya dhammā saṅkhatā saṅkhāra nāma* (DA. ii, 230).

> The elements of existence were regarded as something more similar to energies (*saṁskṛta dhamma* [skr. equivalent for *saṅkhata-dhamma*]) than to substantial elements. ... Since the energies [*saṅkhata-dhamma*] never worked in isolation, but always in mutual interdependence according to causal law, they were called "synergies" cooperators (*saṁskāra* [skr. equivalent for *saṅkhāra*]).[16]

Thus, in certain contexts, conditioned phenomena are synonymous with *saṅkhāra* because they were previously produced, they were conditioned and, most of all, because they do not subsist independently of other *saṅkhata*—they are "cooperators". This definition of *saṅkhāra* is valid for the entire universe: the individual microcosm (the five aggregates) is included in the term[17] and so is the macrocosm, the entire phenomenal world we live in.[18] Therefore, everything but *nibbāna* is *saṅkhāra*. Everything that has been compounded and has a cause is a *saṅkhāra* in the sense of conditioned phenomena (*saṅkhata-dhamma*).

Saṅkhāra as *Paccaya*

Within the complex theory of dependent origination, *saṅkhāra* is inserted as a link between ignorance (*avijjā*) and consciousness (*viññāṇa*).[19] This means that on account of ignorance, *saṅkhāra* come into being and generate a consciousness. It seems that within the *paṭiccasamuppāda* the term *saṅkhāra* has a meaning radically different from the one previously ascribed to "*saṅkhāra* as a *saṅkhata*" since there is no explicit textual evidence of conditioned phenomena producing consciousness.

The *Vibhaṅga* defines *saṅkhāra* produced by ignorance (and implicitly generating a future consciousness) as volition (*cetanā*).[20] The *sutta* literature also has a similar definition of *saṅkhāra*: the *Saṁyutta-*

16 Th. Stcherbatsky, *Buddhist Logic* (New York: Dover, 1962), 1:5.

17 S. iii, 144.

18 The *Sammohavinodanī* correlates the words *anekadhātu-nānādhātuloka* with *upādinnakasaṅkhāraloka* (VbhA. 456).

19 *Avijjāpaccayā saṅkhārā; saṅkhārapaccayā viññāṇa* (S. ii, 5).

20 *Tattha katamo avijjāpaccayā saṅkhāro? Yā cetanā sañcetanā sañcetayitattam, ayam vuccati avijjāpaccayā saṅkhāro* (Vbh. 144; a similar passage is also found at Vbh. 173).

nikāya equates the term with the six groups of volition, which are defined therein with respect to the six sense-doors.[21]

Volition is clearly explained in the *Aṅguttaranikāya*, where the Buddha states that what he calls volition (*cetanā*) is simply *kamma*, and that one who "cetanizes" is one who generates *kamma* either by body, words or mind: "Monks, I say that volition is action. Having "cetanized," one acts by deed, word or thought."[22] Another example of the relation between *saṅkhāra* (or volition) and *kamma* is symbolically exemplified in the *Rathakāravagga* of the *Aṅguttaranikāya*. In this *sutta*, a "wheel-maker" explains to the king that the wheel (and by analogy the *kamma*-concept) "kept rolling as long as the impulse that set the motion (*abhisaṅkhārassa gati*) lasted. It then circled and fell to the ground."[23] The term *abhisaṅkhāra*[24] is a synonym of volition and refers here to the dynamism and momentum usually associated with *kamma*. For this reason, Padmasiri de Silva points out that *saṅkhāra* is often considered synonymous with the concept of volition or *kamma*.[25] These pieces of textual evidence support the relation that the Burmese meditation teacher Sayagyi U Ba Khin drew between *kamma* and *saṅkhāra*:

> In this connection, we should understand that each action—either by deed, word, or thought—leaves behind a force of action, *saṅkhāra* (or *kamma* in popular terminology), which goes to the credit or debit account of the individual, according to whether the action is good or bad. There is, therefore, an accumulation of *saṅkhāra* (or *kamma*) with everyone, which function as the supply-

---

21 *Katamā ca bhikkhave saṅkhārā? Chayime bhikkhave cetanākayā. Rūpa ... sadda ... gandha ... rasa ... phoṭṭhabba ... dhammasañcetanā ime vuccanti bhikkhave saṅkhārā* (S. iii, 60).

22 *Cetanāhaṁ bhikkhave kammaṁ vadāmi; cetayitvā kammaṁ karoti kāyena vācāya manasā* (A. iii, 415).

23 *Taṁ pavattitaṁ samāṇam yāvatikā abhisaṅkhārassa gati tāvatikaṁ gantvā ciṅgulāyitvā bhūmiyaṁ papati* (A. i, 111).

24 The interchangeability of the terms *abhisaṅkhāra* and *saṅkhāra* is evidenced by the *Saṁyuttanikāya* (S. iii, 87) and the *Dīghanikāya* (D. i, 18) where the function of *saṅkhāra* is said to be "*abhisaṅkharoti*."

25 M.W. Padmasiri de Silva, *Buddhist and Freudian Psychology* (Colombo: Lakehouse Investments, 1973), p. 117; also see Aung, *Compendium of Philosophy*, p. 274.

> source of energy to sustain life, which is inevitably followed by suffering and death.[26]

The *Vibhaṅga* further states that *saṅkhāra* produced by ignorance are threefold: meritorious *saṅkhāra* (*puññābhisaṅkhāra*), non-meritorious *saṅkhāra* (*apuññābhisaṅkhāra*) and "unshakable" *saṅkhāra* (*āneñjābhisaṅkhāra*).[27] Meritorious *saṅkhāra* are defined as being profitable volitions—*kamma*—that will yield their results either in the sensual sphere or in the fine material sphere; these meritorious "actions" (of body, speech and mind) consist of charity, morality and meditation.[28] The non-meritorious *saṅkhāra* are explained as being unprofitable *kamma*, the results of which will be reaped only in the sensual sphere.[29] The unshakable *saṅkhāra* are said to be wholesome *kamma* producing a result in any of the four immaterial spheres.[30] This division of *saṅkhāra* into meritorious, non-meritorious and unshakable further stresses the relation between *saṅkhāra* and *kamma*, since the *Vibhaṅga* states that these three divisions constitute the entire field of the *kamma*-process.[31]

The *Vimohavinodanī* elucidates the meaning of *saṅkhāra* as threefold: there are *saṅkhāra* of body, of speech and of mind. The *saṅkhāra* of body are initiated by the body and express themselves through it. The *saṅkhāra* of speech and mind are initiated by speech and the mind and express themselves through them.[32] According to the

---

26 Thray Sithu Sayagyi U Ba Khin, "The Essentials of Buddha-Dhamma in Meditative Practice," in *Sayagyi U Ba Khin Journal: A Collection Commemorating the Teaching of Sayagyi U Ba Khin* (Igatpuri: Vipassanā Research Institute, 1991), p. 31.

27 *Tattha katame avijjāpaccayā saṅkhārā? Puññābhisaṅkhāro apuññābhisaṅkhāro āneñjābhisaṅkhāro* (Vbh. 135).

28 *Tattha katamo puññābhisaṅkhāro? Kusalā cetanā kāmāvacarā rūpāvacarā dānamayā sīlamayā bhāvanāmaya, ayam vuccati puññābhisaṅkhāro* (Vbh. 135).

29 *Tattha katamo apuññābhisaṅkhāro? Akusalā cetanā kāmāvacarā: ayaṁ vuccati apuññābhisaṅkhāro* (Vbh. 135).

30 *Tattha katamo āneñjābhisaṅkhāro? Kusalā cetanā arūpavacarā: ayaṁ vuccati āneñjābhisaṅkhāro* (Vbh. 135).

31 *Tattha katamo kammabhavo? Puññābhisaṅkhāro apuññābhisaṅkhāro ñeñjābhisaṅkhāro: ayaṁ vuccati kammabhavo* (Vbh. 137). The compound *kammabhava* literally means "*kamma*-process." However, this term is used in a technical sense and refers to links eight, nine and ten of the theory of dependent origination. See pp. 110ff. for further discussion of this concept.

32 *Kāyena pavattito, kāyato vā pavatto, kāyassa vā saṅkhāro ti kāyasaṅkhāro. Vacīsaṅkhāra-citta-saṅkhāresu pi es' eva nayo* (VbhA. 142).

Yamaka, the *saṅkhāra* of body are said to originate from breathing in and breathing out; the *saṅkhāra* of speech, from reflection and investigation which "denote the whole mental process of thinking";[33] the mental *saṅkhāra*, from *saññā* and *vedanā* or, in other words, all the principles associated with the mind except reflection and investigation.[34] I do not believe that body-*saṅkhāra* (*kāyasaṅkhāra)* arise from the mere function of respiration, but since breathing is essential for the subsistence of the body and the performance of any other action, it is considered to be the precursor of any further body-*saṅkhāra*. Similarly, reflection and investigation are not inherently speech-*saṅkhāra* (*vacīsaṅkhāra*) but, because these functions precede all verbal activities, they are regarded as the foundation that allows a person to speak and thereby generate speech-*saṅkhāra*. Since the mental *saṅkhāra* are said to arise from *saññā* and *vedanā*,[35] *saṅkhāra* as a *paccaya* is not simply deeds, but also physical, vocal or mental actions that will yield certain consequences in the future. Both of these, the karmically charged action and the future consequences, are *saṅkhāra* in the sense of condtioned phenomena, but only the former can be classified under *saṅkhāra* as a *paccaya*.

Saṅkhāra Used in the Compound *Āyusaṅkhāra*

Another type of *saṅkhāra* is also mentioned in the Pāli canon. The *Kathāvatthu* alludes to the Buddha entering into *parinibbāna* only after he had "let loose" his *āyusaṅkhāra*.[36] The *sutta* literature, particularly in the discourses referring to the Buddha's death, also makes a few allusions to this word.[37] The term *bhavasaṅkhāra* also seems to have been used as a synonym of *āyusaṅkhāra*. The *Aṅguttaranikāya* employs this expression to state that when the Buddha had released his *bhava-*

33 Rhys Davids and Stede, *P.T.S. Pāli-English Dictionary*, p. 620.

34 *Tayo saṅkhārā: kāya-saṅkhāro vacīsaṅkhāro cittasaṅkhāro. Assāsapassāsā kāyasaṅkhāro, vitakkavicārā vacīsaṅkhāro, saññā ca vedanā ca cittasaṅkhāro, ṭhapetvā vitakkavicāre sabbe pi cittasampayuttakā dhammā cittasaṅkhāro* (Ymk. i, 229).

35 Ymk. i, 229.

36 *Cāpāle cetiye āyusaṅkhāro ossaṭṭho, Kusinārāyaṁ Bhagavā parinibbuto ti?* (Kvu. ii, 559).

37 Such as in D. ii, 99; 108.

saṅkhāra, he broke apart the "coat of mail"[38] that originates from one's own person.[39] None of the commentaries explain the meaning of these two terms, yet the words themselves suggest a kind of "life principle," a vital energy which provides the neccessary fuel to produce rebirth and without which life ceases. This is reminiscent of our interpretation of *saṅkhāra* as *paccaya*, where the term *saṅkhāra* was correlated with the dynamism and momentum associated with the concept of *kamma*. The only difference is that the *āyusaṅkhāra* (as well as the *bhavasaṅkhāra*) refers to a specific force—not simply any karmic force, but the one responsible for rebirth. Both *āyusaṅkhāra* and *bhavasaṅkhāra* refer to the force responsible for generating a new existence.

Saṅkhāra Used in the Compounds *Asaṅkhāra* and *Sasaṅkhāra*

The fourth usage of the word *saṅkhāra* is found in the compounds "without *saṅkhāra*" (*asaṅkhāra*) and "with *saṅkhāra*" (*sasaṅkhāra*), the latter appearing in relation to the word *parinibbāyin* in the *sutta* literature, and usually in conjunction with the term *citta* in the *Abhidhamma* texts.

While discussing the different methods of attaining *nibbāna*, the *Saṁyuttanikāya* states that one who eradicates the five fetters of the lower sort attains *nibbāna* "without *saṅkhāra*" and, following a similar procedure, can achieve nibbāna "with *saṅkhāra*."[40] Although the meaning of this sentence is obscure because no textual evidence is implied as to the distinction between the procedures to be followed in order to enter either *nibbāna* "with *saṅkhāra*" or *nibbāna* "without *saṅkhāra*," the meaning of these two terms seems fairly clear. *Asaṅkhāra* means "without *saṅkhāra*," while *sasaṅkhāra* means "with *saṅkhāra*." Therefore, the term *asaṅkhāra* applied to *nibbāna* suggests that *nibbāna* has been reached while the experiencer still possesses a karmic

---

38 *Kavaca*: the *P.T.S. Dictionary* (p. 200) says that the word applies to "existence," probably because the latter is made up of many factors and combinations, or, in other words, that life is the expression of an intricately knitted mail of conditioned phenomena.

39 *Tulan atulañ ca sambhavaṁ bhavasaṅkhāraṁ avassaji muni ajjhattarato samāhito abhindi kavacam iv' attasambhavan ti* (A. iv, 312).

40 *No ce pañcannam orambhāgiyānaṁ saṁyojanānam parikkhayā asaṅkhāraparinibbāyī hoti. Atha pañcannam orambhāgiyānaṁ saṁyoganānam parikkhayā sasaṅkhāraparinibbāyī hoti* (S. v, 70). The same passage is found at A. i, 233.

residue.[41] According to tradition, the Buddha attained *nibbāna* at the age of thirty-five, but remained alive some forty-five more years. Because he "came back" to teach in the *kāmaloka*, we might postulate that he still had certain stock of *kamma* which allowed (or caused) him to come back into this world; he had not yet entered *nibbāna* without residue. When he reached that state, no more karmic residue was present, thus no force could hold him to this world. The problem we encounter is that in the *sutta*, the words *sasaṅkhāra* and *asaṅkhāra* are used not in reference to *nibbāna*, but to *nibbāna* without residue. A further difficulty emerges from the fact that Pāli is a highly inflected language; we often find two or more declined words losing their case endings and being compounded (concatenated) together. Sometimes, it is only through a careful analysis (and often, speculation) that we can unveil the syntactic relation uniting the members of the compounds. The compounds *sa-saṅkhāra-parinibbāyī* and *a-saṅkhāra-parinibbāyī* are extremely ambiguous. From one perspective, the first element (*asaṅkhāra* or *sasaṅkhāra*) could be interpreted as an attribute of the word *parinibbāyī*,[42] hence meaning "one who has attained the state of *parinibbāna* which has (or has no) *saṅkhāra*." Although grammatically correct, this analysis is rejected by the *Sumaṅgalavilāsinī* which holds that an instrumental case relation[43] links *parinibbayi* to *asaṅkhāra* and *sasaṅkhāra*, hence attributing quite a different meaning to the compounds: one who has attained *parinibbāna* from (or because of) *saṅkhāra* (or from the lack of it in the case of *asaṅkhāraparinibbāyī*). The commentator further elaborates by defining *asaṅkhāra* as "without effort, with ease and pleasure," and *sasaṅkhāra* as "with efforts, difficulty and *dukkha*."[44]

The *Abhidhamma* literature strengthens the commentarial definition of *sasaṅkhāra* and *asaṅkhāra* by emphasizing that one who has completely eradicated the fetters and thereby perceives the noble path "without efforts" is called a person who has achieved *parinibbāna*

---

41 The *Atthasālinī* apparently agrees with this interpretation since Buddhaghosa defines *sasaṅkhāra* as "with *saṅkhāra*." *Tass' attho saha saṅkhārenā ti sasaṅkhāro* (DhsA. 156).

42 *Bahuvrīhī* compound.

43 Instrumental *tatpuruṣa*.

44 *Asaṅkhārena appayogena akilamanto sukhena patto asaṅkhāra-parinibbāyī nāma. Sasaṅkhārena sappayogena kilamanto dukkhena patto sasaṅkhāra-parinibbāyī nāma* (DA. iii, 1030); similar definitions are found in the *Sāratthappakāsinī* (SA. iii, 143) and the *Manorathapūraṇī* (AA. ii, 350).

"without efforts"; similarly, one who eradicates the fetters through striving, and thereby perceives the noble path, is called a person who has achieved *parinibbāna* "with efforts".[45] The *Atthāsalinī* further elucidates the meaning of the term *sasaṅkhāra* (which the commentator considers to be a new word in Buddhist terminology)[46] with a narrative. A monk had certain duties to perform, such as sweeping the courtyard, taking care of an elderly monk and listening to the *dhamma*, but was not naturally inclined to fulfill them. Yet, either by self-instigation or by being admonished by another monk, he realized the disadvantages of not performing his duties and the advantages of carrying them out, and ultimately performed what he had to do. This action of his, triggered by instigation and necessitating efforts on his part, is called an action which gives birth to a wholesome mental state because of *saṅkhāra* ("with effort").[47] According to Mrs. Rhys Davids, all the thoughts (*citta*) which are not called *sasaṅkhāra* are implicitly included in the concept of *asaṅkhāra*.[48]

The story of Bāhiya Dārucīriya[49] serves as a good illustration of *asaṅkhāraparinibbayī* within Theravāda Buddhism. The elderly ascetic Bāhiya, who was living in the vicinity of what is now Bombay, decided to travel all the way to Sāvatthi to seek advice from the Buddha. When he arrived in the capital city of Kosala, he met the Buddha and received a few words of inspiration. While he was listening, he suddenly reached enlightenment. Later, the Buddha said that Bāhiya Dārucīriya was the supreme example of those who comprehended the truth instantly (*khippābhiññāṇaṁ*).[50] This story exemplifies the unexpected attainment of *nibbāna*—a realization devoid of proximate conscious striving (*asaṅkhāra*).

Both in the *sutta* and abhidhammic literature, the term *sasaṅkhāra* seems to refer to a thought, action or state attained by instigation or mental efforts that constrain the natural tendencies of the

---

45 *So asaṅkhārena ariyamaggaṁ sañjaneti upariṭ ṭhimānaṁ saññojanānaṁ [saṁyoja-nānaṁ] pahānāya: ayaṁ vuccati puggalo asaṅkhāra-parinibbāyī. ... So sasaṅkhārena ariyamaggaṁ sañjaneti upariṭ ṭhimānaṁ saññojannaṁ pahānāya: ayaṁ vuccati puggalo sasaṅkhāra-parinibbāyī* (Pug. 17).

46 *Imamsiṁ tāva dutiyacittaniddese sasaṅkhārenā ti idam eva apubbaṁ* (DhsA. 156).

47 Dhs. 156.

48 C.A.F. Rhys Davids, *Buddhist Psychology*, p. lxvii.

49 Malasekera, *Dictionary of Pāli Proper Names*, 2:281ff.

50 A. i, 24.

individual, while *asaṅkhāra* points to a thought, action or state that has arisen effortlessly, without instigation, in accord with personal inner tendencies. The *Atthasālinī* offers a list of synonyms of *sasaṅkhāra* ("with energy, with preparation, with effort, with the grasping of a cause"[51]), all of which indicate that the term implies a conscious instigation on the part of the individual. We see that in the context of *sasaṅkhāra* and *asaṅkhāra*, the term *saṅkhāra* also refers to a certain dynamism or force of action, as with *saṅkhāra* as *paccaya*.[52]

General Meaning of the Term *Saṅkhāra*

Now that we have looked at the meaning of *saṅkhāra* within the first four divisions of our fivefold classification, I will attempt to extract the essence of the term and to underline the general meaning of this puzzling concept.

We have seen that *saṅkhāra*, as a *saṅkhata*, refers to all the principles of existence, i.e., everything that exists except, of course, for *nibbāna* which is considered to be an unconditioned phenomenon. In this context, *saṅkhāra* is a synonym of conditioned phenomena since all of them are, by definition, conditioned. As mentioned before, this particular definition of *saṅkhāra* means "the entire universe," within and without; this includes the individual microcosm made up of the five aggregates, and the macrocosm—the entire phenomenal world we live in. In short, *saṅkhāra* as a *saṅkhata* refers to everything that causes and that is caused.

Saṅkhāra as a *paccaya* was defined in terms of two divisions. First we examined the various *saṅkhāra* divided into *puñña, apuñña* and *āneñja*, each being respectively described as meritorious *kamma*, unprofitable *kamma* and wholesome *kamma* producing a result in any of the four immaterial spheres.[53] Then, the word was described in terms of *kāya, vacī* and *citta*, referring to physical, verbal and mental actions. In this context, *saṅkhāra* seems to mean any action that will ultimately bring about a result; here *saṅkhāra* is not different from

51 *Tena sasaṅkhārena saussāhena sappayogena sa-upāyena sappaccayagahaṇenā ti attho* (DhsA. 156).

52 This leads to a further problem: can nibbāna (an *asaṅkhatadhamma*) be produced or caused by anything (such as the practice of the eightfold noble path)?

53 Vbh. 135.

volition, which is often equated with *kamma*.[54] *Saṅkhāra* as a *paccaya* is the initiating action (mental, vocal or physical), and the karmic force that will yield an effect. However, this effect, although not included in *saṅkhāra* as *paccaya*, falls under the definition of *saṅkhāra* as a *saṅkhata*, for the result of a particular *saṅkhāra* (or *kamma*) is nothing but a conditioned phenomenon.

Saṅkhāra as *āyusaṅkhāra* is a synonym of *bhavasaṅkhāra*, the energy which is responsible for sustaining life. Here, it is important to mention that at the instant of death, the *āyusaṅkhāra* is not necessarily extinct. In most cases, it is still present, and manifests itself as the energy that keeps an individual bound to the wheel of birth, death and rebirth. On the other hand, if eradicated, rebirth does not occur and the "person" enters into *nibbāna* without residue. Because the *āyusaṅkhāra* and the *bhavasaṅkhāra* are dependent on other activities, they are conditioned phenomena. And since they constitute the energy that will eventually lead to rebirth, they can also be seen as *saṅkhāra* as a *paccaya*, for they definitely are a force.

Saṅkhāra as it appears in the compounds *asaṅkhāra* and *sasaṅkhāra* is interpreted slightly differently in the *sutta* and abhidhammic literatures. In the former, these compounds are described mainly as attributes of the state of *parinibbāna*, while in the latter, they do not only qualify that state, but any conditioned phenomena as well. Although the qualified term varies depending on the *piṭaka*, the meaning of the qualifier remains the same. *Asaṅkhāra* refers to that which has arisen effortlessly as a result of an individual's inner tendencies. On the other hand, *sasaṅkhāra* points to something brought about by effort or striving. The meaning of *saṅkhāra* in these compounds is "conscious effort or instigation."

Sasaṅkhāra means with effort or instigation, hence produced by. When used as a qualifier to *parinibbāyin*, it means that someone has attained *parinibbāna* through conscious effort. *Asaṅkhāra* means the opposite. Within this context, the actual meaning of *saṅkhāra* implies production, whether it be of *nibbāna* or a conditioned phenomenon.

The four contexts outlined above point to a generic meaning for the term *saṅkhāra*. This underlying meaning is twofold: first, *saṅkhāra* is a productive force, like volition, which outflows from actions (mental, physical or verbal) and produces effects; second, it comprises everything that exists—all compounded things—these are conditioned phenomena.

---

54 A. iii, 415.

Some (such as anger, love, etc.) result from the "productive force" and are likely to become themselves "productive forces." However, some of these conditioned phenomena (such as external objects) are independent of the personal psychological process and can by no means become "productive forces." We can also see this twofold division in terms of a distinction between active and passive. If we say that the meaning of *saṅkhāra* is "everything that is compounded," then we can divide these conditioned phenomena into "active" and "passive" components. The "active" *saṅkhāra* are those associated with the other four constituents of the individual (*pañcakkhandhā*), and are likely to produce more conditioned phenomena. The "passive" *saṅkhāra* (conditioned phenomena) would be those independent from any aggregate and incapable of producing anything except, of course, the process of decaying inherent in all compounded things.

The "mysterious" term *saṅkhāra*, as Stcherbatsky remarked, seems to have two distinct meanings. The first is *saṅkhāra* as "generating" and "producing" and, in this sense, it is a force of action (verbal, mental or physical), relying on the functioning of the four other aggregates (*rūpa, vedanā, saññā* and *viññāṇa*). *Saṅkhāra* in this sense cannot function independently of these four aggregates. The second meaning describes the term as whatever is produced by this force of action; this includes all conditioned phenomena. Let me offer an analogy that may clarify the twofold meaning of the term. *Saṅkhāra* could be compared to cooking. In fact, the verbal root *saṁskṛ* does, in some contexts, refer to food preparation.[55] An analysis of the word for cooking (*pacati*) does indeed shed light on the meaning of *saṅkhāra*. The *Vaiyākaraṇasiddhāntakaumudi*, one of the commentaries to Panīṇī's Sanskrit grammar, explains the meaning of the word *pacati* as a complex activity. According to this Sanskrit text, the action of cooking requires undertaking several minor activities which ultimately lead to a result. For example, cooking rice, the commentary explains, involves putting the rice into the vessel, pouring water over it, washing the rice several times, placing the vessel on the fire with a suitable quantity of water, leaving it over the heat, testing a single rice grain, and so on. When all these minor activities are performed, the actual action of cooking is accomplished and leaves the performer with a specific result: in this case, soft and edible rice (*viklittiḥ*). This rather intricate description of

55 Refer, for example, to Sn. 241 where "well-prepared" (*susaṁkhata*) meat is mentioned.

"cooking" is provided by the commentator to show that the word cooking itself implies two major elements: (1) the bare action of cooking (*kriyā*), including all the major activities it adumbrates, and (2) the result or the effect of these activities (*phala*).[56] Similarly, the term *saṅkhāra* implies these two elements: (1) what is understood as volition or, to be more precise, a conation resulting in a volitional effort and eventually in an action (mental, vocal or physical), and (2) the bare effect, the result outflowing from previous actions. Any action will yield a result so long as it is performed on the basis of craving sensations—in other words, if it is performed as the result of the activity of *saññā*, or as a blind reaction towards the *vedanā*.

Although these two meanings are distinct, our discussion of the four previous categories of *saṅkhāra* could be combined and shaped to form a general meaning. *Saṅkhāra* (as a producing force) generates other *saṅkhāra* (conditioned phenomena). Yet, these conditioned phenomena can, in turn, become a producing force and create more conditioned phenomena. Whenever these conditioned phenomena are associated with the four other aggregates (i.e., when the conditioned phenomena are mental states and not external objects), they may very well become active or productive *saṅkhāra*. But, if independent from the four aggregates, these conditioned phenomena will remain passive *saṅkhāra*.

The *Saṅkhārakkhandha*

Having ascribed a generic meaning to the concept of *saṅkhāra*, we are in a much better position to understand the *saṅkhārakkhandha*. According to the *Vibhaṅga*, *saṅkhāra*, as one of the constituents of the personality, can be seen in many different ways. As "onefold," the *saṅkhārakkhandha* is associated with the mind; as twofold, it is either caused or uncaused; as threefold, it is either positive, negative or neutral.[57] The first approach suggests that *saṅkhāra* are always associated with the mind (*citta*). The *Dhammasaṅgani* supports the *Vibhaṅga* by grouping the different kinds of *saṅkhāra* under three

56 Bhattaji Diksita, ed., *Vaiyākaraṇasiddhāntakaumudi* (Varanasi: Caukhamba Samskrita Sirija Aphisa, 1969), p. 607.

57 *Tattha katamo saṅkhārakkhandho? Ekavidhena saṅkhārakkhandho: cittasampayutto. Duvidhena saṅkhārakkhandho: atthi sahetu, atthi na hetu. Tividhena saṅkhārakkhandho: atthi kusalo, atthi akusalo, atthi avyākato ... pe ... evaṁ bahuvidhena saṅkhārakkhandho* (Vbh. 72; there is also a similar passage at Vbh. 89).

distinct types of mind (*kusala, akusala*, and *avyākata*).[58] This exhaustive listing of *saṅkhāra* classified under the only three possible kinds of mind implies both that *saṅkhāra* are associated with the mind, and that *saṅkhāra* are either good, bad or neutral—the third approach mentioned by the *Vibhaṅga*. (Refer to Table 6 for an overall view of these principles.) All these principles which arise in accordance with the *paṭiccasamuppāda*, and which exclude the *vedanākkhandha*, the *saññākkhandha* and the *viññāṇakkhandha*, fall under the *saṅkhārakkhandha* category.[59] A total number of fifty different principles fall under the category of *saṅkhārakkhandha*. However, it is not necessary to analyze each of these independently here.

The second approach implied by the *Vibhaṅga* states that *saṅkhāra* can either be with or without cause (*hetu*). Here *hetu* refers to "the six roots of action," three being wholesome (non-aversion, non-craving and non-delusion) and three unwholesome (aversion, craving and delusion). This would imply that certain *saṅkhāra* can be "unconditioned," in the sense of not having a cause (*ahetu*). This is problematic, for, as we have seen, all *saṅkhāra* are conditioned. However, in this context, as A.K. Warder has pointed out, *hetu* is closer in meaning to *mūla* (root) than to "cause."[60] *Hetu*, in this specific sense, is one of the twenty-four *paccaya* of the *Paṭṭhāna*;[61] by extension, *ahetu* would refer to whatever is not *hetu*, i.e., the twenty-three remaining *paccaya*. The author of the *Vibhaṅga* likely uses *ahetu* in the sense of the remaining twenty-three *paccaya*; otherwise his statement would contradict the rest of canonical literature.

As we have just seen, the *Dhammasaṅgaṇi* and the *Yamaka* strongly correlate *saṅkhārakkhandha* with the different types of mind, thereby implying that *saṅkhārakkhandha* is an activity restricted to the mental realm. Here we should call attention to our previous discussion

58 See Dhs. 18 for *kusala*, Dhs. 84-85 for *akusala*, and Dhs. 118 for *avyākata*.

59 When the list includes the *saññākkhandha* and the *vedanākkhandha*, the enumeration is known as the list of mental concomittants (*cetasika*); this is not the one exposed here.

60 A.K. Warder, *Indian Buddhism* (Delhi: Motilal Banarsidass, 1980), p. 310.

61 For further clarification on *saṅkhāra* as *hetu*, one of the twenty-four *paccaya*, refer to Ps. i, 50ff.

Table 6
The Fifty Elements of *Saṅkhāra*

Avyākatacitta	*Akusala*	*Kusala*
contact	contact	contact (*phassa*)
volition	volition	volition (*cetanā*)
life	life	life (*jīvita*)
concentration	concentration	concentration (*samādhi*)
fixed thought	fixed thought	fixed thought (*manasikāra*)
thinking about	thinking about	thinking about (*vitakka*)
consideration	consideration	consideration (*vicāra*)
determination	determination	determination (*adhimokkha*)
effort	effort	effort (*viriya*)
joy	joy	joy (*pīti*)
resolution	resolution	resolution (*chanda*)
	delusion (*moha*)	wisdom (non-delusion; *amoha*)
	shamelessness (*ahiri*)	shame (*hiri*)
	unscrupulousness	scrupulousness (*ottappa*)
	agitation (*uddhacca*)	faith (*saddhā*)
	envy (*issā*)	attention (*sati*)
	selfishness (*macchariya*)	balance of mind (*tatramajjhattatā*)
	remorse (*kukkucca*)	non-anger (*adosa*)
	greed (*lobha*)	non-greed (*alobha*)
	views (*diṭṭhi*)	serenity of body (*kāyapassadhi*)
	pride (*māna*)	serenity of mind (*cittapassadhi*)
	sloth (*thīna*)	buoyancy of body (*kāyalahutā*)
	torpor (*middha*)	buoyancy of mind (*cittalahutā*)
	doubt (*vicikicchā*)	flexibility of body (*kāyamudutā*)
	anger (*dosa*)	flexibility of mind (*cittamudutā*)
		alertness of body (... *maññatā*)
		alertness of mind (... *kammaññatā*)
		fitness of body (*kāyapaguññatā*)
		fitness of mind (*cittapaguññatā*)
		straightness of body (*kāyojukatā*)
		straightness of mind (*cittojukatā*)
		refraining from unwholesome bodily conduct (*kāyiduccaritavirati*)
		refraining from unwholesome mental conduct (*vāciduccaritavirati*)
		refraining from wrong livelihood (*micchājīvavirati*)
		compassion (*karuṇā*)
		sympathy (*muditā*)

on *saṅkhāra* as a *paccaya*[62] and correlate *saṅkhārakkhandha* with *saṅkhāra* of mind. In that section, it was stated that "mental" *saṅkhāra* depend on *vedanā* and *saññā*, each being one of the five aggregates. Although there is a connection between *saṅkhārakkhandha* and "mental" *saṅkhāra*, it must be stressed that the realm of *saṅkhārakkhandha* is not restricted to "mental" *saṅkhāra*—it also includes verbal and physical *saṅkhāra*. As I noted above, verbal and physical *saṅkhāra* are both dependent on subtler activities, respectively "reflection and investigation" and "breathing in and breathing out." I would go even further by suggesting that both verbal and physical *saṅkhāra* also depend on "mental" *saṅkhāra*. As the first verse of the *Dhammapāda* indicates, "mind leads all actions" whether physical or verbal.[63] Any verbal or physical activity must be preceded by mental activity. Therefore, although we should understand *saṅkhārakkhandha* as a "mental" *saṅkhāra*, its comprehensive meaning adumbrates the whole realm of *saṅkhāra* as a *paccaya*. *Saṅkhārakkhandha* is the same as *saṅkhāra* as a *paccaya*.

The *Visuddhimagga* further clarifies our understanding of *saṅkhāra* as one of the aggregates by correlating the term with conditioned phenomena. Buddhaghosa holds that the *saṅkhārakkhandha* should be understood as whatever has the characteristic of forming (*abhisaṅkharaṇalakkhaṇa*) and heaping things together.[64] The *Atthasālinī*, while using a different style, defines the term in the same manner.[65] It is in complete accord with these sources to say that the function or energy that gives birth to conditioned phenomena is nothing but the *saṅkhārakkhandha*. Yet the *Yamaka* introduces an important distinction: not all *saṅkhāra* belong to the *saṅkhārakkhandha*. *Rūpa, vedanā, saññā* and *viññāṇa* (the other four aggregates) are *saṅkhāra*, but they are not *saṅkhārakkhandha*.[66] We find a similar distinction introduced in the *sutta* literature itself. The *Saṁyuttanikāya* states that *saṅkhāra* (*-kkhandha*) is thus called for it conditions the five aggregates

62 Refer to the discussion on p. 97 on verbal, physical and mental *saṅkhāra*.

63 *Manopubbaṅgamā dhammā manoseṭṭhā manomayā; manasā ce paduṭṭhena bhāsati vā karoti vā; tato naṁ dukkham anveti cakkaṁ va vahato padaṁ* (Dh. i, 1).

64 *Yaṁ pana vuttaṁ, yaṁ kiñci abhisaṅkharaṇalakkhaṇaṁ sabban taṁ ekato katvā saṅkhārakkhandho veditabbo ti, ettha abhisaṅkharaṇalakkhaṇaṁ nāma rāsikaraṇalakkhaṇaṁ* (Vsm. 462).

65 *Rāsaṭṭhena abhisaṅkharaṇaṭṭhena eko va saṅkhārakkhandho* (DhsA. 154).

66 Ymk. 16.

of the next moment, or the next existence.[67] Although the *saṅkhāra-kkhandha* is associated with all the other *saṅkhāra*, these two groups have to be seen as distinct. This distinction elucidates the difference between *saṅkhāra* as an aggregate and *saṅkhāra* in general. The former is an active force, producing and gathering together the conditioned phenomena (*saṅkhāra* as a *saṅkhata*) while the latter is more comprehensive and consists of any of the five aggregates, as well as any of the conditioned phenomena.

The *saṅkhārakkhandha* is definitely a *saṅkhāra* in the sense of conditioned phenomena since it has been formed and conditioned. Yet not all *saṅkhāra* are *saṅkhārakkhandha*, since they are not all endowed with the capacity of "forming" or generating more conditioned phenomena. It seems to me that a conditioned phenomena—this term, of course, also includes *saṅkhārakkhandha*—can only produce other conditioned phenomena when working in conjunction with *viññāṇa*, *vedanā*, *saññā* and *rūpa*; in other words, only the *saṅkhārakkhandha* (which, by definition, is closely connected to the other four aggregates) can produce conditioned phenomena. This implies that *saṅkhāra* as a *paccaya* is simply a paraphrase of *saṅkhārakkhandha*. They both refer to a force that will generate an effect. The effect, however, although being *saṅkhata* in the sense that it has been caused, is not necessarily a *paccaya* or a *saṅkhārakkhandha* for it may not generate a further effect.

Correlation between the *Saṅkhārakkhandha* and the *Paṭiccasamuppāda*

Each of the aggregates discussed so far has been directly correlated with distinct links of the theory of dependent origination. The *rūpakkhandha* was equated with the six sense-doors (*saḷāyatanā*) and with contact (*phassa*), the *vedanākkhandha* with *vedanā*, and the *saññākkhandha* was introduced between *vedanā* and craving (*taṇhā*). As for the *saṅkhāra-kkhandha*, we can establish a relation between this particular aggregate and the second link of the *paṭiccasamupāda*, *saṅkhāra*, for we have seen

67 *Kiñca bhikkhave saṅkhāre vadetha? Saṅkhataṁ abhisaṅkharontīti bhikkhave tasmā saṅkhārā ti vuccanti. Kiñ ca saṁkhataṁ abhisaṅkharonti? Rūpaṁ rūpattāya saṅkhatam abhisaṅkharonti. Vedanaṁ ... Saññaṁ ... Saṅkhāre ... Viññāṇaṁ ...* (S. iii, 87). A similar distinction is found in Vasubandhu's *Abhidharmakośa*: "Les saṁskāras, c'est tout ce qui est conditionné, mais on réserve le nom de saṁskāraskandha aux conditionnés qui ne rentrent ni dans les *skandhas* de *rūpa*, de *vedanā*, de *saṁjñā* et de *vijñāna*" (La Vallée Poussin, *Abhidharmakośa*, 1:15).

in this chapter that *saṅkhārakkhandha* is the same as *saṅkhāra* as *paccaya*; both are forces that will generate a result. This work is primarily concerned with the eight middle links of the theory of dependent origination, the links that are traditionally held to be representative of the present life. Since the *saṅkhārakkhandha* is one of the five aggregates characterizing human existence, its function must also express itself within these eight links, in the present.

According to the commentarial tradition of Theravāda Buddhism, the *paṭiccasamuppāda*, as well as the whole process of existence, is usually divided in two: (a) the *kamma*-process (*kammabhava*) or the karmically active aspect of existence, which is the cause of rebirth, and (b) the regenerating or rebirth-process (*uppattibhava*) or the karmically passive aspect of existence, which arises due to the first process (*kammabhava*).[68] The active aspect of existence (*kammabhava*) determines the passive aspect (*uppattibhava*).[69] The first five links of the present period of the *paṭiccasamuppāda*—links three to seven: *viññāṇa, nāmarūpa, saḷāyatanā, phassa* and *vedanā*—are part of the passive aspect, while the last three links of the present period—links eight to ten: *taṇhā, upādāna* and *bhava*—are part of the active aspect of existence. This is illustrated in Table 7.

According to this, craving, clinging and becoming are part of the *kamma*-process of the present existence. Since we have previously defined *kamma*-process as the *saṅkhārakkhandha*, we can state with confidence that the *kamma*-process is identical with craving, clinging and becoming, and arrive at a distinct correlation between these three links and the *saṅkhārakkhandha*.

This appears to present a problem: according to the *Vibhaṅga*, becoming is itself defined as being composed of *kamma*-process and of rebirth-process[70] and its commentary explains the terms in the same way as they have been defined here.[71] This seems to imply that the *saṅkhārakkhandha* is only part of the concept of becoming, the one that is *kamma*-process.

---

68 Vsm. 200; 579.

69 Aung, *Compendium of Philosophy*, p. 43.

70 *Tattha katamo upādānapaccayā bhavo? Duvidhena bhavo: atthi kammabhavo, atthi uppattibhavo* (Vbh. 136; 137).

71 VbhA. 183.

Table 7
The *Paṭiccasamuppāda* at a Glance

Past	1.	*avijjā*	ignorance	*Kammabhava*
	2.	*saṅkhāra*	(as a *paccaya*)	
	3.	*viññāṇa*	consciousness	
	4.	*nāmarūpa*	mind and matter	
	5.	*saḷāyatana*	6 sense-doors	*Uppattibhava*
Present	6.	*phassa*	contact	
	7.	*vedanā*	sensation	
	8.	*taṇhā*	desire	
	9.	*upādāna*	clinging	*Kammabhava*
	10.	*bhava*	becoming	
Future	11.	*jāti*	(re-) birth	*Uppattibhava*
	12.	*jarāmaraṇā* ...	old age, death ...	

If we refer back to the list of fifty types of *saṅkhāra* on p. 107, we see that thinking about and consideration are both included in *saṅkhāra*. These two terms are precursors to the concept of obsessions previously discussed;[72] without any of these three, craving could not arise because, as the *Sakkapañhasutta* states, envy (*issā*) and avarice (*macchariya*), as well as desire (*chanda*)[73] have their origin in obsessions.[74] The commentarial tradition is correct in affirming that the three links of craving, clinging and becoming belong to the *kamma-*

72 As evidenced by the causal chain of the *Majjhimanikāya*: *Cakkhuṇ c'āvuso paṭicca rūpe ca uppajjati cakkhuviññāṇaṁ tiṇṇaṁ saṅgati phasso, phassapaccayā vedanā, yaṁ vedeti taṁ sañjānāti, yaṁ sañjānāti taṁ vitakketi, yaṁ vitakketi taṁ papañceti, yaṁ papañceti tato nidānaṁ purisaṁ papañcasaṅkhā samudācaranti atītānāgata-paccuppannesu cakkhuviṇṇeyyesu rūpesu*. Visual consciousness arises on account of visual forms and the eye. The meeting of these three is contact (*phassa*); on account of contact there is a sensation; what one senses (as a sensation), one recognizes; what one recognizes, one "thinks about" (*vitakka*); what one thinks about, one is obsessed with; what obsesses one is the cause of the number of obsessions which assail a person in regard to past, present or future visual forms cognizable by the eye (M. i, 111-12; similar occurrences of the formula also appear at M. i, 259 and S. iv, 67).

73 *Chanda* is equated by the commentary of the text with *taṇhā*, desire, craving.

74 D. ii, 277-78.

process, for thinking about and consideration both precede craving, and these two elements are included in *saṅkhāra*.[75] However, this statement does not reject the theory that becoming can itself be divided into *kamma*-process and rebirth-process. Logically, there is no reason why *kamma*-process could not occupy a certain place within becoming, while extending to more than one link of the *paṭiccasamuppāda*. *Kamma*-process (or the *saṅkhārakkhandha*) can and does belong to becoming and to craving and clinging.

In this chapter, we have seen that not all *saṅkhāra* belong to the *saṅkhārakkhandha*, since they are not all endowed with the capacity for forming or generating more conditioned phenomena. A conditioned phenomenon can only produce other conditioned phenomena when working in conjunction with *viññāṇa, vedanā, saññā* and *rūpa*; in other words, only the *saṅkhārakkhandha* can produce conditioned phenomena. This implies that *saṅkhāra* as a *paccaya* is simply a paraphrase of *saṅkhārakkhandha*. They both refer to a force that will generate an effect. The effect, however, although being *saṅkhata* in the sense that it has been caused, is not necessarily a *paccaya* or a *saṅkhārakkhandha* for it might not generate a further effect.

We have also situated the *saṅkhārakkhandha* within the present period of the *paṭiccasamuppāda*, namely, taking the place of the three links of craving, clinging and becoming. The next chapter discusses the element that is generated by this active force.

75 Refer to the list of elements belonging to *saṅkhāra* on p. 107.

Chapter 6

The *Viññāṇakkhandha*

In the traditional enumeration of the aggregates, *viññāṇa* is fifth and is commonly translated as "consciousness." As with the previous four aggregates, six kinds of *viññāṇa* exist, with each designation dependent upon the sense organ through which the faculty performs its function.[1] Therefore, we find *viññāṇa* associated with each of the six sense-doors. The canonical definition of this aggregate is, again, as obscure as those of the previous *khandha*. The Pāli canon tells us that *viññāṇa* is so called because it "viññāṇizes."[2] This definition could make sense only to native speakers of Pāli who had already interiorized through linguistic and cultural reinforcement the significance of "to viññāṇize." Unfortunately, most of us are left without the slightest hint as to its meaning.

In looking elsewhere for clues that will help define this aggregate, we find that *viññāṇa* displays the characteristics of all conditioned phenomena: namely the truths of impermanence and selflessness. For example, the *Cullavedallasutta* condemns the attempt to regard not only *viññāṇa* but any of the five aggregates as the seat of individuality (*atta*),[3] while the *Alagaddūpamasutta* stresses that *viññāṇa* itself is impermanent.[4] And it is mentioned elsewhere that those who believe that *viññāṇa* has a destiny of its own, distinct from the other four *khandha*, are misled as to its true nature.[5] Therefore, it is clear that within the realm of Pāli Buddhism, neither *viññāṇa* nor any of the

---

1 *Chayime āvuso viññāṇakāyā: cakkhuviññāṇaṁ sotaviññāṇaṁ ghānaviññāṇaṁ jivhāviññāṇaṁ kāyaviññāṇaṁ manoviññāṇaṁ* (M. i, 53; also M. i, 259; iii, 216, 281).

2 *Vijānāti vijānātīti kho āvuso, tasmā viññānan ti vuccatīti* (M. i, 292).

3 *Sutavā ariyasāvako ... na rūpaṁ attato samanupassati ... na vedanaṁ ... na saññaṁ ... na saṅkhāre ... na viññāṇaṁ attato samanupassati, na viññāṇavantaṁ attānaṁ, na attani viññāṇaṁ na viññānasmim attānaṁ* (M. i, 300).

4 *Taṁ kiṁ maññatha bhikkhave. Viññāṇaṁ niccam va aniccaṁ vā ti? Aniccaṁ bhante* (M. i, 138; also S. iv, 67-68).

5 *Yo bhikkhave evaṁ vadeyya: aham aññatra rūpā aññatra vedanāya aññatra saññāya aññatra sakkhārehi viññāṇassa āgatiṁ vā gatiṁ vā cutiṁ vā upapattiṁ vā vuddhiṁ vā virūḷhiṁ vā vepullaṁ vā paññāpessāmi ti n'etaṁ ṭhānam vijjati* (S. iii, 53.)

other aggregates can be considered as permanent or as occupying the place of an everlasting self.

Yet scholars such as Mrs. Rhys Davids[6] argue that textual evidence does not always portray *viññāṇa* as an impermanent element. Their main argument is that *viññaṇa* is often approached as the seat of individuality, the residing place of the self, or of a permanent entity. They support their theory by canonical evidence which, according to them, refers to *viññāṇa* in the sense of "self." There are at least two of these occurrences.[7] After the death of certain monks who had reached arahanthood (Bhikkhu Godhika and Vakkhali), the evil spirit Māra searched in vain for their *viññāṇa* since the latter had utterly ceased to arise. According to Mrs. Rhys Davids, this definitely indicates that after death, the *viññāṇa* of a non-liberated person is expected to go somewhere before being "reborn"—therefore implying the existence of some sort of permanent entity which travels from body to body. Mrs. Rhys Davids also notes that the verb "to arise" (*uppajjati* or *uppatti*), usually used in reference to *viññāṇa*, is occasionally replaced by "to descend" (*avakkhanti*).[8] Once again, she interprets this as alluding to a permanent entity, a kind of "soul" which descends into the body. Viewed in this manner, these few examples contradict the core doctrine of impermanence in general, the changing nature of *viññāṇa* itself,[9] and the view that the body is existing permanently (*sakkāyadiṭṭhi*).[10] Mrs. Rhys Davids suggests that, therefore, the notion of a transmigrating entity must have been an intrusion of popular belief into Buddhism—mere "folklore speech"[11]—for, when contrasted with the emphasis given to the concepts of *anicca* and *sakkāyadiṭṭhi* throughout the entire realm of Buddhist literature, these pieces of evidence are far too scarce to be taken seriously.

However, her interpretation of these passages is, I believe, a result of a misunderstanding of the concept of impermanence and of the core theory of dependent origination. *Viññāṇa* is characterized by impermanence in the sense that it arises and passes away at every

6 C.A.F. Rhys Davids, trans., *Buddhist Psychology: An Inquiry into the Analysis and Theory of Mind in Pāli Literature* (London: Luzac, 1924), p. 22.

7 S. iii, 124; S. i, 121.

8 Rhys Davids, *Buddhist Psychology*, p. 22.

9 S. ii, 94; iv, 67; D. i, 21.

10 M. i, 300.

11 Rhys Davids, *Buddhist Psychology*, p. 22.

moment. Yet Buddhism stresses that new instances of *viññāṇa* continually arise in an unbroken causal sequence. As Richard Hayes remarks: "Accepting that a continuum of moments of mental events moves from one physical body to another, or even lives outside a physical body for a while, does not commit one either to a view of permanence or to a view that the continuum is a self."[12] A continuing sequence of causally related *viññāṇa* needs not imply, as Rhys Davids suggests, any kind of permanence. This leaves us with no substantial grounds for affirming that the passages mentioned above represent an "intrusion of folklore speech." Furthermore, other passages are congruent with the mainstream canonical interpretation of *viññāṇa*. As Lilian Silburn explains:

> C'est autour de *vijñāna* [*viññāṇa*] que graviteront les erreurs de la continuité personnelle, à commencer par celle de Sāti, un des disciples du Buddha, jusqu'à celle des Bouddhologues occidentaux qui s'acharnent à découvrir une personne qui dure et transmigre dans un *vijñāna* que tant de textes pourtant décrivent comme conditionné et évanescent ... à chaque instant apparaît un *vijñāna* conditionné par un *vijñāna* précédent; il y a une certaine continuité parce que les moments de conscience dépendent de leurs conditions et se succèdent sans interruption; mais il n'y a pas de continuité d'un principe qui demeurerait essentiellement le même en dépit de ces changements.[13]

This concept of ever-changing *viññāṇa*, of "non-entity," seems also to be in complete accord with William James' understanding of consciousness:

> To deny plumply that "consciousness" exists seems so absurd on the face of it—for undeniably "thoughts" do exist—that I fear some readers would follow me no further. Let me then immediately explain that I mean only to deny that the word stands for an entity, but to insist most emphatically that it does stand for a function.[14]

---

12 Electronic-mail message, received from Richard Hayes on March 12, 1992.

13 Lilian Silburn, *Instant et cause: le discontinu dans la pensée philosophique de l'Inde* (Paris: Librairie Philosophique J. Vrin, 1955), pp. 207-208.

14 William James, *Essays in Radical Empiricism* (London: Longmans, Greens, 1912), p. 4.

Therefore, to elucidate the meaning of *viññāṇa* we should, as James recommends, approach it as an abstract function, an intangible mental operation, just as we have approached all the other mental aggregates.

The Function of *Viññāṇa*

Many scholars hold that the function of *viññāṇa* merely consists of apprehending the bare phenomenal world, "the immediately known thing which on the mental side is in opposition with the entire brain process."[15] Stcherbatsky's interpretation is typical:

> It [*viññāṇa*] represents pure consciousness, or pure sensation, without any content. Its content is placed in the objective part which contains the definite sensation (*sparśa*), feelings (*vedanā*), ideas (*saṁjña*), volition (*cetanā*). ...[16]

He continues:

> ... *vijñāna* and its synonyms, *cittā*, *manaḥ*, represent pure sensations, the same as the *kalpanāpoḍha pratyakṣa* of Diṅnāga, and *saṁjña* corresponds to definite ideas. Every construction (*kalpanā*), every abstraction (*udgrahana*), every definite (*parichinna*) representation, such as blue and yellow, long and short, male and female, friend and enemy, happy and miserable—this is all brought under the head of ideas (*saṁjña*) as distinguished from *vijñāna* = pure sensation.[17]

Stcherbatsky's theory receives support from other scholars such as E.R. Sarathchandra, who advocates that when the term *viññāṇa* was "applied to the psychology of perception, it meant not full cognition, but bare sensation, a sort of anoetic sentience that occurs before the object is completely apprehended."[18] Jayatilleke also agrees, quoting the *Vibhangāṭṭhakatha*, to the effect that visual consciousness means mere visual perception.[19]

---

15 William James, *Principles of Psychology* (New York: Dover, 1950), p. 142.

16 Stcherbatsky, *The Central Conception of Buddhism*, p. 13.

17 Ibid., p. 16.

18 Sarathchandra, *Buddhist Theory of Perception*, p. 4.

19 *Cakkhuviññāṇam pan' ettha dassanamattam viññāṇa eva hoti* (Jayatilleke, *The Early Buddhist Theory of Knowledge*, p. 436).

The theory that correlates *viññāṇa* with bare sensations devoid of any content seems to be inconsistent with certain passages of the Pāli canon, since the *Majjhimanikāya* indicates that the function of *viññāṇa* is to "viññāṇize" what is pleasant, unpleasant and neither pleasant nor unpleasant.[20] If, as Stcherbatsky and Sarathchandra propose, *viññāṇa* is pure sensation without any content, then it would be impossible for the *viññāṇa* to "viññāṇize" anything pleasant, unpleasant or neutral. This would be possible only if the pleasantness, etc., that the faculty viññāṇizes were intrinsic to the object (be it sensation or mere external form) being approached. Nevertheless, if the pleasantness were intrinsic to the object, then no difference would be found between *viññāṇa* and *vedanā*, which is also said to be pleasant, unpleasant or neutral.

The Pāli canon also explains *viññāṇa* differently. As Sarathchandra mentions, "*viññāṇa* in the earliest texts was almost synonymous with *saññā*."[21] One of the items of canonical evidence supporting this theory states that *viññāṇa* is so called because it viññāṇizes flavours as sour and bitter, acid and sweet, salty and bland.[22] Recalling our definition of *saññā* (see p. 77), it is the recognition of a certain colour as blue, red or yellow which can be extended to the recognition of a certain sound as flute, drum or trumpet, or a certain flavour as sour, bitter or sweet, and so on. Hence, according to this interpretation, *viññāṇa* seems almost identical to *saññā*.

These numerous different interpretations of *viññāṇa* have confused scholars who have attempted to circumscribe the meaning of the term. The general meaning of *viññāṇa* is pure consciousness, mere attention, but what remains obscure is whether this consciousness or attention is of pure percepts devoid of any categorization, of something pleasant, unpleasant or neutral, or of a certain categorization. By examining these three possible definitions for *viññāṇa*, we notice that (1) pure percepts refer to our definition of secondary matter or of

20 *Kiñ ca vijānāti: sukhan ti pi vijānāti, dukkhan ti pi vijānāti, adukkhamasukhan ti pi vijānāti* (M. i, 292; M. iii, 242).

21 Sarathchandra, *Buddhist Theory of Perception*, p. 16.

22 *Kiñca bhikkhave viññāṇaṁ vadetha. Vijānātīti kho bhikkhave tasmā viññāṇan ti vuccati. Kiñca vijānāti. Ambilam pi vijānāti. Tittakam pi vijānāti. Kaṭukam pi vijānāti madhukam pi vijānāti. Khārikam pi vijānāti. Akhārikam pi vijānāti. Loṇakam pi vijānāti. Aloṇakam pi vijānāti. Vijānātīti kho bhikkhave tasmā viññāṇan ti vuccati* (S. iii, 87).

contact (see p. 49), (2) something pleasant, unpleasant or neutral can be correlated with our interpretation of *vedanā*, and (3) the categorization is in line with our explanation of *saññā*. I feel that it would be a mistake to assign the function of *viññāṇa* to only one of these three possibilities. *Viññāṇa* can be applied to contact, *vedanā* and *saññā*. The "mystical" sense of *viññāṇa* may be elucidated if looked at as a function which is applied throughout the mind and matter phenomenon. *Viññāṇa* is probably the faculty needed for the cognition of pure percept, of sensation and of conceptualization as well; it is not independent of any of these three aggregates. Since none of the aggregates has the capacity of being self-conscious, only *viññāṇa* can be considered as performing the function of consciousness or attention.

In our discussion of contact (see p. 49ff.), we saw that in order for a stimulus to be perceived, the presence of three elements is required. There must be a sense-object (*visaya*), a sense-organ (*indriya*) and attention or consciousness (*viññāṇa*). Only when these three elements come together can a stimulus be perceived. This implies, however, that *viññāṇa* itself is present before the stimulus has appeared, and that the former is independent of the latter. *Viññāṇa* as pure consciousness or mere attention does not necessarily need to be conscious of or attentive to something in order to exist.

As pointed out by Jayatilleke,[23] another aspect of *viññāṇa* is its similarity to wisdom (*paññā*). The *Mahāvedallasutta*[24] correlates wisdom with *viññāṇa* since the former is also characterized by cognition, but in this case, the objects cognized are restricted to the four Noble Truths. However, the same source mentions a difference between the two terms: "while *viññāṇa* needs to be thoroughly understood, wisdom needs to be developed."[25] As Jayatilleke concludes, this fifth aggregate "seems to be the general term for 'cognition,' while *paññā* is more or less restricted in connotation to the cognition of spiritual truths."[26] Therefore, when I translate the term *viññāṇa* as "consciousness," it is essential to bear in mind that although the function of what we call "consciousness" is mere cognition, what is cognized is either pure percepts (*rūpa*), percepts loaded with either pleasant, unpleasant or

---

23 Jayatilleke, *The Early Buddhist Theory of Knowledge*, p. 434.

24 M. i, 292.

25 *Paññā bhāvetabbā viññāṇaṁ pariññeyyaṁ, idaṁ nesaṁ nānākaraṇaṁ* (M. i, 293).

26 Jayatilleke, *The Early Buddhist Theory of Knowledge*, p. 435.

neutral connotations (*vedanā*), or conceptualizations resulting from the activy of *saññā* on the sense-data.

Finally, there are two conditions without which "consciousness" cannot appear. As the *Majjhimanikāya* states:

> Whenever there is a functioning sense-organ (eye, ear, tongue, nose, body and mind), a sense-object (visual form, sound, taste, smell, touch and thought) entering into the field of the sense-organ then, with these brought together, there is the manifestation of the part of consciousness referring to the specific sense-organ.[27]

From this same Pāli passage, Jayatilleke reads three conditions: to the two we have mentioned, he adds "an appropriate act of attention on the part of the mind" which, he says, is the English equivalent of *tajjo samannāhāro hoti*.[28] His elaboration of three conditions refutes the references found in the *sutta* literature, which mentions only two conditions, namely the sense-door and a respective sense-object.[29] Furthermore, while the *Pāli Text Society Dictionary* renders *samannāhāro* as "bringing together," Jayatilleke stretches the meaning to an "appropriate act of attention." Even if his English rendering of *samannāhāro* were correct, what would this "mind" which applies the "act of attention" be? No "entity" shapes the individual other than the five aggregates, and, because of our systematic discussion of the *khandha*, we know that neither *rūpa*, *vedanā*, *saññā* or *saṅkhāra* is responsible for anything that resembles "an appropriate act of attention." Rather, it seems that the "act of attention" is precisely the function of *viññāṇa*.

Viññāṇa and *Mano*

Many canonical and commentarial passages equate the terms *viññāṇa* and *mano*. For example, the *Brahmajālasutta* and the *Visuddhimagga* indicate that *citta* and *mano* are both synonyms of *viññāṇa*.[30] Bhikkhu

---

27 *Yato ca kho āvuso ajjhattikañ c'eva cakkhuṁ aparibhinnaṁ hoti bāhirā ca rūpā āpāthaṁ āgacchanti tajjo ca samannāhāro hoti, evaṁ tajjassa viññāṇabhāgassa pātubhāvo hoti* (M. i, 190).

28 Jayatilleke, *The Early Buddhist Theory of Knowledge*, p. 435.

29 *Cakkhuñ ca paṭicca rūpe ca uppajjati cakkhuviññāṇam* (S. iv, 86; M. i, 259).

30 *Cittan ti va mano ti va viññāṇaṁ ti* (D. i, 21). *Viññāṇaṁ cittaṁ, mano ti atthato ekaṁ* (Vsm. 452).

Nārada in the introduction to his translation of the *Abhidhammattha-saṅgaha* says that "*citta, ceta, cittuppāda, nāma, mana, viññāṇa* are all used as synonymous terms in Abhidhamma. Hence, from the Abhidhamma standpoint no distinction is made between mind and consciousness."[31] However, I would be more inclined to say that within the *sutta* literature, these terms were used more or less synonymously and that only in later abhidhammic and commentarial sources did the distinctions between them become more important. Yet, we must acknowledge that even in the *sutta* an implicit distinction is established between these terms.[32]

Since the concept of *mano* has already been discussed (see p. 40), I shall only stress the difference between the "mental sense-organ" (*mano*) and *viññāṇa* itself here. In the discussion of "secondary matter," we saw that matter, in general, forms the six sense-objects: touch (*phoṭṭhabbāyatana*), sound (*saddāyatana*), taste (*rāsāyatana*), smell (*gandhāyatana*), visual form (*rūpāyatana*) and thought (*dhammāyatana*). There are also six faculties or sense-organs that allow us to perceive them: the tactile organ (*kāyāyatana*), the auditory organ (*sotāyatana*), the gustatory organ (*jivhāyatana*), the olfactory organ (*gandhāyatana*), the visual organ (*cakkhāyatana*), and finally, the mental sense-organ (*manāyatana*). However, we have seen that such perception is only possible when there is a contact between the sense-object, the sense-organ and the respective consciousness (*viññāṇa*). *Manāyatana* on its own, without the function of *viññāṇa*, cannot induce perception. Like the other five sense-organs, *manāyatana* is dependent on *viññāṇa* to bring the object to the attention of the subject. *Manāyatana* is purely a sense-organ that cannot function without *viññāṇa*. However, there is a substantial difference between *manāyatana* and the other sense-organs: while the latter can only apprehend their respective sense-objects, *manāyatana* apprehends only mental objects (*dhammāyatana*)—yet these very thoughts are derived from the contact of other sense-objects with their respective sense-doors. As Kalupahana elucidates this point:

> In fact, its [*mano*'s] function is to assist in bringing back the impression produced by the other sense faculties and, as such,

31 Nārada, *A Manual of Abhidhamma*, p. 9.

32 For a more detailed study of the distinction between *mano*, *viññāṇa* and other Pāli and Sanskrit concepts often translated by the English words "consciousness" or "mind," refer to Herbert V. Guenther, *Philosophy and Psychology in the Abhidharma* (Delhi: Motilal Banarsidass, 1974), pp. 15-49.

> constitutes a form of "reflection." *Mano*, therefore, has "concept" (*dhammā*) as its objects, and these are generally considered substitutes for percepts. ... While *mano* is performing this special function, consciousness (*viññāṇa*) continues to flow uninterrupted like a stream fed by all the faculties including *mano*.[33]

The *Uṇṇābho Brāhmaṇo Sutta* of the *Saṁyuttanikāya* explains the function of *mano*. According to this text, each of the first five sense-organs has a different scope and range, none of which are interchangeable. In other words, the eye cannot perceive smell. Yet *mano* is common to them all in the sense that it is able to interact with all the other sense-organs.[34] The text does not imply that *mano* perceives smells, visual forms, etc., but only that it can perceive the concept (*dhamma*) that was derived from the percept apprehended by one of the first five sense-doors. Table 8 will help further clarify the distinction of *manāyatana* and *viññāṇa*. It shows that *mano* is endowed with a special function distinct from that of all the other sense-doors: *mano* has the ability to survey the fields (*gocara*) of the other senses. The term "field" does not refer to the sense-object itself, but to the actual contact between the sense-object, the sense-door and the respective *viññāṇa*. The sense-object as such is merely a potential object of perception, and, as long as it has not been apprehended by the senses and the consciousness, it cannot become an object of *mano*. Once contact has taken place, a percept arises. This percept may be either visual, auditory, olfactory, gustatory or tactile. In its turn, the percept becomes a potential object of *mano*, potential in the sense that not all percepts come in contact with both *mano* and a *viññāṇa*. However, when it does come in contact with these two other faculties, the percept itself is technically termed *dhammāyatana* for it becomes the direct object of *mano*.

The main distinction between *viññāṇa* and *mano*, however, is summed up in the following statement by Bhikkhu Ñāṇamoli:

33 Kalupahana, *Principles of Buddhist Psychology*, p. 30.

34 *Pañcimāni brāhmaṇa indriyāni nānāvisayāni nānāgocarāni na aññāmaññassa gocaravisayaṁ paccanubhonti. Katamāni pañca? Cakkhundriyaṁ. pe ... Kāyindriyaṁ. Imesaṁ kho brāhmaṇa pañcannam indriyānaṁ nānāvisayānaṁ nānāgocarānaṁ na aññamaññassa gocaravisayam paccanubhontānam mano paṭisaraṇam mano ca nesaṁ gocaravisayam paccanubhotī ti* (S. v, 218).

> *Viññāṇa* (rendered by "consciousness") is, loosely, more or less a synonym of *mano* and *citta*; technically, it is bare cognition considered apart from feeling [*vedanā*], perception [*saññā*] or formations [*saṅkhāra*]. *Mano* (rendered by "mind"), when used technically, is confined to the sixth internal base for contact.[35]

Mano is often employed as synonym of *viññāṇa* or *citta*,[36] yet it seems that a slight nuance can be implied by these terms. *Viññāṇa* is often associated with sense cognition in general, while *mano* frequently refers to the intellectual activity triggered by the contact of the mental objects and *viññāṇa*[37]—a function similar to that of *manas* in Nyāya philosophy where it is "the instrument through which the objects of sense affect the soul."[38]

Table 8
Mano* and *Viññāṇa

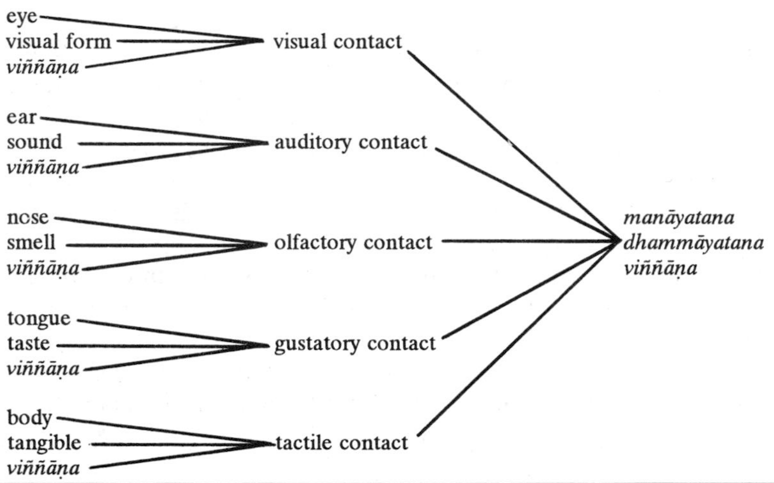

35 Ñāṇamoli, *The Path of Purification*, p. 507, n. 35.

36 Such as in S. ii, 94: *cittaṁ iti pi mano iti pi.*

37 Refer to our previous discussion of *mano* on p. 40.

38 Apte, *The Practical Sanskrit English Dictionary*, p. 1233.

Viññāṇa as Rebirth and Death Consciousness

In later Buddhist scholasticism, *viññāṇa* is often interpreted as being either a rebirth-consciousness (*paṭisandhiviññāṇa*) or a death-consciousness (*cuticitta*)—more literally, a "departing" consciousness.[39] The death-consciousness constitutes the last consciousness of one's life, whereas the rebirth-consciousness consists of the very first consciousness of a being. It is the factor that triggers the stream of consciousness which characterizes one's existence and is wholly conditioned by previous *saṅkhāra* and *kamma* from previous lives. As Bhikkhu Nārada explains: "Dependent on past conditioning activities [*saṅkhāra*] arises relinking or rebirth consciousness in a subsequent birth. It is so called because it links the past with the present, and is the initial consciousness one experiences at the moment of conception."[40] This idea of rebirth-consciousness may be misleading; it is not a permanent entity transferred from one body to another. As Venerable Nāgasena explains to King Milinda, that which transmigrates from one life to another is neither the same nor another.[41] In the *Visudhimagga*, Buddhaghosa explains this "transmigration" of consciousness very clearly:

> But it should be understood that it [the *viññāṇa*] has neither come here from the previous becoming nor has it become manifest without the kamma, the formations, the pushing, the objective field, etc., as a cause. And here, let the illustration of this consciousness be such things as an echo, a light, a seal, a seal impression, a looking-glass image, for the fact of its not coming here from the previous becoming and for the fact that it arises owing to causes that are included in past becomings. For just as an echo, a light, a seal impression, and a shadow, have respectively sound, etc., as their cause and come into being without going elsewhere, so also this consciousness.[42]

The *cuticitta* and *paṭisandhiviññāṇa* respectively stand for the death-consciousness and the rebirth-consciousness. However, their

39 The term *citta* has been used instead of *viññāṇa* in the expression *cuticitta*. However, in this specific context, both terms are synonymous. With regard to the interchangeability of these two terms, see p. 119, particularly n. 30.

40 Nārada, *A Manual of Abhidhamma*, p. 422.

41 *Na ca so na ca añño* (Mil. 40).

42 Ñāṇamoli, *The Path of Purification*, p. 639.

meaning is not limited to these two particular types of consciousness, for *viññāṇa* in general is also subject to the three characteristics of existence. At every moment, each consciousness arises and passes away, continually yielding its place to a new one. Thus every consciousness must have the quality of both rebirth-consciousness, in the sense that it arose from the previous consciousness, and death-consciousness, in the sense that the rebirth-consciousness that has arisen must also die. The quality of this latter *viññāṇa* (which becomes a death-consciousness at the moment of death) will engender a new rebirth-consciousness. Birth, death and rebirth do not occur only at the beginning and the end of life. From a microcosmic point of view, the cycle repeats itself at each and every moment and each time a new consciousness is engendered.

Correlation between *Viññāṇa* and the *Paṭiccasamuppāda*

Like the four previous aggregates, *viññāṇa* holds a specific place in the theory of dependent origination. As one of the links of the *paṭicca-samuppāda*, *viññāṇa* is the third link of the chain, preceding mind and matter, the six sense-doors and contact; the last two being part of the *rūpakkhandha*. I will leave the explanation as to why *viññāṇa*, which is the fifth member in the traditional enumeration of the aggregates, occupies a place that precedes all the other aggregates in the *paṭicca-samuppāda* for the next chapter. Here I will explain the function of *viññāṇa* in the *paṭiccasamuppāda* and describe its relation to the *viññāṇakkhandha*.

We have to note that the explanation of the *viññāṇa*-link is often limited to the first consciousness that enters the mother's womb,[43] which would be a rebirth-consciousness. To my knowledge, no such statement is found in the *sutta* literature itself. In later literature, however, we find that the *viññāṇa*-link is associated not only with the nineteen types of rebirth-consciousnesses,[44] but also with the other types of consciousness that may arise from this "original" consciousness. The *Vibhaṅga*, for example, defines the *viññāṇa*-link as consciousness (*citta, mano, viññāṇa, manoviññāṇadhātu*), the mind base (*manāyatana*), the controlling faculty of mind (*manindriya*), and the *viññāṇakkhandha*

43 See for example Nyānatiloka, *Buddhist Dictionary*, pp. 121-22.

44 Nārada, *A Manual of Abhidhamma*, p. 361. These nineteen types of consciousness are described in Anuruddha's *Abhidhammatthasaṅgaha* (ed. T.W.S. Rhys Davids, *Journal of the P.T.S.* [1884]: 21-23).

itself.[45] Therefore, the third link of the *paṭiccasamuppāda* includes the whole *viññāṇakkhandha* and not merely the *paṭisandhiviññāṇa*.

In this chapter, we have seen that *viññāṇa* is variously translated. Some scholars hold that it means "bare sensation," some, "pure consciousness" and others, "the cognition of something pleasant, unpleasant or neutral." However, none of these theories seems to be completely accurate, since *viññāṇa* is responsible for the cognition of all of these. Hence we defined the term as mere consciousness, whether that consciousness is of *rūpa*, *vedanā* or *saññā*. We have also seen the difference between *mano*—one of the six sense-organs—and *viññāṇa* itself. Both are necessary for perception of thoughts or concepts (*dhamma*), but only the latter is necessary for the apprehension of stimuli from any of the other sense-organs. Finally, we have established a correlation between the third link of the *paṭiccasamuppāda*—the *viññāṇa*-link—and the *viññāṇakkhandha*. Now that we have discussed the function of each of the five aggregates, let us turn to a discussion of their interrelation.

45 *Tattha katamaṁ saṅkhārapaccayā viññāṇaṁ? Yaṁ cittaṁ mano mānasaṁ hadayaṁ paṇḍaraṁ mano manāyatanaṁ manindriyaṁ viññāṇaṁ viññāṇakkhandho tajjā manoviññāṇadhātu: idaṁ vuccati saṅkhārapaccayā viññāṇaṁ* (Vbh. 144).

Chapter 7

Interrelation of the Aggregates

In the previous chapters we discussed each of the five aggregates separately, without attempting to establish a detailed correlation between them. However, simply understanding the purport of these aggregates gives us merely a superficial insight into Buddhist psychology. The knowledge that *rūpa* is equated with the six sense-doors and bare perception, *vedanā* with sensation, *saññā* with recognition, *saṅkhāra* with any type of actions that will produce an effect, and *viññāṇa* with consciousness fails to shed much light on either the workings of the mind or the path leading to salvation. On the other hand, this understanding of the relationship between each of the aggregates will considerably increase our insights into Buddhist psychology.

The order in which the five aggregates have been presented so far reflects their typical canonical enumeration. To my knowledge, canonical literature does not offer a different order for the aggregates.[1] Unfortunately, aside from the traditional order in which the aggregates are enumerated, no hint as to their interrelation is given in the *sutta* literature. We must, then, deduce their operational process from the core theories of Buddhism. I will argue that the function of each of the aggregates, in their respective order, can be directly correlated with the theory of dependent origination—especially with the eight middle links. Three of the aggregates—*saṅkhāra*, *viññāṇa* and *vedanā*—as well as the entire psycho-physical phenomenon termed *nāmarūpa*, are included in the chain of dependent origination, indicating the intimate relation

---

1 Rhys Davids and Stede state in their *Pāli Text Society Pāli-English Dictionary* (p. 233) that one incidence of a different enumeration has been found in the *Saṁyuttanikāya*: *Rūpaṁ vedayitaṁ saññaṁ viññāṇaṁ yañca saṅkhataṁ neso ham asmi netam me* (S. i, 112). Yet, while the aggregate *saṅkhāra* seems *prima facie* to have been placed after *viññāṇa*, we must stress that the term *saṅkhataṁ* in this particular context comprises the four preceding elements. As the translation of this passage shows: "Matter, sensation, recognition, consciousness, that which is conditioned, is not I." Therefore, we could hardly say that this particular passage offers a different sequence in the enumeration of the aggregates. It simply states that matter, sensations, recognition and consciousness and that which is conditioned cannot be identified with the self.

between the latter and the five aggregates. In this chapter, I will first address the "order problem" that presents itself when trying to establish a correlation with the five aggregates and the eight middle links of the *paṭiccasamuppāda*. Second, I will examine each of the middle links of the *paṭiccasamuppāda* and point out which of the five aggregates can be correlated with them. This investigation will demonstrate that all the aggregates but *saññā* play an obvious role in this middle division. Third, I will attempt to adduce evidence supporting the implicit, yet crucial, presence of *saññā* between the two links of *vedanā* and *taṇhā*. Finally, I will briefly explain the workings of the five aggregates within *vipassanā* meditation.

The Position of *Viññāṇa* in the Enumeration of the *Pañcakkhandhā*

In the traditional enumeration of the *pañcakkhandhā, viññāṇa* appears as the last aggregate. This is puzzling, for how can the functions of *rūpa, vedanā, saññā* and *saṅkhāra* be accomplished if no prior consciousness is present to cognize and to come in contact with the external world? This would imply the impossibility of having either "mere perception," a sensation, or even a recognition imposed on sense-data, for nothing would have been cognized by a *viññāṇa*. The curious point remains as to why *viññāṇa* is listed as the final constituent of the five aggregates throughout the bulk of canonical literature. I believe, however, that there is a simple explanation.

The concept of re-evolution, which finds an expression in the theory of rebirth, is central to Buddhism. According to this theory, death is a natural and unavoidable sequence to birth, and it is inevitably followed by another birth—unless, of course, one has escaped the saṁsāric cycle by becoming an *arahant*. In many Buddhist enumerations—such as the five strengths (*bala*) and the eightfold noble path—the final element revolves and comes back to condition or reinforce the first member. However, there has been a controversy among scholars on whether the different elements of these enumerations are to be construed sequentially or cyclically.[2] It is not my intent to prove that a

2 K.N. Jayatilleke, in his work *Early Buddhist Theory of Knowledge*, deals with the concept of *saddhā* (trust) as the first member of the five strengths and shows that two distinct interpretative trends can be observed. Tilmann Vetter (*The Ideas and Meditative Practices of Early Buddhism*), on the other hand, offers evidence that the eightfold noble path can be construed both cyclically and sequentially.

cyclical perspective is definitively at work within the five strengths or the eightfold noble path. Such an approach is plausible, but establishing it would require a more exhaustive study. Moreover, whether the five strengths or the eightfold noble path can be approached from a cyclical perspective is not crucial for this study, since textual references indicate that the five aggregates are definitely subject to such an approach. This implies, therefore, that the last element of the five aggregates would also become the first, that *viññāṇa* revolves from its "last" position to become the "first" of the aggregates (see Table 9).

Table 9
The Wheel of the Five Aggregates

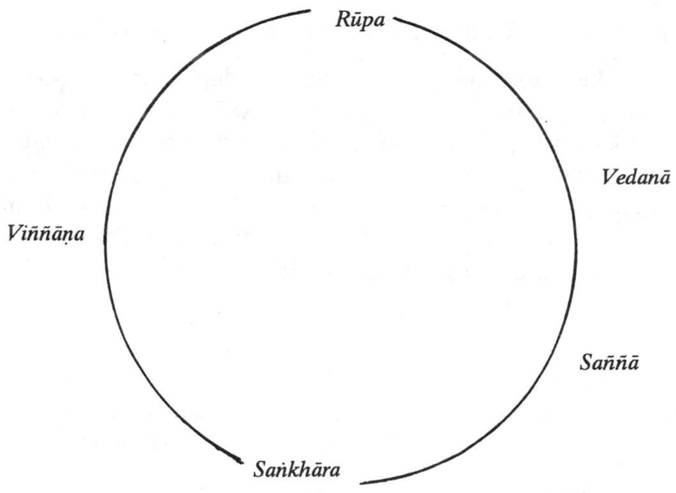

This theory finds support in the *paṭiccasamuppāda* itself, wherein *viññāṇa* is placed before the mind and matter link. The five aggregates themselves constitute the category of mind and matter. Since the last of the aggregates is *viññāṇa*, it will again engender a new set of aggregates until one breaks the chain of *saṃsāra*. The fact that consciousness "engenders" mind and matter emphasizes the cyclical aspect of the five aggregates. This theory is further evidenced by two major canonical passages. The first is found in the *Saṁyuttanikāya*, where Sāriputta—the Buddha's disciple known as the commander-in-chief of Dhamma (*Dhammasenapatti*)[3]—explains to Mahākoṭṭhita that mind and matter are conditioned by *viññāṇa* and that the *viññāṇa* is also conditioned by mind and matter.[4] The second passage is from the *Dīghanikāya* where the Bodhisattva Vipassī is said to have reflected on the nature of consciousness (*viññāṇa*) and of mind and matter. The result of his reflection is the same as that of Sāriputta: *viññāṇa* conditions mind and matter, and vice versa.[5] This clearly shows that *viññāṇa* can either be approached as the last aggregate, as portrayed in the standard enumeration of the *pañcakkhandhā*, or as the first, for *viññāṇa* is necessary for the arising of the other four aggregates. Having shown that *viññāṇa* can be placed as the first or last member of the *pañcakkhandhā*, we may begin our actual analysis of the *paṭiccasamuppāda*.

Correlation between Four Aggregates and the *Paṭiccasamuppāda*

In Table 10, the twelve links of the chain of dependent origination are divided into three traditional categories—past, present and future. Each of these divisions represents an alternative means of explaining the concept of mind and matter when taken in its largest sense, inclusive of the five aggregates.[6] For the purpose of this book, I will limit my analysis to the second division, where the presence of the five aggregates is clearest, and I will clearly demonstrate the presence of the

---

3 The *Anupadasutta* offers a long eulogy of Sāriputta by the Buddha (M. iii, 25ff.). Sāriputta is also known as chief among the disciples (*aggasāvaka*).

4 *Apica* [*sic*] *viññāṇapaccayā nāmarūpanti. ... Api ca nāmarūpapaccayā viññāṇanti* (S. ii, 113).

5 *Atha kho bhikkhave Vipassissa Bodhisattassa etad ahosi: "Kimhi nu kho sati nāmarūpaṁ hoti, kim paccayā nāmarūpan ti?" Atha kho bhikkhave Vipassissa Bodhissattassa yonisomanasikārā ahu paññāya abhisamayo: "Viññāṇe kho sati nāmarūpaṁ hoti, viññāṇapaccayā nāmarūpan ti." Atha kho bhikkhave Vipassissa Bodhisattassa etad ahosi: "Kimhi nu kho sati viññāṇaṁ hoti, kiṁ paccayā viññāṇan ti?" Atha kho bhikkhave Vipassissa Bodhissattassa yonisomanasikārā ahu paññāya abhisamayo: "Nāmarūpe kho sati viññāṇaṁ hoti, nāmarūpapaccayā viññāṇan ti"* (D. ii, 32). It is interesting to note that this reflection of the Bodhisatta Vipassī involves a slightly different formula of the theory of dependent origination. This formula includes only ten links instead of twelve, excluding ignorance (*avijjā*) and karmic activities (*saṅkhāra*)—the first two links of the more well-known formula—from its list. A similar formula is also found at S. ii, 104.

6 See discussion on p. 9.

aggregates within these eight links. The eight elements linked in this second group can be considered a mere rewording or a more detailed explanation of the psychosomatic process set in motion by mind and matter.

Table 10
The *Paṭiccasamuppāda* from a Mind and Matter Perspective

	1. *avijjā* (ignorance)	
Mind and matter	2. *saṅkhāra* (karmic activities)	Past
	3. *viññāṇa* (consciousness)	
	4. *nāmarūpa* (mind and matter)	
	5. *saḷāyatanā* (six sense-doors)	
	6. *phassa* (contact)	
Mind and matter	7. *vedanā* (sensation)	Present
	8. *taṇhā* (craving)	
	9. *upādāna* (clinging)	
	10. *bhava* (becoming)	
	11. *jāti* (birth; rebirth)	Future
Mind and matter	12. *jarāmaraṇa* (old age and death)	

The first link enumerated in the middle group of the theory of dependent origination is *viññāṇa*. While *viññāṇa* is the last member of the *pañcakkhandhā*, it can also very well be considered the first. According to the traditional interpretation of the theory of dependent origination, consciousness, as a member of the chain, is nothing but a rebirth-consciousness.[7] But as we have seen, every consciousness is a rebirth-consciousness at the moment of its emergence, and a death-consciousness at the moment of its dissolution. As soon as the consciousness emerges, however, mind and matter arise.[8]

7 Vsm. 528. For clarification on the term *paṭisandhi*, see p. 123.

8 *Idha paṭisandhi viññāṇaṁ okkanti nāmarūpaṁ* ... (Ps. i, 52; also found at Vsm. 600). "Here [in this present life] there is a relinking which is consciousness, there is an appearance which is *nāmarūpa*." The word *okkanti* literally means descent, but can

Many passages explain the second link of the middle group, mind and matter (*nāmarūpa*), as that which comprises all the five aggregates. The term *nāmarūpa* itself was already employed in pre-Buddhist philosophical systems. As Sarathchandra has pointed out:

> The expression *nāmarūpa*, borrowed from the earlier upanishadic literature, possessed two meanings. In one sense it referred to the empirical individual who, in the Upanishads too, enjoyed only a relative reality. But sometimes it was used as a comprehensive term which included the entire phenomenal worlds comprising mind and matter.[9]

Buddhism also ascribes these two meanings to the term. In the context of the *paṭiccasamuppāda*, however, the meaning of the term is limited to the psycho-physical structure of the individual. The authors of the *Pāli Text Society Dictionary*[10] note that the commentary on the *Dhammapada* states that the four mental aggregates plus the material aggregate constitute mind and matter.[11] Throughout Pāli literature,[12] numerous passages support this statement. Yet, oddly enough, we also find repeated an explicit contradiction of this definition of mind and matter. This has been noted by Étienne Lamotte who remarked that "*par mentalité* [nāma], *il faut entendre les trois* skandha *mentaux à l'exclusion du* vijñāna."[13] Although matter is always characterized by the *rūpakkhandha*, the mind (*nāma*), in certain passages, is defined only in terms of three aggregates—*vedanā, saññā* and *saṅkhāra*—instead of

---

also imply appearance; certain translators such as Ñāṇamoli have juxtaposed the phrase "into the mother's womb" to the term. This addition was probably inspired by a sentence of the *Dīghanikāya* where it is explicitly stated that if a *viññāṇa* does not enter the mother's womb, mind and matter cannot be engendered: *Viññāṇaṁ va hi Ānanda mātu kucchiṁ na okkamissatha, api nu kho nāmarūpaṁ mātu kucchismiṁ samucchissathāti* (D. ii, 63).

9 Sarathchandra, *Buddhist Theory of Perception*, p. 7.

10 Rhys Davids and Stede, *P.T.S. Pāli-English Dictionary*, p. 350.

11 *Vedanādijaṁ catunnaṁ rūpakkhandhassa cā ti pañcannaṁ khandhānaṁ vasena pavattaṁ nāmarūpaṁ* (DhA. iv, 100).

12 *Nāman ti cattāro arūpakkhandhā, rūpan ti rūpakkhandha* (AA. ii, 154); a similar statement is also found at DhsA. 392.

13 Lamotte, *Histoire du bouddhisme indien*, p. 40.

four.[14] This particular interpretation excludes *viññāṇa* from the mental category. Although there is an apparent contradiction, the problem might not be as serious as it seems, because the simple presence of the material aggregate along with the first three mental aggregates implies *viññāṇa*. Since *saṅkhāra* is listed as one of the mental aggregates, *viññāṇa* must naturally follow for, according to the *paṭiccasamuppāda*, *saṅkhāra* gives rise to *viññāṇa* (*saṅkhārapaccayā viññāṇaṁ*). Moreover, as we have previously seen, the mind and matter category itself conditions *viññāṇa*. Perhaps certain sources exclude *viññāṇa* from the definition of mind and matter simply in order to avoid duplication,[15] or perhaps they assume its presence to be so self-evident that it does not warrant mentioning. Whether consciousness is explicitly mentioned in the list or not, its function is always and undoubtedly present: on the one hand, mind and matter arise on the ground of *viññāṇa*, and on the other, *saṅkhāra* inevitably generates a *viññāṇa*. Therefore, the mind and matter category must contain all five aggregates.

The third link of this middle group is the six sense-doors (*saḷāyatanā*), usually described as the six organs of cognition; namely, the visual, auditory, olfactory, gustatory, tactile and thinking organs. Each of these sense-doors is then further divided into internal (*ajjhatta*) and external (*bāhira*). However,[16] within the *paṭiccasamuppāda* formula itself, the term *saḷāyatanā* includes only the six sense-organs (*ajjhatta*) and not their respective objects. We can therefore establish a direct correlation with the six sense-doors link of the *paṭiccasamuppāda* and the five sense-organs that partly constitute the *rūpakkhandha*.

The fourth link of the middle group, contact (*phassa*), arises from the six sense-doors. But as we saw, contact is bare sensory experience devoid of any subjective content. We can establish a further correlation here between the sense-objects (*bāhirasaḷāyatanā*) and the

---

14 For example, the *Vibhaṅga* excludes *viññāṇa* from *nāma*: *Vedanākkhandho saññākkhandho saṅkhārakkhandho: idaṁ vuccati viññāṇapaccayā nāmaṁ* (Vbh. 144). The *Visuddhimagga* also states that *nāma* only includes the three aggregates starting with *vedanā*: *nāman ti ārammaṇābhimukhaṁ namanato vedanādayo tayo khandhā* (Vsm. 558). This view is not shared by Vasubandhu who stated in his *Abhidharmakośa* that "les quatre *skandhas* immatériels, *vedanā, saṁjñā, saṁskāras, vijñāna*, sont nommés *nāman*, car *nāman* signifie 'ce qui se ploie', *namatīti nāma*" (La Vallée Poussin, *Abhidharmakośa*, 2:94).

15 Although duplication was not a technique that the compilers of the Pāli canon frowned upon.

16 See p. 48.

rūpakkhandha. The sense-objects, which belong to the *rūpakkhandha*, are potential objects of perception. But because of the congregation of consciousness, sense-organs and sense-objects, they become actual objects of perception and are termed contact.

Contact conditions the fifth link of the middle group, *vedanā*. To describe *vedanā* as one of the links is not necessary, since it has already been discussed as one of the aggregates, and we can rightly assume that the meaning of the term is the same in both contexts.

The sixth and seventh links which follow the *vedanā*-link are craving (*taṇhā*) and clinging (*upādāna*). As Bhikkhu Ñāṇamoli points out in his translation of the *Nettippakaraṇaṁ*, the literal translation of *taṇhā* is "thirst," but the term *taṇhā* itself is never used in Pāli literature to refer to "thirst" as such. Instead, the word *pipāsa* is employed when thirst is intended.[17] Moreover, our common understanding of craving may be misleading, since *taṇhā* refers to both craving and aversion. According to Buddhism, craving reflects our discontentment with the present moment, with reality as it is. We desire or crave something because of a deep inner dissatisfaction and because of our inability to accept reality as it presents itself. Craving is nothing but aversion towards our immediate situation. Similarly, aversion manifests itself as the craving for a better condition. The word *taṇhā* refers to both craving and aversion and henceforth, whenever the word craving is employed, aversion is also intended since both are the two faces of the same coin. Clinging is usually defined as an intensified form of craving.[18] *Taṇhā* and *upādāna* can be dealt with together since both represent craving at different levels of intensity. Craving always expresses itself first at the mental level, but it only rarely remains confined to that realm; through verbal and physical deeds, craving shapes life. Since *taṇhā* cannot express itself without a mental, verbal or physical action, we can equate both *taṇhā* and *upādāna* with part of *saṅkhāra*, namely the activity that arises from a mental conation. To return to the simile used to describe *saṅkhāra*,[19] craving would correspond to the activity of cooking, but would not include the final cooked product.

---

17 Ñāṇamoli, *The Guide* (*Nettippakaraṇaṃ*), p. 15, n. 42.

18 According to the *Visuddhimagga*, "Clinging is characterized by 'seizing' (*gahaṇa*), its property is not to release, and it manifests itself as a strong craving and as *diṭṭhi*." *Gahaṇalakkhaṇaṁ upādānaṁ, amuñcanarasaṁ, taṇhādaḷhatta-diṭṭhipaccupaṭṭhānaṁ* (Vsm. 528).

19 See p. 104.

The *sutta* literature mentions that craving is the conduit to becoming (*bhavanetti*);[20] therefore craving leads us to the eighth link in our investigation—becoming (*bhava*). However, a distinction should be made between becoming as a general concept and becoming as one of the links of the *paṭiccasamuppāda*. According to Pāli literature, becoming in the general sense is divided into *kamma*-process and rebirth-process.[21] The former refers to all actions that lead to becoming—what Nyānātiloka explains as "the karmically active side of existence ... while the latter refers to the ... karma-produced Rebirth or Regenerating Process, i.e. [*sic*] the karmically passive side of existence consisting in the arising and developing of the karma-produced and therefore morally neutral mental and bodily phenomena of existence."[22] Thus the rebirth-process is the result, the effect which outflows from the *kamma*-process and reproduces the five aggregates by generating a new *viññāṇa*.[23] Yet becoming, as one of the links of the *paṭiccasamuppāda*, does not include what we described as rebirth-process, for it is only the *kamma*-process that is a condition for birth.[24] Furthermore, the *kamma*-process is not restricted to the eighth link (*bhava*), but includes the two previous links of the chain of dependent origination, craving and clinging,[25] for all the *kamma* leading to the general concept of becoming are included in *kamma*-process.[26]

Here, again, there is an evident correlation with the *pañca-kkhandhā*: the *saṅkhārakkhandha* is connected to the concept of *bhava*. As we saw on p. 103, the underlying meaning of *saṅkhāra* is twofold. It is defined as a productive force and as whatever is compounded. The first aspect of *saṅkhāra* can be correlated with the *kammabhava*, i.e., to

---

20 S. iii, 190; v, 432.

21 Vsm. 571; also Vbh. 137.

22 Nyānātiloka, *Buddhist Dictionary*, p. 28.

23 The *sutta* state that the five aggregates have craving or desire as their root. *Ime kho, bhikkhave, pañc' upādānakkhandhā chandamūlakā ti* (M. iii, 16); also at S. iii, 100. Furthermore, Buddhaghosa briefly explains the *uppattibhava* as the [five] aggregates generated by *kamma*. *Uppattibhavo pana saṅkhepato kammābhinibbattā khandhā pabhedato navavidho hoti* (Vsm. 571).

24 *Bhavo ti pan'ettha kammabhavo va adhippeto, so hi jātiyā paccayo, na uppattibhavo* (Vsm. 575).

25 Vsm. 581.

26 *Sabbam pi bhavagāmikamman ti iminā pana cetanā sampayuttā abhijjhādayo vutta* (Vsm. 571).

craving, clinging and the link of becoming itself, while the second aspect is nothing but the *uppattibhava*.

Through this simple analysis of the middle group of the *paṭicca-samuppāda*, we have now assigned four of the aggregates to the eight links of the chain: with consciousness (*viññāṇa*), we have correlated the *viññāṇakkhandha*; with mind and matter, the five aggregates; with the six sense-doors (*saḷāyatanā*), matter (*rūpa*); with contact (*phassa*), matter as well; with *vedanā*, sensation; and with craving (*taṇhā*), clinging (*upādāna*) and becoming (*bhava*), *saṅkhāra*. The only aggregate that has not been included is *saññā*. Although it is not mentioned as a member of the chain of dependent origination, nor even alluded to by the twelve links, its implicit presence plays a crucial role.

Inclusion of *Saññā* in the *Paṭiccasamuppāda* Formula

My work has already demonstrated[27] that *saññā* comes in contact with sensations after they have arisen, and that *saññā* plays an important role in the emergence of craving, attachment and becoming—the three links of the *paṭiccasamuppāda* that are correlated with *saṅkhāra*. This claim was based upon two major arguments. The first is supported by the canonical statement that unwholesome *saññā* leads to "obsessions" (*papañca*),[28] a concept similar to that of [*micchā-*] *diṭṭhi*,[29] and by Buddhaghosa's statement that clinging (*upādāna*) is manifested as [*micchā-*] *diṭṭhi*.[30] It is important to stress that only unwholesome *saññā* (*kilesasaññā*) produce *papañca*.[31] Since *papañca* is basically interchangeable with *micchādiṭṭhi*, we could easily paraphrase Buddhaghosa's statement and say that clinging is manifested as *papañca*. And, as the *Suttanipāta* affirms, unwholesome *saññā* is responsible for the arising of *papañca*. Therefore *saññā* must precede clinging. Since *saññā* always follows *vedanā*,[32] it must perform its function between *vedanā* and *upādāna*. Yet, we still ought to clarify whether *saññā* occurs between *vedanā* and craving, or between craving and clinging.

---

27 Refer to pp. 87ff.

28 Sn. 874.

29 Refer to p. 80.

30 Vsm. 528. Previously quoted in n. 18 on p. 134.

31 This was discussed on p. 80, and evidenced by the *Sāratthappakāsini* (SA. ii, 382).

32 *Taṁ vedeti taṁ sañjānāti* (M. i, 111).

This is where we used the second argument which is grounded in the causal chain of the *Majjhimanikāya*,[33] a psychological theory that E.R. Sarathchandra has qualified as one of the earliest Buddhist formulas of sense-consciousness.[34] According to this formula,[35] "visual consciousness (*cakkhuviññāṇa*) arises on account of visual forms (*rūpa*) and the eye (*cakkhu*). The meeting of these three elements is contact (*phassa*)" which is a necessary condition for the arising of the next link: *vedanā*. The formula continues by stating that "whatever is felt (*vedeti*) as a sensation is recognized (*sañjānāti*)," thus explicitly supporting our statement that *saññā* follows *vedanā*. Furthermore, this same formula affirms that "*saññā* is followed by three mental functions (*vitakka, papañca* and *papañcasaṅkhā*)" that fall into the category of *saṅkhāra-kkhandha*. Therefore, this also implies that *saññā* operates precisely between the *vedanākkhandha* and the *saṅkhārakkhandha*. Since *taṇhā* belongs to the *saṅkhārakkhandha*,[36] the activity of the *saññākkhandha* must take place before *taṇhā* and after *vedanā*. The commentary on the *Dhammasaṅgaṇi* further supports this claim, for it places the activity of *saññā* between *vedanā* and *cetanā*,[37] a synonym of *saṅkhāra*.[38] Stcherbatsky provides a diagram which clearly shows that the function of *saññā* is activated after the emergence of sensation (see Table 11).[39]

As the chapter on *vedanā* demonstrates,[40] sensation in and of itself does not necessarily lead to craving. The *sutta* themselves distinguish between two kinds of sensations: those that are impure

---

33 M. i, 111-12. Similar occurrences of the formula also appear at M. i, 259; S. iv, 67, etc. Previously discussed on p. 81.

34 Sarathchandra, *Buddhist Theory of Perception*, p. 63. Sarathchandra quotes Mrs. Rhys Davids from *Buddhist Psychology* (p. 63) and includes in parentheses that this formula "is one of the earliest."

35 *Cakkhuñ c'āvuso paṭicca rūpe ca uppajjati cakkhuviññāṇaṁ tiṇṇaṁ saṅgati phasso, phassapaccayā vedanā, yaṁ vedeti taṁ sañjānāti, yaṁ sañjānāti taṁ vitakketi, yaṁ vitakketi taṁ papañceti, yaṁ papañceti tato nidānaṁ purisaṁ papañcasaṅkhā samudācaranti atītānāgatapaccuppannesu cakkhuviññeyyesu rūpesu* (M. i, 111-12).

36 See p. 110.

37 *Phassena pana phusitvā vedanāya vediyati saññāya sañjānati cetanāya ceteti* (DhsA. 107).

38 As seen on p. 95.

39 I have translated Stcherbatsky's Sanskrit terms into Pāli, and replaced some of the English equivalents by those that were used in this work (Stcherbatsky, *Buddhist Logic*, 2:311).

40 See p. 71.

(*āmisā*) or belonging to the householder (*gehasitā*) and others which are pure (*nirāmisā*) or belonging to the renouncer (*nekkhammasitā*). The difference is that the former act as potential agents in the future arising of craving while the latter do not. A certain *vedanā* may engender craving only if it is accompanied by unwholesome *saññā*, for the latter is likely to give rise to obsessions. Because of this particular faculty of recognition, pleasant sensations are approached as likeable or unlikeable, and individuals very soon find themselves generating craving or aversion towards these sensations. Craving in turn generates more *saṅkhāra* and keeps the cycle of life and death rotating.

Table 11
The Emergence of Sensation (*Vedanā*)

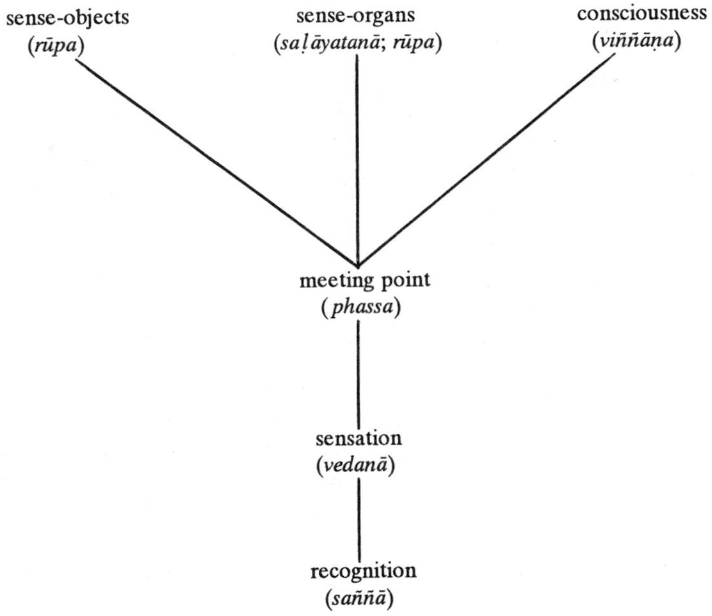

The position traditionally attributed to *saññā* within the *pañcakkhandhā* is of crucial importance, since the relation between *vedanā* and *saññā* is responsible for human bondage as well as for liberation. The *saññā* of an ordinary person (*puthujjana*) interprets and approaches the sensations as one's own property, considers them responsible for one's sorrow or happiness, and sets in motion the wheel of becoming; this would be what the *Sāratthappakāsini* terms unwholesome *saññā*,[41] which in themselves constitute thegiri *saññākkhandha*. The *Aṅguttaranikāya* indirectly states that a wise person utilizes [wholesome] *saññā* to develop wisdom[42] and, not being misled as to the nature of sensations, does not generate craving or aversion, therefore putting a halt to the cycle of life and death. This distinction between unwholesome and wholesome *saññā* is implicitly supported by many passages of the *Majjhimanikāya*. The function of *saññā*, as we may recall, is to recognize and interpret perceptions through their signs (*nimitta*) and minor characteristics (*anubyañjana*). The texts state that those established in the noble discipline, when seeing a form with the eye, hearing a sound with the ears, etc., do not hold on to their signs and minor characteristics (*anubyañjana*) because doing so would lead to the arising of desire,[43] discontent and unwholesome states of mind.[44]

Since the function of *saññā* is precisely to hold to the signs and minor characteristics, we could say, therefore, that unwholesome *saññā* is propitious to the emergence of desire. This is evidenced by another passage of the *Majjhimanikāya*:

> When he has seen a material shape (*rūpa*) through the eye, he feels attraction for agreeable material shapes, he feels repugnance for disagreeable material shapes; and he dwells without mindfulness aroused as to the body with a mind that is limited (*parittacetaso*), and he does not comprehend that freedom of mind (*cetavimutti*) and that freedom through intuitive wisdom (*paññāvimutti*) as they really are, whereby those evil unskilled states (*akusalā dhammā*) of his are stopped without remainder. Possessed thus of compliance and antipathy, whatever feelings

41 A. ii, 382.

42 According to the *Girimānandasutta*, *paññā* is equated with the ten recognitions such as *aniccasaññā, anattasaññā, asubhasaññā*, and so on (A. v, 109).

43 The word used is *abhijjā* which, according to the *Pāli Text Society Dictionary*, is synonymous with *lobha* and is closely connected with *taṇhā* and *upādāna*.

44 M. i, 180-81; i, 270; i, 273; iii, 34-35.

> (*vedanā*) he feels—pleasant or painful or neither painful nor pleasant—he delights (*abhinandati*) in that feeling, welcomes (*abhivadati*) it and persists in cleaving (*ajjhosāya tiṭṭhati*) to it. From delighting in that feeling of his, from welcoming it, from persisting in cleaving to it, delight (*nandī*) arises; whatever is delight amid those feelings, that is grasping; conditioned by grasping is becoming; conditioned by becoming is birth; conditioned by birth, old age and dying, grief, sorrow, suffering, lamentation and despair come into being. Such is the arising of this entire mass of anguish.[45]

This passage clearly suggests that when a person generates attraction or repugnance to sensations (*vedanā*), craving—or actually, *nandī*—and clinging arise, and the rest of the links of the *paṭiccasamuppāda* are automatically called in. What is important to notice is that attraction or repugnance are directly linked to the activity of *saññā*. When *saññā* is primarily focussed on the signs and minor characteristics of the object, it is very likely that attraction or repugnance will be generated, and that craving and attachment will then follow. This is what is meant by unwholesome *saññā*. Tilmann Vetter, commenting on the above passage suggested that

> One should not dwell on these impressions and thoughts a moment longer than is necessary to orientate oneself. If one goes too deeply into the signs of what is presented, or into minor features, then one cannot avoid the arising of desires and dejection and it will take a long time before these conditions disappear again.[46]

However, Vetter seems to ignore the positive aspect of *saññā*. The *Aṅguttaranikāya* clearly states that greed (*rāga*) cannot arise in one who is totally focussed on the signs of *asubha*[47]—as we have seen, *asubha* is one of the ten *saññā* described in the *Girimānandasutta*. Although Vetter interprets the concept of *nimitta* as the signs of an object, it must be stressed that the principal marks of any phenomenon are the three characteristics of existence—*anicca, anattā* and *dukkha*. Vetter uses the

---

45 M. i, 266. Translation from Horner, *The Collection of the Middle Length Sayings*, 1:322-23.

46 Vetter, *The Ideas and Meditative Practices of Early Buddhism*, p. 24.

47 *Asubhanimittan ti'ssa vacanīyaṁ. Tassa asubhanimittaṁ yoniso manasikarato anuppanno c'eva rāgo n'uppajjati uppanno ca rāgo pahīyatī ti* (A. i, 200-201).

term *nimitta* in the sense of outward appearance, while its signification also includes other characteristics. In this sense, Vetter is correct: one focussing on the signs which only reflect the outside appearance of an object will eventually generate desire. However, one focussing on the essential characteristics of every object—the three characteristics of existence and the other "positive *saññā*"—will eradicate greed.

Therefore, when *saññā* is primarily focussed on these three characteristics of existence, craving cannot be generated, for the person will understand the true nature of the object as well as the danger of associating any form of delight (*abhinandati*) with it. The recognition of these three marks of existence, as well as the other characteristics described in the *Girimānandasutta*, is the function of *saññā* that we termed wholesome. We must stress, however, that these wholesome *saññā* do not belong to the *saññākkhandha* as such. As we saw on p. 87, the essential function of the *saññākkhandha* is to apprehend a *nimitta* (sign). The fact that the three characteristics of existence—*anicca, anattā* and *dukkha*—are never considered *nimitta* and that, furthermore, they are classified as *animitta*, implies that the wholesome *saññā* does not apprehend *nimitta* and, therefore, does not belong to the *saññākkhandha*. It becomes clear that *saññā*, as unwholesome or wholesome, plays a crucial role between *vedanā* and craving; craving will or will not arise depending on the kind of *saññā* present. The inclusion of *saññā* between these two links of *vedanā* and craving further clarifies the emergence of *saṅkhāra*.

As we have hitherto suggested, the first part of *saṅkhāra* does not refer to all activities, but only to actions that have previously been conditioned by the *saññā*. In other words, any action performed with craving or aversion as its foundation—craving which arose due to the activity of *saññā*—results in a *saṅkhāra*, since *saññā* predisposes a blind reaction to the sensations. However, actions performed with wisdom as their foundation do not result in *saṅkhāra* since sensations approached as impermanent cannot give rise to craving and aversion.

Thus, a simple analysis of the eight middle links of the *paṭiccasamuppāda* explains each one of the *pañcakkhandhā*. Table 12 shows which elements of the middle link of the *paṭiccasamuppāda* are correlated with which aggregate.

We have seen, then, that each of the five aggregates finds a specific place in the theory of dependent origination. We have also explained that the *saññākkhandha* plays a critical role in the multiplication of misery, for it seems to be the faculty that is indirectly responsible for transforming *vedanā* into craving. When *vedanā* is coloured by the faculty of recognition, craving and attachment arise.[48] Yet, if one deactivates the inherently unwholesome *saññākkhandha*, or transforms it into the ten recognitions mentioned in the *Girimānanda-sutta*, craving is no longer produced, because wisdom—and not wrong views (*micchādiṭṭhi*)—arises from the activity of this wholesome *saññā*. The chain of dependent origination is thus broken and the final goal of enlightenment is ultimately reached. We will now explore how this theory is applied to Theravāda meditation practice as taught in Burma, Sri Lanka and Thailand.

Table 12
Correlation between the *Paṭiccasamuppāda* and the Aggregates

Elements of the *Paṭiccasamuppāda*		Corresponding Aggregate
viññāṇa (consciousness)		*viññāṇa*
nāmarūpa (mind and matter)		the five aggregates
saḷāyatanā (the six sense-doors)		*rūpa*
phassa (sensory stimuli)		*rūpa*
vedanā (sensation)		*vedanā*
	<------------------------------------	*saññā*
taṇhā (craving)		*saṅkkhāra*
upādāna (clinging)		*saṅkhāra*
bhava (becoming)		*saṅkhāra*

Vipassanā and the *Pañcakkhandhā*

The *paṭiccasamuppāda* constitutes a fundamental tenet of Buddhism, indispensable for realizing and understanding the implications of the Buddhist goal, *nibbāna*. Since this complex chain of causation is always said to give rise to suffering,[49] the deactivation of any of the twelve links of this chain is bound to break the causal process and eliminate suffering. The theory of dependent origination in its reverse order (*paṭiloma*) is consequently one version of the path leading to the eradication of misery. In fact, the meditation practice in Theravāda

48 See pp. 79ff.

49 "This [the *paṭiccasamuppāda*] is the origin of the entire mass of suffering." *Evam etassa kevalassa dukkhakkhandhassa samudayo hoti.*

countries is traditionally known to be an application of the process described by this reverse order. The five aggregates being nothing but a paraphrase of the theory of dependent origination, their function must therefore be apparent in the Buddhist meditation process.

Before tackling the subject, I need to clarify what is meant by meditation. The term meditation has a vast panoply of meanings within the Theravāda tradition, let alone the Buddhist tradition at large. However, since this study is solely focussed on the Theravāda, I will refer to the meditation technique most widely practised in Theravāda countries: *vipassanā*. Although there are differences in the various techniques labelled *vipassanā*, all their proponents link them unanimously to the *Satipaṭṭhānasutta*, the discourse in which four modes of attention are described: attention towards the body (*kāya*), sensation (*vedanā*), mind (*citta*) and mental contents (*dhamma*). In essence, the technique consists in observing objectively these four objects of attention. Some teachers may lay more emphasis on one than another, but in most cases, observation of breathing[50] and of sensations are prevailing.

Through the observation of sensations, the practitioner becomes increasingly aware of the fleeting nature of existence; every sensation that arises eventually passes away. This awareness is the ground from which sprouts a certain understanding of the two other characteristics of existence; namely, suffering and selflessness. The transience of sensations and of the entire psycho-physical structure enables a meditator to become experientially acquainted with selflessness. Realization of impermanence also strengthens the belief that attachment to any sensation is doomed to produce misery, for that sensation will sooner or later pass away. Therefore, one attempts to simply observe the sensations objectively, without generating any form of desire or aversion towards them:

> Here a *bhikkhu*, when feeling a pleasant sensation understands, "I am feeling a pleasant sensation"; when feeling a painful sensation, he understands, "I am feeling a painful sensation"; when feeling a neutral sensation, he understands, "I am feeling a neutral sensation." Now this awareness is firmly established in the present moment. This awareness develops to the extent that there is mere observation and mere understanding, nothing else, and he

50 Observation of breathing (*ānāpāna*) is one of the numerous practices included in the first mode of attention (*kāyānupassanā*).

> dwells in a state where he does not grasp anything, and there is nothing for him to grasp in the frame-work of the body. This is how a *bhikkhu* dwells observing bodily sensation in bodily sensation itself.[51]

From a purely technical perspective, this attitude comes within the scope of the *paṭiccasamuppāda*. When sensations are observed with equanimity, *saññā* is no longer active and craving is not generated. When the habit pattern of the mind is broken and sensations are perceived as impermanent, they are no longer approached as desirable or undesirable. In fact, having replaced *saññā* by wisdom (*paññā*), one does not react to the sensations, and new *saṅkhāra* cannot arise.

Of course, this process of liberation is gradual in the sense that liberation is not necessarily attained the instant that one ceases to generate *saññā* and begins to develop wisdom. Even when a person observes sensations with the understanding of their true nature (*anicca, anatta* and *dukkha*) and does not generate new cravings, the wheel of birth and death keeps turning. The force that activates the motion of the wheel results from *saṅkhāra*. Even when one does not produce new ones, old *saṅkhāra* will still continue to bear fruit in the form of new *viññāṇa*, *rūpa*, and *vedanā*. However, by failing to react or impose particular evaluations on these newly arisen *vedanā*, one does not generate new *kamma*, and so the fruits of the old *saṅkhāra* are eradicated. In the presence of constant awareness, keen diligence and strong wisdom arising from wholesome *saññā*, new *saṅkhāra* cannot arise from sensations, since unwholesome *saññā* no longer exist to react to sensations with craving and aversion. The old *saṅkhāra* will eventually all come up to the surface and pass away. As the Buddha told Ānanda: "Indeed, all karmic activities are transient. Arising and passing away is their true nature. Having arisen, they are eradicated; the tranquillity attained from such eradication is the real happiness."[52]

Earlier, we compared *saṅkhāra* with cooking;[53] I now wish to extend the metaphor further by correlating the process of eradication of *saṅkhāra* with that of fasting. If one ceases to give food to the body,

---

51 D. ii, 298.

52 *Aniccāvata saṅkhārā uppādavaya dhammino; uppajjitvā nirujjhanti, tesaṃ vūpasamo sukho ti* (D. ii, 199). This same passage was uttered by Sakka in the *Mahāparinibbānasutta* at D. ii, 156.

53 See p. 104.

one does not die immediately after the first meal is missed. Rather, one can survive without eating for perhaps two or three months. This is possible even though the body has to feed itself at every moment, because the body is able to break down and digest the old stock of food, all the fat and muscle previously accumulated. Not until this storage of nutriment has been consumed and only skin and bones remain will the body finally die, no more sustenance being available. In a similar manner, the mind and matter phenomenon needs to be fed at every moment by *saṅkhāra* which are constantly resulting from craving and aversion towards *vedanā*.[54] But if one remains in a state of equanimity characterized by wisdom, and does not react to sensations, the past *saṅkhāra* that are responsible for the arising of these very sensations dissolve, and a time comes when not a single *saṅkhāra* is left to propel the cycle. It is at this moment only that one attains or enters into *nibbāna* without residue, the final goal of true liberation.

From the perspective of the five aggregates, this process might be more easily understood by referring to Table 9 (see p. 129) where they are presented from a cyclical perspective. *Saṅkhāra* is responsible for the arising of *viññāṇa*; *viññāṇa* for *ṛūpa*; *rūpa*, for *vedanā*; *vedanā* for *saññā*; and *saññā* for *saṅkhāra*, upon which another re-evolution of the constantly repeated cycle is begun. If, however, one deactivates *saṇṇā*, new *saṅkhāra* are not created and the chain is broken. This constitutes the attainment of *nibbāna* with residue. The individual is still alive and the five aggregates are still present, as in the case of the Buddha and all the *arahant* mentioned in the Pāli texts. The five aggregates are still present, for old *saṅkhāra* that were produced in the past continue to the surface and yield their fruits in the form of the four other aggregates. At this stage, the individual has transformed *saññā* into *paññā* and further *saṅkhāra* cannot be generated. The five aggregates—or the individual's life—are maintained simply by dint of the previously accumulated *saṅkhāra*, and this keeps the wheel rolling

---

54 The *Majjhimanikāya* supports our simile by mentioning that four kinds of substance are found; namely, material food, *phassa, saṅkhāra* and *viññāṇa*. *Kabaḷiṅkāro āhāro oḷāriko vā sukhumo vā, phasso dutiyo, manosaṃcetanā tatiyo, viññāṇaṃ catuttho* (M. i, 48). Although the term *saṅkhāra* is not used explicitly in this text, the word used (*manosaṃcetanā*) can be directly related to *saṅkhāra*. Such is the description of *manosaṃcetanā* of the *Paramatthamañjūsā* (VsmA. 335; reported by Bhikkhu Ñāṇamoli in his translation of the *Visuddhimagga*, *The Path of Purification*, p. 372, n. 2).

as long as the impulse that set the motion lasts.[55] This motion stops when all *saṅkhāra*—past and present—have been eradicated. From then onwards, none of the five aggregates can arise; this is the attainment of *nibbāna* without residue, achieved upon the death of the *arahant*.

This exact same process can also be understood from the perspective of the *paṭiccasamuppāda*. If one has totally transformed *saññā* into *paññā*, sensations cannot be the grounds for the arising of further craving. Therefore, clinging, becoming and (re-)birth, all being necessarily dependent upon the presence of craving, cannot arise either. Although one may keep living for a certain period, rebirth is no longer possible. The life of such an individual is temporarily maintained by *saṅkhāra*—the link that precedes the eight middle links which characterize the present. When these past *saṅkhāra* are totally eradicated, the switch from *nibbāna* with residue to without residue can occur.

Whether we approach Buddhist soteriology from the angle of the *paṭiccasamuppāda* or of the five aggregates, it has become clear that the same process is at work: from the Theravāda texts that were analyzed in this work, the deactivation of *saññā* is the primary factor for the attainment of enlightenment. Of course, this deactivation can be expressed in different ways, such as the destruction of ignorance, the cessation of craving or the eradication of *saṅkhāra*, but they all necessarily imply an objective observation of sensations (mental or physical) which will not produce craving or *saṅkhāra*.

55 The wheel "kept rolling as long as the impulse that set the motion (*abhisaṅkhārassa gati*) lasted. It then circled and fell to the ground." *Taṁ pavattitaṁ samāṇam yāvatikā abhisaṅkhārassa gati tāvatikaṁ gantvā ciṅgulāyitvā bhūmiyaṁ papati* (A. i, 111).

Conclusion

Although many scholars have referred to the five aggregates in their works on Buddhism, none have thoroughly explained their respective functions. By clarifying the importance of this previously untreated subject, this study has circumscribed the meaning and the role of each of the five aggregates and has established a correlation between each of the aggregates and certain links of the *paṭiccasamuppāda*.

In the chapter on the *rūpakkhandha*, I argued that the many classifications of this aggregate could be condensed and divided into two major categories: those elements belonging to the sense-organs, and those pertaining to the sense-objects. When approached from these two categories, the *rūpakkhandha* can be integrally correlated to two links of the *paṭiccasamuppāda*; namely, the six sense-doors and contact. All the sense-organs except the mental organ (*mano*) belong to the six sense-doors, while the sense-objects along with the mental organ are included in contact (*phassa*). When these sense-objects are actually perceived, they, along with consciousness and the sense-organs, constitute contact: bare sensory experience, devoid of any subjective inclination. Contact can potentially become a sensation *vedanā*.

I also suggested that no distinction is found between the *vedanākkhandha* and *vedanā* as a member of the chain of dependent origination. By exploring how *vedanā*, like *rūpa*, was also classified according to different schemes—such as pure (*nirāmisā*), belonging to the renouncer (*nekkhamasitā*), impure (*āmisā*) and belonging to the householder (*gehasitā*)—I came to the conclusion that a certain way of approaching *vedanā* would transform them into *nirāmisā* or *nekkhammasitā vedanā*—of an inoffensive nature—while an alternative approach would transform the *vedanā* into *āmisā* or *gehasitā vedanā*—endowed with a negative connotation because this type of sensation may act as an agent bringing about the future arising of craving and aversion. I have presented evidence which supports the idea that the factor responsible for this second approach to *vedanā* is the next aggregate: *saññā* (recognition). It is *saññā* that will transform the sensation into *nirāmisā* (or *nekkhamasitā*) or *āmisā* (or *gehasitā*), a transformation which will become responsible for generating or eradicating craving.

The main function of the *saññākkhandha* is to recognize and interpret sensations through the imposition of certain categories. Yet not all *saññā* belong to the *saññākkhandha*. To clarify this nuance, it was again necessary to elaborate a scheme dividing *saññā* into two categories. The wholesome *saññā* are, in short, recognitions of the three characteristics of existence. These do not belong to the *saññākkhandha* as such for they do not apprehend signs (*nimitta*). The unwholesome *saññā*, on the other hand, are simply certain interpretations of reality through the major signs. The latter type of *saññā* is not conducive to insight; it generates obsessions, and essentially constitutes the *saññā-kkhandha*. Upon realizing the presence of the *saññākkhandha* between the two links of *vedanā* and craving, the major function assigned to this aggregate in the arising of craving and aversion became evident: unless an individual's faculty of recognition is governed by the wholesome *saññā*, that person is likely to generate craving, clinging and becoming, all of which fall under the next aggregate: *saṅkhāra*.

The *saṅkhārakkhandha* was also analyzed in terms of different schemes. I came to the conclusion that the *saṅkhārakkhandha* is definitely a *saṅkhāra* in the sense of conditioned phenomena since it has been formed and conditioned. Not all *saṅkhāra*, however, belong to the *saṅkhārakkhandha*, for they are not all endowed with the capacity of forming or generating more conditioned phenomena. A conditioned phenomenon can only produce other conditioned phenomena when working in conjunction with *viññāṇa, vedanā, saññā* and *rūpa*; in other words, only the *saṅkhārakkhandha*, which, by definition, is closely connected to the four other *khandha*, can produce conditioned phenomena. This implies that *saṅkhāra* as a *paccaya* is simply a paraphrase of *saṅkhārakkhandha*. Both these terms refer to a force that will generate an effect. The effect, however, although being *saṅkhata* in the sense that it has been caused, does not necessarily belong to the *paccaya* or the *saṅkhārakkhandha* categories, for it might not generate a further effect. I have also correlated the *saṅkhārakkhandha* with three of the links of the *paṭiccasamuppāda*: craving, clinging and becoming—the three links responsible for the emergence of a new existence, a new consciousness (*viññāṇa*).

We have seen that *viññāṇakkhandha* is variously translated. Some scholars hold that it means bare sensation, some, pure consciousness, and others, the cognition of something pleasant, unpleasant or neutral. Since the *viññāṇakkhandha* is responsible for the cognition of all of these, however, none of these suppositions is totally accurate. Consequently, the term was defined as "mere consciousness," whether that consciousness be of *rūpa*, *vedanā* or *saññā*. The difference between the mental organ and *viññāṇa* itself was also examined. Both are necessary for perception of phenomena (*dhamma*), but only the latter is necessary for the apprehension of stimuli from any of the other sense-organs. A correlation between the third link of the *paṭicca-samuppāda—viññāṇanidāna*—and the *viññāṇakkhandha* was finally established.

By correlating the five aggregates, in the order they traditionally appear,[1] with the theory of dependent origination, I have presented evidence supporting the significance of their traditional nomenclature. The traditional order of the five aggregates is in perfect harmony with the theory of dependent origination. If the order of the aggregates were arranged differently, there would be a definite contradiction between the two theories. Having correlated these two theories, I emphasized that *viññāṇa*, which can cyclically manifest itself as either the first or last member, is a necessary condition for the arising of matter, which in turn conditions sensations. Sensation is necessary for the emergence of *saññā*, which might lead to *saṅkhāra* if the *saññā* is unwholesome (and therefore belongs to the *saññākkhandha*)—or to wisdom (*paññā*) if the *saññā* is wholesome. If a *saṅkhāra* is generated, then the grounds for the arising of a new *viññāṇa* are prepared. Thus, the cycle is complete: from *viññāṇa* to *viññāṇa*. Beings are trapped within a quasi-eternal round of birth, death and rebirth.

The Buddhist tradition usually explains the process that binds beings to *saṁsāra* by the use of the twelvefold chain of dependent origination in direct order (*anuloma*). This same process when viewed in the reverse order (*paṭiloma*) is perceived as a soteriological indicator by virtue of the implication that the chain can be broken. Thus the doctrine of dependent origination plays an irrevocably crucial role in Buddhism: it elucidates not only the process that binds beings to *saṃsāra*, but also the one necessary for attaining enlightenment. It is probably for this reason that canonical literature states that "whoever understands the *paṭiccasamuppāda* understands the *dhamma*, and whoever understands the *dhamma* understands the *paṭicca-samuppāda*."[2] While the theory of dependent origination has been allotted such great importance, the five aggregates have never received

1 With the sole exception of *viññāṇa* which appears as the last member and was moved to the first place, for reasons explained on pp. 127ff.

2 *Yo paṭiccasamuppādaṁ passati so dhammaṁ passati, yo dhammaṁ passati so paṭiccasamuppādaṁ passatīti* (M. i, 190-1).

much emphasis in terms of the process that leads to *nibbāna*. Nevertheless, the *paṭiccasamuppāda* is a process that takes place within every individual, and since Buddhism describes the individual as constituted of the five aggregates, these aggregates must mirror the process hinted at by the *paṭiccasamuppāda*. Similarly, the five aggregates are reflecting a process of interdependence which must necessarily be in accordance with the *paṭiccasamuppāda*. By correlating the five aggregates with the theory of dependent origination, I have presented evidence that shows, on the one hand, the interdependence of the two theories and, on the other hand, how the process which binds beings to *saṁsāra* is reflected in the five aggregates, thus transposing Buddhist soteriology into a more concrete Buddhist psychological framework.

Glossary

The main purpose of this glossary is to refer the reader to the English equivalents of the Pāli or Sanskrit terms used in this book. Using the index, one may then locate the passage where the term is analyzed.

ajjhattta	internal
ākāsa	space
āmisā	pure (vegeterian)
anāgāmin	non-returner
anāpānasati	contemplation of breath
anatta	selflessness
anuloma	normal order (of the *paṭiccasamuppāda*)
anupādisesa	without residue (*nibbāna*)
apāya	four states of misery
āpodhādu	water, water element
appaṭighaṃ	unresisting
arahant	liberated person
arahattaphalasamāpatti	attainment of the fruits of arahantship
arūpāvacara	immaterial realm
asaṅkhata	unconditioned
asaṅkhatadhamma	unconditioned phenomenon (in the Theravāda tradition, *nibbāna* is the only phenomenon)
āsava	bias
āvacara	realm
āyatana	base; sense-organs
bahiddhā	external
bala	strength (the five strengths, powers)
bhava	becoming
bhikkhu	monk
cetanā	volition
cetasika	mental factors
citta	consciousness
cittavṛttinirodha	cessation of mental activities
cuticitta	death-consciousness
dhamma	phenomenon of existence; teaching
dhammāyatana	mental objects

dhātu	element
diṭṭhi	views (wrong-views)
diṭṭhisaññā	recognition of views
dūre	far
dukkha	suffering
gehasitā	belonging to the householder
gotrabhū	change of lineage
hadayavatthu	heart basis
hetu	cause
indriya	sense-organ
itthindriya	femininity
jhāna	absorptions
kāmāvacara	realm of sensuality
kammabhava	*kamma*-process
kammavipāka	*kamma*-result
khandha	aggregate
khandhaparinibbāna	total extinction of the five aggregates
khaya	destruction
kusala	wholesome
lobha	greed
lokuttara	transcendental realm
maggaphala	levels of realization
mahābhūta	primary elements (4)
mano	mental organ
manussaloka	human realm
nāmarūpa	mind and matter
navalokuttaradhammā	nine supramundane elements
nekkhamasitā	belonging to the renouncer
nidāna	link of the paṭiccasamuppāda
nimitta	sign
nirāmisā	impure (non-vegetarian)
nirodha	eradication
nirupādisesa nibbāna	nibbāna without residue
oḷārika	gross
pañcakkhandhā	five aggregates
paññā	wisdom
papañca	obsession
paramatthasacca	highest truth

paṭhavīdhātu	earth, earth element
paṭiccasamuppāda	dependent origination
paṭiloma	reverse order
paṭisandhiviññāṇa	rebirth-consciousness
phassa	contact
phoṭṭhabbāyatana	bodily impression
puthujjana	ordinary people
rūpa	matter
rūpāvacara	material realm
saḷāyatanā	six sense-doors
sabhāvadhamma	phenomenon which exists by itself
sagga	celestial realm
sakādāgāmin	once-returner
sakkāyadiṭṭhi	view that the body is existing [permanently]
samādhi	concentration
samāpatti	attainments (4)
samatha	concentration
sammutisacca	conventional truth
saṃsāra	cycle of birth, death and rebirth
saṅkhāra	karmic activities [compounded phenomena]
saṅkhata	conditioned
saṅkhatadhamma	conditioned phenomena
saññā	recognition
saññākkhandha	recognition aggregate
saññāvedayitanirodha	extinction of recognition and sensation
santike	near
sappaṭighaṃ	resisting
sīla	morality
sopādisesa	with residue (nibbāna)
sotāpanna	stream-enterer
sukhuma	subtle
sutta	discourse
taṇhā	craving
tejodhātu	fire, fire element
ucchedadiṭṭhi	annihilation view
upādāna	clinging
upādānakkhandhā	clinging-aggregate
upādārūpa	secondary matter
uppattibhava	rebirth-process

vāyadhātu	air, air element
vedanā	sensation
vedanākkhaya	state of destruction of sensations
vimutti	release
viññāṇa	consciousness
vipassanā	discriminative insight; one of the theravāda medition techniques
visaya	sense-object
vitakka	thinking about
voharasacca	conventional truth

Bibliography

Primary Sources (Pāli and Sanskrit Texts)

Abhidhammattasaṅgaha. T.W.S. Rhys Davids, ed., *Journal of the Pali Text Society* (1884) 1:1-48

Abhidharmakośa and Bhāsya with Sphutārthā Commentary of Ācārya Yośomittra. Swāmī Dwārikādās Śastri, ed. Varanasi: Bauddha Bharati, 1981.

Aṅguttaranikāya. R. Morris and E. Hardy, eds. 2 vols. London: Pali Text Society (P.T.S.), 1961.

Atthasālinī. E. Müller, ed. London: P.T.S., 1979.

BUDSIR. Entire Pāli Canon on CD-ROM. Designed at Mahidol University, Bangkok: 1989.

Chandogyopanishadbhashya. Siromani Uttamur T. Viraraghavacharya, ed. Tirupati: Sri Venkatesvara Oriental Institute, 1952.

Dhammapada and Khuddakapāṭha. C.A.F. Rhys Davids, ed. London: P.T.S., 1931.

Dhammapada Commentary. H.C. Norman, ed. London: P.T.S., 1906-14.

Dhammasaṅgaṇi. E. Müller, ed. London: P.T.S., 1987.

Dhātukathā with Commentary. E.R. Gooneratne, ed. London: P.T.S., 1963.

Dīghanikāya. T.W.S. Rhys Davids and J.E. Carpenter, eds. 3 vols. London: P.T.S., 1910.

Itivuttaka. E. Windisch, ed. London: P.T.S., 1890.

Kathāvatthu. A.C. Taylor, ed. London: P.T.S., 1979.

Majjhimanikāya. V. Trenckner and R. Chalmers, eds. 3 vols. London: P.T.S., 1902.

Manorathapūraṇī. M. Walleser and H. Kopp, eds. 4 vols. London: P.T.S., 1973.

Milindapañhapāli. Swāmī Dwārikādās Śastri, ed. Varanasi: Bauddha Bharati, 1979.

Mohavicchedanī. A.K. Warder, ed. London: P.T.S., 1961.

Nettipakaraṇa. E. Hardy, ed. London: P.T.S., 1902.

Niddesa (Mahā). L. de La Vallée Poussin and E.J. Thomas, eds. London: P.T.S., 1978.

Pañcappakaraṇatthakathā. C.A.F. Rhys Davids, ed. *Journal of the P.T.S.* 6. 1910-12.

Papañcasūdanī. J.H. Woods, D. Kosambi and I.B. Horner, eds. 4 vols. London: P.T.S., 1977.

Paṭisambhidāmagga. A.C. Taylor, ed. London: P.T.S., 1979.

Paṭisambhidāmagga Commentary. C.V. Joshi, ed. 3 vols. London: P.T.S., 1979.

Puggalapaññatti. R. Moris, ed. London: P.T.S., 1883.

Saddhammappakāsinī. C.V. Joshi, ed. 3 vols. London: P.T.S., 1947.
Samantapāsādikā. J. Takakusu and M. Nagai, eds. 7 vols. London: P.T.S., 1947.
Saṁyuttanikāya. L. Feer, ed. 4 vols. London: P.T.S., 1898.
Sāratthappakāsinī. F.L. Woodward, ed. 3 vols. London: P.T.S., 1937.
Sumaṅgalavilāsinī. T.W.S. Rhys Davids, J.W. Carpenter and W. Stede, eds. 3 vols. London: P.T.S., 1971.
Suttanipāta. Dines Andersen and Helmer Smith, eds. London: P.T.S., 1913.
Suttanipāta Commentary. Helmer Smith, ed. 3 vols. London: P.T.S., 1918.
Theragāthā and Therīgāthā. H. Oldenberg and R. Pischel, eds. London: P.T.S., 1966.
Udāna. Paul Steinthal, ed. London: P.T.S., 1948.
Vaiyākaraṇasiddhāntakaumudi. Bhattaji Diksita, ed. Varanasi: Caukhamba Samskrita Sirija Aphisa, 1969.
Vibhaṅga. C.A.F. Rhys Davids, ed. London: P.T.S., 1904.
Vibhaṅga commentary (Sammohavinodanī). Ven. A.P. Buddhadatta, ed. London: P.T.S., 1923.
Vinayapiṭaka. H. Oldenberg, ed. 4 vols. London: P.T.S., 1883.
Visuddhimagga. C.A.F. Rhys Davids, ed. 2 vols. London: P.T.S., 1975.
Yamaka. C.A.F. Rhys Davids, ed. 2 vols. London: P.T.S., 1913.

Translations

L'Abhidharmakośa de Vasubandhu. 6 vols. Louis de La Vallée Poussin, trans., Étienne Lamotte, ed. Bruxelles: Institut Belge des Hautes Études Chinoises, 1980.
The Book of Analysis: A Translation of the Vibhaṅga from the Abhidharmapiṭaka. Ven. U Thittila, trans. London: P.T.S., 1969.
The Book of the Discipline (Vinayapiṭaka). 6 vols. I.B. Horner, trans. The Sacred Books of the Buddhists Series (vols. 10, 11, 13, 14, 20, 25). London: P.T.S., 1982-86.
The Book of the Gradual Sayings (Anguttaranikāya). 5 vols. F.L. Woodward, trans. of vols. 1, 2 and 5; E.M. Hare, trans. of vols. 3 and 4. London: P.T.S., 1979-86.
The Book of the Kindred Sayings (Saṁyuttanikāya). 5 vols. C.A.F. Rhys Davids, trans. of vols. 1 and 2; F.L. Woodward, trans. of vols. 3, 4 and 5. London: P.T.S., 1917-22.
Buddhist Psychology: A Buddhist Manual of Psychological Ethics. A Translation of the Dhammasaṅgaṇi from the Abhidharmapiṭaka. C.A.F. Rhys Davids, trans. Delhi: Oriental Books Reprint Corporation, 1975.
The Collection of the Middle Length Sayings (Majjhimanikāya). 3 vols. I.B. Horner, trans. London: P.T.S., 1959.
Compendium of Philosophy (Abhidhammatthasaṅgaha). Shwe Zan Aung, trans.; C.A.F. Rhys Davids, rev. and ed. London: P.T.S., 1967.

Dialogues of the Buddha (Dīghanikāya). 3 vols. C.A.F. Rhys Davids, trans., F. Max Müller, ed. Sacred Books of the Buddhists Series (vols. 2-4). London: Luzac, 1969.

Discourse on Elements: A Translation of the Dhātukathā from the Abhidharmapiṭaka. Mahā Thera Nārada, trans. London: P.T.S., 1962.

The Discourse on the All-Embracing Net of Views: The Brahmajāla Sutta and Its Commentarial Exegesis. Bhikkhu Bodhi, trans. Kandy: Buddhist Publication Society (B.P.S.), 1978.

The Discourse on the Root of Existence: The Mūlapariyāya Sutta and Its Commentarial Exegesis. Bhikkhu Bodhi, trans. Kandy: B.P.S., 1980.

Eight Upaniṣads. With the Commentary of Śaṅkharācārya. 2 vols. Swāmī Gambhīrānanda, trans. Calcutta: Advaita Ashrama, 1986.

Elder's Verses (Theragāthā and Therīgāthā). 2 vols. K.R. Norman, trans. London: P.T.S., 1969.

The Expositor (Atthasālinī). Pe Tin Maung, trans. London: P.T.S., 1976.

The Great Discourse on Causation: The Mahānidāna Sutta and Its Commentarial Exegesis. Bhikkhu Bodhi, trans. Kandy: B.P.S., 1984.

The Group of Discourses (Suttanipāta). K.R. Norman, trans., with alternative translations by I.B. Horner and Walpola Rahula. London: P.T.S., 1984.

The Guide (Nettippakaraṇaṁ). Bhikkhu Ñāṇamoli, trans. London: P.T.S. 1977.

Maitrāyaṇīya Upaniṣad: A Critical Essay. With Text, Translation and Commentary. J.A.B. Buitenen, trans. The Hague: Mouton, 1962.

A Manual of Abhidhamma: Abhidhammatthasaṅṅaha. By Anuruddha. Mahā Thera Nārada, trans. Rangoon: Printed by the Buddha Sasana Council, 1970.

Milinda's Questions (Milindapañha). I.B. Horner, trans. Sacred Books of the Buddhists, 22, 23. London: P.T.S., 1964.

The Minor Readings (Khuddakapāṭha). Ven. Ñāṇamoli, trans. London: P.T.S., 1978.

The Nighaṇṭu and the Nirukta: The Oldest Indian Treatise on Etymology, Philology and Semantics. By Yakṣa. Lakśman Sarup, ed. and trans. Delhi: Motilal Banarsidass, 1977.

The Path of Discrimination (Paṭisambhidāmagga). Ven. Ñāṇamoli, trans. London: P.T.S., 1982.

The Path of Purification (Visuddhimagga) by Bhadantācariya Buddhaghosa. Ven. Ñāṇamoli, trans. Kandy: B.P.S., 1979.

Points of Controversy or Subjects of Discourse: A Translation of the Kathāvatthu from the Abhidharmapiṭaka. Shwe Zan Aung and C.A.F. Rhys Davids, trans. London: P.T.S., 1979.

The Suttanipāta. H. Saddhatissa, trans. London: Curzon Press, 1985.

The Thirteen Principal Upanishads. Robert Ernest Hume, trans. Delhi: Oxford University Press, 1985.

Thus Have I Heard: The Long Discourses of the Buddha (Dīghanikāya). Maurice Walshe, trans. London: Wisdom Publications, 1987.

Secondary Sources

Apte, Vaman Shivaram. *The Practical Sanskrit English Dictionary*. Revised and enlarged ed. Kyoto: Rinsen Book Company, 1986.

Bhattacharya, Kamaleswar. "*Upadhi-*, *upādi-* et *upādāna-* dans le canon bouddhique pāli." In *Mélanges d'indianisme à la mémoire de Louis Renou*. Paris: Publications de l'institut de civilisation indienne, 1967.

Bodhi, Bhikkhu. "Khandha and Upādānakkhandha." *Pali Buddhist Review* 1(1) (1976): 91-102.

Boisvert, Mathieu. "A Brief Survey of the Relation between the *Paṭiccasamuppāda* and the *Pañcakkhandhā*." In Vol. 2, *Contact Between Cultures; South Asia*, ed. K.I. Koppedrayer. Lewiston: Edwin Mellen Press, 1992.

———. "A Comparison of the Early Forms of Buddhist and Christian Monastic Traditions." *Journal of Buddhist-Christian Studies* (November 1992).

———. "Le Processus métaphorique du *Milindapañhapāli*." *Religiologiques* (April 1993).

———. "*Saññāvedayitanirodha:* An Endless Controversy." *The Pacific World: Journal of the Institute of Buddhist Studies* 9 (New Series) (1993).

———. "La Contemplation de la mort dans le bouddhisme Theravāda." *Actes du 1er Congrès international de psychiatrie transculturelle (Le processus de guérison: par-delà la souffrance ou la mort)*. Québec: Éditions HWM (1994).

———. "*Maraṇasati*: Texutal Interpretation and Contemporary Practice." *Buddhist Studies Review* (forthcoming).

Brahmachari, Silananda. *An Introduction to Abhidhamma: Buddhist Philosophy and Psychology*. Calcutta: Jadab Barua Publications, 1979.

Buddhadatta, A.P. *Concise Pāḷi English Dictionary*. Colombo: The Colombo Apothecaries Co., 1968.

Carrithers, Michael, Steven Collins and Steven Lukes, eds. *The Category of the Person: Anthropology, Philosophy, History*. New York: Cambridge University Press, 1985.

Chang, Jui-Liang. "An Analytic Study on Three Concepts of 'Skandha,' 'Āyatana' and 'Dhātu'" (in Chinese: "Che hs[e]ueh lun p[v]ing"). *Philosophical Review* 8 (January 1975): 107-21.

Collins, Steven. *Selfless Persons: Imagery and Thought in Theravāda Buddhism*. Cambridge: Cambridge University Press, 1982.

Cousins, L.S. "Buddhist Jhāna: Its Nature and Attainment According to the Pali Sources." *Religion, A Journal of Religion and Religions* 3 (1973): 115-31.

Dasgupta, Surendranath. *A History of Indian Philosophy*. 4 vols. Delhi: Motilal Banarsidass, 1975.

Demiéville, Paul. "L'Origine des sectes bouddhiques d'après Paramartha." In *Mélanges chinois et bouddhiques*. Vol. 1. Bruxelles: Institut Belge des Hautes Études Chinoises, 1932.
Foucher, A. *La Vie du Bouddha d'après les textes et les monuments de l'Inde*. Paris: J. Maisonneuve, 1987.
Gabaude, Louis. *Une herméneutique bouddhique contemporaine de Thaîlande: Buddhadasa Bhikkhu*. Paris: Publications de l'École Française d'Extrême-Orient, 1988.
Gethin, R.M. "The Five Khandhas: Their Theatment [*sic*] in the Nikāyas and Early Abhidhamma." *Journal of Indian Philosophy* 52 (1986): 35-53.
Govinda, Anagarika Brahmacari. *The Psychological Attitude of Early Buddhist Philosophy*. London: Rider, 1961.
Griffiths, Paul. "Concentration and Insight: The Problematic of Theravāda Buddhist Meditation-Theory." *Journal of the American Academy of Religion* 49 (1981): 606-24.
———. *On Being Mindless: Buddhist Meditation and the Mind-Body Problem*. Illinois: Open Court, 1986.
Guenther, Herbert V. *Philosophy and Psychology in the Abhidharma*. Delhi: Motilal Banarsidass, 1974.
———. *Ecstatic Spontaneity*. Berkeley: Asian Humanities Press, 1993.
———. *Wholeness Lost and Wholeness Regained*. Albany: State University of New York Press, 1994.
Gyatso, Tenzin. *Freedom in Exile: The Autobiography of the Dalai Lama*. New York: HarperCollins, 1990.
Hayes, Richard P. *Dignaga on the Interpretation of Signs.* London: Kluwer Academic Publishers, 1988.
Hume, Robert Ernest. *The Thirteen Principal Upanishads*. Delhi: Oxford University Press, 1985.
James, William. *Essays in Radical Empiricism*. London: Longmans, Greens, 1912.
———. *Principles of Psychology*. New York: Dover, 1950.
Jayatilleke, K.N. *The Early Buddhist Theory of Knowledge.* Delhi: Motilal Banarsidass, 1980.
Johansson, Rune E.A. *The Psychology of Nirvana*. London: George Allen and Unwin, 1969.
Kalupahana, David J. *Buddhist Philosophy: A Historical Analysis*. Honolulu: University Press of Hawaii, 1976.
———. *The Principles of Buddhist Psychology.* Albany: State University of New York Press, 1987.
———. *A History of Buddhist Philosophy: Continuities and Discontinuities*. Honolulu: University Press of Hawaii, 1992.
Karunadasa, Y. *Buddhist Analysis of Matter*. Colombo: Department of Cultural Affairs, 1967.

Kāśyapa, Jagadīśa, Bhikkhu. *The Abhidhamma Philosophy: or, The Psycho-Ethical Philosophy of Early Buddhism.* Delhi: Bharatiya Vidya Prakashan, 1982.

King, Winston Lee. "The Stucture and Dynamics of the Attainment of Cessation in Theravada Meditation." *Journal of the American Academy of Religion* 45 (1977): 707-25.

———. *Theravāda Meditation: The Buddhist Transformation of Yoga.* University Park: Pennsylvania University Press, 1980.

Krishan, Y. "Buddhism and Belief in *Ātma.*" *Journal of the International Association of Buddhist Studies* 7(2) (1984): 117-36.

Lamotte, Étienne. "Conditioned Co-Production and Supreme Enlightenment." In *Buddhist Studies in Honour of Walpola Rahula*, ed. O.H. de A. Wijesekera, pp. 118-39. London: Gordon Fraser, 1980.

———. *Histoire du bouddhisme indien: des origines à l'ère Śaka.* Louvain: Institut Orientaliste, 1967.

———. "Textual Interpretation in Buddhism." In *Buddhist Hermeneutics*, ed. Donald S. Lopez, pp. 11-28. Honolulu: University of Hawaii Press, 1988.

La Vallée Poussin, Louis de. "Le Nirvāṇa d'après Āryadeva." In *Mélanges chinois et bouddhiques.* Vol. 1. Bruxelles: Institut Belge des Hautes Études Chinoises, 1932.

———. "Musīla et Nārada: Le chemin du nirvāṇa." In *Mélanges chinois et bouddhiques.* Vol. 3. Bruxelles: Institut Belge des Hautes Études Chinoises, 1937.

———. *The Way to Nirvana: Six Lectures on Ancient Buddhism as a Discipline of Salvation.* Cambridge: Cambridge University Press, 1979.

Madanayake, Bandu W. "The Concept of Saññā in Theravāda Buddhism." M.A. diss. University of Toronto, 1978.

———. "The Study of Saṅkhāras in Early Buddhism." Ph.D. diss., University of Toronto, 1987.

Malasekera, G.P. *Dictionary of Pāli Proper Names.* 2 vols. London: P.T.S., 1974.

Masefield, Peter. "The Nibbāna-Parinibbāna Controversy." *Religion, A Journal of Religion and Religions* 9 (1979): 215-30.

Matthews, Bruce. *Craving and Salvation: A Study in Buddhist Soteriology.* Waterloo: Wilfrid Laurier University Press, 1983.

Ñāṇananda, Bhikkhu. *Concept and Reality in Early Buddhist Thought.* Kandy: B.P.S., 1986.

Nārada, Mahā Thera. *The Buddha and His Teaching.* Kandy: B.P.S., 1980.

Nyanaponika, Thera. *The Heart of Buddhist Meditation: A Handbook of Mental Training Based on the Buddhist Way of Mindfulness with an Anthology of Relevant Texts Translated from the Pali and Sanskrit.* York Beach: n.p., 1984.

Nyānātiloka. *Buddhist Dictionary: Manual of Buddhist Terms and Doctrines*. Colombo: Frewin, 1956.

———. *Guide Through the Abhidhamma Piṭaka*. Colombo: n.p., 1933.

Potter, Karl H. *Presuppositions of India's Philosophies*. Connecticut: Greenwood Press, 1963.

Rahula, Walpola. *What the Buddha Taught*. Bedford: Gordon Fraser, 1967.

Reat, Ross N. *Origins of Indian Psychology*. Berkeley: Asian Humanities Press, 1990.

Rhys Davids, C.A.F. *Buddhist Psychology: An Inquiry into the Analysis and Theory of Mind in Pāli Literature*. London: Luzac, 1924.

Rhys Davids, T.W. and William Stede. *The Pāli Text Society Pāli-English Dictionary*. London: P.T.S., 1979.

Rogers Macy, Joanna. "Dependent Co-Arising: The Distinctiveness of Buddhist Ethics." *Journal of Religious Ethics* 7(1) (1979): 38-52.

Ruegg, D. Seyfort. "Ahimsa and Vegetarianism in the History of Buddhism." In *Buddhist Studies in Honour of W. Rahula*, ed. O.H. de A. Wijesekera, pp. 234-41. London: Gordon Fraser, 1980.

Sadaw, Ledy. "Some Points in Buddhist Doctrine." *Journal of the Pāli Text Society* (1914): 115-69.

Sarathchandra, E.R. *Buddhist Theory of Perception*. Colombo: Ceylon University Press, 1958.

Sayadaw, Ledi. *L'enseignement de Ledi Sayadaw*. Paris: Editions Albin Michel, 1961.

———. *The Requisites of Enlightenment*. Kandy: B.P.S., 1983.

Schumann, Hans Wolfgang. *Bedeutung und Bedeutungsentwicklung des Terminus Samkhāra im frühen Buddhismus*. Ph.D. diss., Rheinishchen Friedrich-Wilhelms-Universität, Bonn, 1957.

Silburn Lilian. *Instant et cause: le discontinu dans la pensée philosophique de l'Inde*. Paris: Librairie Philosophique J. Vrin, 1955.

Silva, M.W. Padmasiri de. *Buddhist and Freudian Psychology*. Colombo: Lakehouse Investments, 1973.

———. "Kamma and Vedanānupassanā." In *The Importance of Vedanā and Sampajañña* (no. ed.) Igatpuri: Vipassanā Research Institute, 1990.

Sinha, Braj. "The Abhidharmika Notion of *Vijñāna* and its Soteriological Significance." *Journal of the International Association of Buddhist Studies* 3(1) (1980): 54-67.

Stcherbatsky, Th. *Buddhist Logic*. 2 vols. New York: Dover Publications, 1962.

———. *The Conception of Buddhist Nirvāṇa*. Varanasi: Bharatiya Vidya Prakashan, 1968.

———. *The Central Conception of Buddhism and the Meaning of the Word "Dharma."* Delhi: Motilal Banarsidass, 1970.

Tanaka, Kenneth K. "Simultaneous Relation (*sahabhū-hetu*): A Study in Buddhist Theory of Causation." *Journal of the International Association of Buddhist Studies* 8(1) (1985): 91-111.

Thomas, E.J. *The History of Buddhist Thought*. London: P.T.S., 1933.
U Ba Khin, Thray Sithu Sayagyi. "The Essentials of Buddha-Dhamma in Meditative Practice." In *Sayagyi U Ba Khin Journal: A Collection Commemorating the Teaching of Sayagyi U Ba Khin* (no ed.). Igatpuri: Vipassanā Research Institute, 1991, pp. 31-35.
Vetter, Tilmann. *The Ideas and Meditative Practices of Early Buddhism*. Leiden: E.J. Brill, 1988.
Warder, A.K. "The Concept of a Concept." *Journal of Indian Philosophy* (1971).
———. *Indian Buddhism.* Delhi: Motilal Banarsidass, 1980.
———. *Introduction to Pali*. London: Pali Text Society, 1984.
Wayman, A. "Regarding the Translation of the Buddhist Technical Terms *Saññā/ Saṁjñā, Viññāṇa/Vijñāna*." In *Malasakera Commemoration Volume*, ed. O.H. de A. Wijesekera. Colombo, 1976, pp. 324-36.
Welbon, Guy Richard. *The Buddhist Nirvāna and Its Western Interpreters*. Chicago: University of Chicago Press, 1968.
Wiltshire, Martin G. *Ascetic Figures before and in Early Buddhism: The Emergence of Gautama as the Buddha*. New York: Mouton de Gruyter, 1990.
Winternitz, Maurice. *History of Indian Literature*. Delhi: Motilal Barnasidass, 1983.

Index

absorptions 24, 28, 32, 58, 59, 61, 64, 70
aggregate ix, 1-6, 8-13, 16-18, 20-32, 43, 50, 53-57, 62-63, 65-67, 69, 76, 86, 89, 93, 95, 102, 104-105, 108-110, 113-14, 118, 127-30, 132-36, 141-42, 145-47, 148-49, 150
air 31, 34, 35, 42, 44, 47
annihilation view 66, 67
attainment of the fruits of arahantship 24
attainments 28, 53, 58, 59, 61

base 68, 122, 124
bases 3, 12, 56
becoming 7, 10, 89, 110-12, 123, 128, 131, 134-36, 138, 139, 142, 146, 148
belonging to the householder 74, 137, 147
belonging to the renouncer 74, 137, 147
biases 20, 22, 23, 25-27, 29, 30
bodily impression 41, 42, 44, 47, 48

change of lineage 25, 26
clinging 6-8, 10, 12, 18, 20-27, 29-31, 55, 56, 66, 67, 89, 110-12, 131, 134, 135, 136, 140, 142, 146, 148
clinging-aggregate 29-31
concentration 17, 52, 64, 70, 107
conditioned x, 1, 8, 15, 73, 93-95, 99, 102, 103, 104-106, 108, 109, 112, 113, 123, 127, 130, 139-41, 148
conditioned phenomena 1, 15, 94, 95, 99, 102-103, 104, 105, 108, 109, 112, 113, 148
consciousness ix, 2, 4, 5, 7, 10, 12, 16, 19, 21, 22, 25, 27, 29, 32, 33, 49, 50, 54, 55, 59, 62, 66, 67, 77, 81, 95, 111, 113, 115-25, 127-31, 133, 135, 137, 138, 142, 147, 148
contact ix, 7, 10, 41, 46-51, 58, 62, 70, 72, 78, 81, 107, 109, 111, 118, 120, 121, 122, 124, 128, 131, 133, 134, 136, 137, 147
conventional truth 3, 6
craving ix, 7, 10, 23, 27, 28, 70-73, 76, 77, 79-83, 86, 88, 89, 105, 106, 109-112, 131, 134-42, 144-48
cycle of birth, death and rebirth 8, 12, 66

death-consciousness 123, 124, 131
dependent origination vii, 3, 6-11, 21, 30, 48, 49, 53, 71, 77, 86, 91, 95, 97, 109, 110, 114, 124, 127, 130, 131, 135, 136, 141, 142, 147, 149
desire ix, 42, 80, 81, 111, 134, 135, 139, 140, 143

Series Published by Wilfrid Laurier University Press for the Canadian Corporation for Studies in Religion / Corporation Canadienne des Sciences Religieuses

Editions SR

1. *La langue de Ya'udi : description et classement de l'ancien parler de Zencircli dans le cadre des langues sémitiques du nord-ouest*
   Paul-Eugène Dion, O.P.
   1974 / viii + 511 p. / OUT OF PRINT
2. *The Conception of Punishment in Early Indian Literature*
   Terence P. Day
   1982 / iv + 328 pp.
3. *Traditions in Contact and Change: Selected Proceedings of the XIVth Congress of the International Association for the History of Religions*
   Edited by Peter Slater and Donald Wiebe with Maurice Boutin and Harold Coward
   1983 / x + 758 pp. / OUT OF PRINT
4. *Le messianisme de Louis Riel*
   Gilles Martel
   1984 / xviii + 483 p.
5. *Mythologies and Philosophies of Salvation in the Theistic Traditions of India*
   Klaus K. Klostermaier
   1984 / xvi + 549 pp. / OUT OF PRINT
6. *Averroes' Doctrine of Immortality: A Matter of Controversy*
   Ovey N. Mohammed
   1984 / vi + 202 pp. / OUT OF PRINT
7. *L'étude des religions dans les écoles : l'expérience américaine, anglaise et canadienne*
   Fernand Ouellet
   1985 / xvi + 666 p.
8. *Of God and Maxim Guns: Presbyterianism in Nigeria, 1846-1966*
   Geoffrey Johnston
   1988 / iv + 322 pp.
9. *A Victorian Missionary and Canadian Indian Policy: Cultural Synthesis vs Cultural Replacement*
   David A. Nock
   1988 / x + 194 pp. / OUT OF PRINT
10. *Prometheus Rebound: The Irony of Atheism*
    Joseph C. McLelland
    1988 / xvi + 366 pp.
11. *Competition in Religious Life*
    Jay Newman
    1989 / viii + 237 pp.
12. *The Huguenots and French Opinion, 1685-1787: The Enlightenment Debate on Toleration*
    Geoffrey Adams
    1991 / xiv + 335 pp.
13. *Religion in History: The Word, the Idea, the Reality / La religion dans l'histoire : le mot, l'idée, la réalité*
    Edited by/Sous la direction de Michel Despland and/et Gérard Vallée
    1992 / x + 252 pp.
14. *Sharing Without Reckoning: Imperfect Right and the Norms of Reciprocity*
    Millard Schumaker
    1992 / xiv + 112 pp.

15. *Love and the Soul: Psychological Interpretations of the Eros and Psyche Myth*
James Gollnick
1992 / viii + 174 pp.
16. *The Promise of Critical Theology: Essays in Honour of Charles Davis*
Edited by Marc P. Lalonde
1995 / xii + 140 pp.
17. *The Five Aggregates: Understanding Theravada, Psychology and Soteriology*
Mathieu Boisvert
1995 / xii + 166 pp.
18. *Mysticism and Vocation*
James R. Horne
1995 / 152 pp. est. / FORTHCOMING

Comparative Ethics Series / Collection d'Éthique Comparée

1. *Muslim Ethics and Modernity: A Comparative Study of the Ethical Thought of Sayyid Ahmad Khan and Mawlana Mawdudi*
Sheila McDonough
1984 / x + 130 pp. / OUT OF PRINT
2. *Methodist Education in Peru: Social Gospel, Politics, and American Ideological and Economic Penetration, 1888-1930*
Rosa del Carmen Bruno-Jofré
1988 / xiv + 223 pp.
3. *Prophets, Pastors and Public Choices: Canadian Churches and the Mackenzie Valley Pipeline Debate*
Roger Hutchinson
1992 / xiv + 142 pp.

Dissertations SR

1. *The Social Setting of the Ministry as Reflected in the Writings of Hermas, Clement and Ignatius*
Harry O. Maier
1991 / viii + 230 pp.
2. *Literature as Pulpit: The Christian Social Activism of Nellie L. McClung*
Randi R. Warne
1993 / viii + 236 pp.

Studies in Christianity and Judaism / Études sur le christianisme et le judaïsme

1. *A Study in Anti-Gnostic Polemics: Irenaeus, Hippolytus, and Epiphanius*
Gérard Vallée
1981 / xii + 114 pp. / OUT OF PRINT
2. *Anti-Judaism in Early Christianity*
Vol. 1, ***Paul and the Gospels***, edited by Peter Richardson with David Granskou
1986 / x + 232 pp.
Vol. 2, ***Separation and Polemic***
Edited by Stephen G. Wilson
1986 / xii + 185 pp.
3. *Society, the Sacred, and Scripture in Ancient Judaism: A Sociology of Knowledge*
Jack N. Lightstone
1988 / xiv + 126 pp.
4. *Law in Religious Communities in the Roman Period: The Debate Over* **Torah** *and* **Nomos** *in Post-Biblical Judaism and Early Christianity*
Peter Richardson and Stephen Westerholm with A. I. Baumgarten, Michael Pettem and Cecilia Wassén
1991 / x + 164 pp.

5. ***Dangerous Food: 1 Corinthians 8-10 in Its Context***
Peter D. Gooch
1993 / xviii + 178 pp.
6. ***The Rhetoric of the Babylonian Talmud, Its Social Meaning and Context***
Jack N. Lightstone
1994 / xiv + 317 pp.

The Study of Religion in Canada / Sciences Religieuses au Canada

1. ***Religious Studies in Alberta: A State-of-the-Art Review***
Ronald W. Neufeldt
1983 / xiv + 145 pp.
2. ***Les sciences religieuses au Québec depuis 1972***
Louis Rousseau et Michel Despland
1988 / 158 p.
3. ***Religious Studies in Ontario: A State-of-the-Art Review***
Harold Remus, William Closson James and Daniel Fraikin
1992 / xviii + 422 pp.
4. ***Religious Studies in Manitoba and Saskatchewan: A State-of-the-Art Review***
John M. Badertscher, Gordon Harland and Roland E. Miller
1993 / vi + 166 pp.
5. ***The Study of Religion in British Columbia: A State-of-the-Art Review***
Brian J. Fraser
1995 / 128 pp. est. / FORTHCOMING

SR Supplements

1. ***Footnotes to a Theology: The Karl Barth Colloquium of 1972***
Edited by and Introduced by Martin Rumscheidt
1974 / viii + 151 pp. / OUT OF PRINT
2. ***Martin Heidegger's Philosophy of Religion***
John R. Williams
1977 / x + 190 pp. / OUT OF PRINT
3. ***Mystics and Scholars: The Calgary Conference on Mysticism 1976***
Edited by Harold Coward and Terence Penelhum
1977 / viii + 121 pp. / OUT OF PRINT
4. ***God's Intention for Man: Essays in Christian Anthropology***
William O. Fennell
1977 / xii + 56 pp. / OUT OF PRINT
5. ***"Language" in Indian Philosophy and Religion***
Edited and Introduced by Harold G. Coward
1978 / x + 98 pp. / OUT OF PRINT
6. ***Beyond Mysticism***
James R. Horne
1978 / vi + 158 pp. / OUT OF PRINT
7. ***The Religious Dimension of Socrates' Thought***
James Beckman
1979 / xii + 276 pp. / OUT OF PRINT
8. ***Native Religious Traditions***
Edited by Earle H. Waugh and K. Dad Prithipaul
1979 / xii + 244 pp. / OUT OF PRINT
9. ***Developments in Buddhist Thought: Canadian Contributions to Buddhist Studies***
Edited by Roy C. Amore
1979 / iv + 196 pp.
10. ***The Bodhisattva Doctrine in Buddhism***
Edited by Introduced by Leslie S. Kawamura
1981 / xxii + 274 pp. / OUT OF PRINT

11. ***Political Theology in the Canadian Context***
Edited by Benjamin G. Smillie
1982 / xii + 260 pp.
12. ***Truth and Compassion: Essays on Judaism and Religion in Memory of Rabbi Dr. Solomon Frank***
Edited by Howard Joseph, Jack N. Lightstone and Michael D. Oppenheim
1983 / vi + 217 pp.
13. ***Craving and Salvation: A Study in Buddhist Soteriology***
Bruce Matthews
1983 / xiv + 138 pp. / OUT OF PRINT
14. ***The Moral Mystic***
James R. Horne
1983 / x + 134 pp.
15. ***Ignatian Spirituality in a Secular Age***
Edited by George P. Schner
1984 / viii + 128 pp. / OUT OF PRINT
16. ***Studies in the Book of Job***
Edited by Walter E. Aufrecht
1985 / xii + 76 pp.
17. ***Christ and Modernity: Christian Self-Understanding in a Technological Age***
David J. Hawkin
1985 / x + 181 pp.
18. ***Young Man Shinran: A Reappraisal of Shinran's Life***
Takamichi Takahatake
1987 / xvi + 228 pp. / OUT OF PRINT
19. ***Modernity and Religion***
Edited by William Nicholls
1987 / vi + 191 pp.
20. ***The Social Uplifters: Presbyterian Progressives and the Social Gospel in Canada, 1875-1915***
Brian J. Fraser
1988 / xvi + 212 pp. / OUT OF PRINT

Available from / en vente chez :
WILFRID LAURIER UNIVERSITY PRESS
Waterloo, Ontario, Canada N2L 3C5